THE INFLUENCE OF HISTORY ON MAHAN:

The Proceedings of a Conference
Marking the Centenary of
Alfred Thayer Mahan's
The Influence of Sea Power Upon History, 1660-1783

ATTENDEES AT THE MAHAN CENTENNIAL CONFERENCE
NAVAL WAR COLLEGE NEWPORT, RHODE ISLAND
29 APRIL - 1 MAY 1990

ATTENDEES AT THE MAHAN CENTENNIAL CONFERENCE
NAVAL WAR COLLEGE NEWPORT, RHODE ISLAND
29 APRIL - 1 MAY 1990

1. Dr. Marc Milner 2. Prof. Philip A. Crowl 3. Dr. Andrew L. Ross 4. RADM J.C. Wylie, USN (ret.)
5. CAPT G. Montenegro, ARN 6. Prof. Barry Hunt 7. Dr. Robert L. Scheina 8. Dr. Malcolm H. Murfett
9. Prof. Gerald Wheeler 10. Prof. John B. Hattendorf 11. Prof. Paul Halpern 12. Dr. Robert S. Wood
13. Prof. Daniel A. Baugh 14. Dr. Dean C. Allard 15. Dr. William J. Morgan 16. Dr. Jon T. Sumida
17. Dr. Nicholas Tracy 18. Prof. William Braisted 19. Dr. William S. Dudley 20. Dr. John Maurer
21. Mr. Frank Uhlig 22. Dr. David Trask 23. Prof. George Baer 24. Dr. W.A.B. Douglas
25. CAPT Dr. Werner Rahn, FGN 26. CAPT Wayne P. Hughes, Jr., USN (ret.) 27. Prof. James A. Field
28. Prof. Donald M. Schurman 29. Prof. Roger Dingman 30. LCDR Reo Leslie, CHC, USN
31. Dr. Norman Friedman 32. Prof. Kenneth Hagan 33. Dr. Sari Hornstein 34. Prof. William Still
35. Prof. Holger Herwig 36. Prof. Richard Turk 37. CAPT Timothy Somes, USN (ret.)
38. Prof. Raymond G. O'Connor 39. Prof. Barry Gough 40. CAPT James A. Barber, USN (ret.)
41. Prof. George C. Quester 42. Dr. Christopher C. Harmon 43. Dr. Mark R. Peattie
44. Prof. Robert Seager II 45. Dr. J. Kenneth McDonald 46. Dr. Lawrence Allin
47. Prof. Clark G. Reynolds 48. Prof. Richard Megargee

THE INFLUENCE OF HISTORY ON MAHAN

The Proceedings of a Conference
Marking the Centenary of
Alfred Thayer Mahan's
The Influence of Sea Power Upon History, 1660-1783

Edited by

John B. Hattendorf
Ernest J. King Professor of Maritime History
Naval War College

NAVAL WAR COLLEGE PRESS
Newport, Rhode Island

1991

Library of Congress Cataloging-in-Publication Data

The influence of history on Mahan: the proceedings of a conference, marking the centenary of Alfred Thayer
   Mahan's The Influcence of sea power upon history, 1660-1783 / edited by John B. Hattendorf with
   John C. Benigno.
       p.   cm. — (U.S. Naval War College historical monograph series : no. 9)
   Includes bibliographical references.
       1. Sea-power—Congresses. 2. Mahan, A. T. (Alfred Thayer), 1840-1914—Congresses. I. Hatten-
   dorf., John B. II. Benigno, John C. III. Mahan, A. T. (Alfred Thayer), 1840-1914. Influence of sea
   power upon history, 1660-1783. IV. Series.
   V25.I54 1991   91-33383
   909'.6—dc20   CIP

CONTENTS

ACKNOWLEDGEMENTS

Many people contributed to the Mahan Centennial Conference which was held at the Naval War College, 30 April and 1 May 1990. Professor George Baer was the first to suggest such a conference, chairing a session on the subject at the American Historical Association's annual meeting in San Francisco in December 1988. In parallel, Dr. William Dudley suggested that the U.S. Navy should officially mark the occasion with a scholarly gathering and promoted the idea of a joint enterprise by the Naval Historical Center and the Naval War College. With the approval of Rear Admiral Ronald J. Kurth, President of the Naval War College, Dr. Robert S. Wood, Dean of the Center for Naval Warfare Studies, enthusiastically agreed to sponsor the joint conference as part of the work of the Center.

Many contributed to the administrative support for the conference which was effectively managed by Lieutenant Commander Chris Benigno, U. S. Navy, with the assistance of Ensign Lindsey Möhle, U.S. Naval Reserve. Mrs Barbara Prisk took great initiative in timely preparation of all the papers for the conference as well undertaking a full range of other activities from travel arrangements, contract preparation and transcription. Tony Nicolosi and Bob Cembrola at the Naval War College Museum prepared the exhibition on Mahan, parts of which are illustrated in this volume. At their request, numerous institutions around the country lent items for the exhibit which remained in place for several months. The staff of the Commissioned Officers Mess (Open) assisted with arrangements for lunch and the final social hour of the conference. Beyond the shores of Coasters Harbor Island, The Treadway Inn, The Viking Hotel and the Newport Historical Society made major contributions to the conference. The Naval War College Foundation generously contributed to both the conference and to the publication of this volume.

John B. Hattendorf
Conference Director

PART I: THEN AND NOW

Rear Admiral Ronald J. Kurth, President of the Naval War College, 1987-1990, making the opening remarks at the Mahan Centennial Conference in Mahan Hall.
Participants shown, left to right: Robert S. Wood, Evelyn Cherpak, Raymond G. O'Connor, John Hattendorf, Malcolm Murfett, John Mauer, Donald Schurman, Robert Seager II, George Baer.

Chapter 1

Opening Remarks

Rear Admiral Ronald J. Kurth, U.S. Navy

It is a great pleasure for me to welcome you here to the Mahan Centennial Conference which we are sponsoring in co-operation with the Naval Historical Center in Washington. I am particularly pleased that our two institutions have worked together so successfully for this occasion, and I want to thank Dr. Dean Allard, the Director of Naval History, for his fine co-operation. Working together, we have planned a conference that is the U.S. Navy's official, centenary commemoration marking the publication of Alfred Thayer Mahan's most famous book, *The Influence of Sea Power Upon History, 1660-1783.*

One hundred years ago this week, Mahan received the advance copies of the book and it began its literary life as one of the most influential American books of the 19th century. It is appropriate that this meeting today is held at the Naval War College, for the book began as Mahan's classroom lectures here and it is appropriate that this group today is a group of historians, naval thinkers and naval strategists. For Mahan was the first in the U.S. Navy to combine all three of those attributes and to reach the pinnacle of fame.

Mahan is no forgotten figure in the U.S. Navy. We have named three ships for him, as well as several buildings, including the one we are now in. Thus, our purpose today is not to commemorate someone who might otherwise have been forgotten. Perhaps, the situation is the reverse and we deal here with a man whose name everyone in the Navy has heard, but very few have fully understood. With this in mind, those outside the Navy still allude, with damning effect, to Secretary of War Stimson's remark about "the peculiar psychology of the Navy Department, which frequently seemed to retire from the realm of logic into a dim religious world in which Neptune was God, Mahan his prophet, and the United States Navy the only true church." If that attitude exists, or has ever existed in the navy, (John Hattendorf would now have me go on to say) it is time to dispel it; there is no better place or time to do it than here and now.

It's funny as I say these words to you I reflect on my experience with talking to Admiral Gorshkov in Moscow about his book, *Morskaya Moshch Gosudarstva* [*The Sea Power of the State*], in which I told him that he sounded very Mahanian. And he said, "And why not? The man was eminently sensible."

Many of you here have already made substantial contributions in this field and these will stand as the foundation stones of our discussions here this week. Yet, I sense that the subject of Mahan and his work has much of value that still needs to be explored. As we have made progress in our understanding of naval power and come to see it, not just as an isolated factor, but as a complementary one within a wide spectrum of national power, we can begin to identify more clearly the extent and nature of Mahan's contribution to thinking about defense issues. With the span of a century behind us, we can see trends in ideas developing and maturing across a substantial period of time. From our vantage point, we can see the various intellectual forces and practical experiences which had an impact on Mahan's thought. We can come to appreciate fully the extent of his contribution and we can begin to discern, too, how his ideas have operated within the context of differing national institutions and national cultures. Since much recent progress has been made in understanding the historical events which Mahan studied, we can judge more accurately how valid his conclusions were. We may well judge some of them wrong by modern standards, and thus we need to correct some of our own theoretical understanding. At the same time, even while we may find them wrong in the light of modern understanding, we can still come to appreciate why his logic and his interpretations of history on those very same points might have been powerful factors to others before our time. Today, however, we seem to have entered a new phase in history; the context of international relations in our time is rapidly changing. As we move forward, we need to think clearly about our intellectual origins and to understand their strengths and their limitations. It is no easy task. It involves being critical about one's own assumptions and one's own traditions, but it is a task that needs to be done. We may even prove Mr. Stimson wrong.

All of you are widely recognized students of naval history and naval affairs who know Mahan's work and of what he wrote. I can think of no better group to deal with this issue. I am particularly pleased to welcome back so many distinguished scholars who have at one time or another been members of our faculty here and I am particularly pleased to have so many distinguished scholars join us from other countries. It is particularly good to have so large a delegation from Canada; you who share our Anglo-American heritage can help us to understand it better with the insight from your own national perspective. And it is a special pleasure to welcome Captain Dr. Rahn of Germany and Captain Montenegro of Argentina. Your views, from outside the English language context of the subject, will make an especially valuable contribution to the deliberations of this conference.

By tomorrow afternoon, when Professor George Baer (our newly appointed Mahan Professor of Strategy) summarizes the papers and discussions of this conference, I hope that you may have found a new consensus about Admiral Mahan's contribution. The time has come to see Mahan, anew, in the context of his own time, in comparison and in contrast to other thinkers, and to define his contribution and his place in the evolution of naval thinking. With such an improved historical understanding among historians and strategists, we, in the Navy, can proceed more effectively. Mahan's work forms an important part of our intellectual heritage. That alone justifies our consideration of it. Yet today, in the context of a changing world, we need more than ever to evaluate correctly to what degree our heritage can guide us in the future. For those reasons, your discussions here are valuable and important. The proceedings of this conference, with the range and nature of your discussions about Mahan and his ideas, may well have an important impact on the way in which the U.S. Navy of the future looks at its own intellectual heritage. This is a task of great intellectual responsibility; let it begin now.

Original photograph of Little, Brown & Company, Boston, the publisher of Mahan's first sea power book, as it appeared in 1894, four years after the book appeared in print. Little Brown published 15 of Mahan's 20 books.

Courtesy of Little, Brown & Company.

Chapter 2

The Influence of History on Mahan

Barry M. Gough

All too rarely comes the opportunity, one of a lifetime, for an historian to celebrate the centenary of a remarkable genius in a field of mutual endeavor. Many have gone before in assessing the work and influence of Captain Alfred Thayer Mahan, U.S. Navy, and many will follow, for his influence transcends time. But new perspectives, even a new look at old evidence, are welcome, and they can provide fresh insights into the man, his thought, and his influence. More, they can provide new viewpoints for modern strategic thinkers, who, pondering as they must the roles of force in peace as in war, are obliged to consider past practices in present circumstances and how, in turn, present circumstances may shape future developments.

The year 1990 marks the hundredth anniversary of the appearance in print of Mahan's *Influence of Sea Power Upon History, 1660-1783,* the first of a series of published Naval War College lectures. This constitutes one of the most remarkable books in the annals of human progress, a distinguished contribution to letters, and arguably the most seminal work in the naval and strategic thought of modern history. True it is that Mahan has come in for some close and valid criticism in recent years, and many persons would say deservedly so.[1] However, like the greats of the profession before him, including Thucydides, Herodotus, Michelet, Carlyle, Parkman and Prescott, he has acquired an indelible place on the pages of human activity over time. As with his fellow-countrymen Frederick Jackson Turner and Charles Beard he has been much challenged, but he is never ignored, or if so, at peril. Mahan is etched in time. He was the principal philosopher of sea power of the late nineteenth century, a naval Mohammed. He was a journeyman historian in

---

[1] For a survey of these, see Barry M. Gough, "Maritime Strategy: The Legacies of Mahan and Corbett as Philosophers of Sea Power," *The Royal United Services Institute for Defence Studies Journal,* Winter 1988, pp. 55-57. See also, John B. Hattendorf, "Alfred Thayer Mahan and his Strategic Thought," and Donald M. Schurman, "Mahan Revisited," [1982], in Hattendorf and Robert S. Jordan, eds. *Maritime Strategy and the Balance of Power: Britain and America in The Twentieth Century* (New York, 1989), pp. 83-94 and 95-109 respectively.

research and writing skills, besides being a capable synthesist of secondary
historical works, who conceived of a series of books explaining the role that
naval affairs at sea had played in the shaping of the world to his time of
writing. Besides these capabilities, which are significant in themselves, he
was imaginative enough to write persuasively, or more correctly publicly and
popularly, so that statesmen and boards of admiralty would endeavor to seize
the moment, and to try to grasp the Trident of Neptune, or at least give their
own particular nation cause to believe that they, too, shared the powerful
purpose of those who could contest the sovereignty of the seas and the might
of the main.

For many years Mahan bestrode the naval-strategic world like a colossus,
writing a phenomenal body of literature constituting a sum total of 20 books
and 160 articles, besides numerous academic and public literary contributions
of a comparatively minor sort.[2] His work was published by the leading English
and American houses, and his key books were translated into French, German,
Russian, Japanese and other languages. Just as a publishing phenomenon
Mahan was remarkable. He was on call to the leading statesmen of his time.
The naval arms race leading up to August 1914 may partly be attributed to
him: he accentuated or at least was contemporaneous with numerous naval
bills of his own government, and of all the key naval states besides. The
diplomatic historian Sir Charles Webster used to tell his students that Mahan
was one of the causes of the First World War.[3] Certainly President Woodrow
Wilson blamed "navalism" for causing the war, and he sought to eradicate
it in his Points of Peace. How much he would put the blame on his fellow-
countrymen is not known but the connection is certainly suggestive even so,
the Great War did not harm Mahan's shining armor; indeed it may have
polished it. As the United States became a world naval power in the later
years of that war, and throughout the interwar period, the legacy of Mahan's

[2] See the most recent list of Mahan's publications, including translations: John B. Hattendorf and Lynn
C. Hattendorf, compilers, *A Bibliography of the Works of Alfred Thayer Mahan* (Newport, Rhode Island: Naval
War College Press, Naval War College Historical Monograph Series No. 7, 1986).
[3] I owe this observation to my mentor Gerald S. Graham. See his *Politics of Naval Supremacy: Studies in
British Maritime Ascendancy* (Cambridge, 1965), p. 5. Graham's discussion of Mahan comes under the heading
of "command of the sea." To my knowledge Graham never wrote specifically on Mahan, though he used
to say "Mahan is dead." What he meant by that is, that Mahan was premature in his conclusions about
maritime power, or the role that sea power played in history, for he never considered the economic
foundations of imperial and maritime influence (which was Graham's *forte*), nor did he address himself
to the diplomatic aspects of employing naval power to fulfill national objectives including the pursuit
of peace, another (though lesser *initially*) of Graham's themes.. Some of these arguments may be traced
in *Ibid.*, pp. 4-6, but see also his discussion of Mahan in Clark G. Reynolds and William J. McAndrew,
eds., *University of Maine at Orono 1971 Seminar in Maritime and Regional Studies* (Orono, Maine, 1972), pp.
86-90. As to whether or not "navalism" was a cause of the war, I am of the opinion that it was not
a *cause* but a *representation of the political circumstances that led to that war*. On this point, see Michael Howard,
The Causes of Wars and Other Essays (Cambridge, Mass., 1983), pp. 18-19.

thought grew, and so the legend itself was lengthened.[4] America's rise to world power was a destiny in need of a supporting cast of heroes, and in these circumstances Mahan took on an added *persona* of one who truly understood the role that the seas could play in human history.

At this time we rightly celebrate the totality of his achievement, mindful as we are of his frailties and his misconceptions. We take it as axiomatic that a great theorist is open to critique. He must survive all sorts of cross examination. He must suffer abuse from those who know him not, and the scorn of those who dismiss him unthinkingly. Here, it is a special mission, indeed a unique obligation, to treat this particular subject with a cautious reverence combined with an academic objectivity. This is no enviable task. But it is one required in any composite assessment of Mahan, such as this occasion demands. It is, besides, a window of opportunity through which to view the larger changes of the writing of naval history over several centuries and Mahan's well earned position as the principal philosopher of sea power in modern times.[5]

I would hazard a guess that the great men who were influenced by the reading of Mahan's 1890 work confined their attention almost solely to three parts: the Preface, the Introductory, and the opening chapter entitled "Discussion of the Elements of Sea Power." Apart from the last several paragraphs of the last chapter, "Critical Discussion of the Maritime War of 1778", there is little comment given to the general strategic conditions and objectives of a maritime war; rather, the whole is given over the details of waging a war at sea. In short, the theoretical issues must have attracted the armchair strategist, not the nuts and bolts.

In and of itself, this section, which may be classified as preliminary to the book, and, more, to the trilogy that took his narrative from 1660 to 1815, constitutes a strategic analysis or proscription of naval warfare. And inasmuch as this is the focus of sustained interest it is here treated in considerable detail, to the necessary exclusion of discussion of other books and essays of Mahan.

"The definitive object proposed in this work," Mahan explained in his Preface, "is an examination of the general history of Europe and America with particular reference to the effect of sea power upon the course of that

---

[4] The high point was reached by Margaret Sprout in her "Mahan: Evangelist of Sea Power," in Edward M. Earle, *Makers of Modern Strategy: Military Thought from Machiavelli to Hitler* (Princeton, 1943), pp. 415-45. See also Harold and Margaret Sprout, *The Rise of American Naval Power* (rev. ed., Princeton, 1942) and Margaret Sprout, *Toward a New Order of Sea Power: American Naval Policy and the World Scene, 1918-1922* (1943, reprint, New York, 1969), pp. 1-34 for the influence of Mahan on American naval history.

[5] The critiques of Mahan continue to be prodigious. A highly recommended introduction to this subject to the eve of the centenary of Mahan's principal work is Philip A. Crowl, "Alfred Thayer Mahan: The Naval Historian," in Peter Paret with Gordon A. Craig and Felix Gilbert, *Makers of Modern Strategy: Machiavelli to the Nuclear Age* (Princeton, 1986), pp. 444-77 and 904-905.

history."⁶ Thus did Mahan launch his enterprise. "Historians generally have been unfamiliar with the conditions of the sea, having as to it neither special interest nor special knowledge, and the profound determining influence of maritime strength upon great issues has consequently been overlooked. This is even more true of particular occasions than of the general tendency of sea power." Now he warmed to his theme: "It is easy to say in a general way, that the use and control of the sea is and has been a great factor in the history of the world; it is more troublesome to seek out and show its exact bearing at a particular juncture." Then he terminated his opening paragraph by remarking, in his time-honored warning: "Yet, unless this be done, the acknowledgement of general importance remains vague and unsubstantial, not resting, as it should, upon a collection of special instances in which the precise effect has been made clear, by an analysis of the conditions at the given moments." By this is meant that unless history be viewed in the particular the whole makes little sense, and that it is equally necessary to look at the causes as much as the developments.

Also in his Preface Mahan attacked the tendency of historians to slight the maritime aspects of human endeavors when writing the annals of nations and of mankind. This was notoriously so in England where national greatness rested on the use and control of the sea. Citing historians Arnold and Creasy as to how success in arms on land had brought ascendancy, Mahan complained that in neither of these episodes—that is, Hannibal striving against Rome or Napoleon against England—did historians note that "the mastery of the sea rested with the victor." In fact, wrote Mahan, Roman sea power obliged Hannibal to undertake a perilous march through Gaul thereby wasting half his veterans, and enabled the elder Scipio to intercept Hannibal's communications, and to return to wage a war on land. Meanwhile, legions passed to and fro by water between Italy and Spain unmolested, unwearied, while Roman sea power sealed off the enemy's approaches by salt water, obliging them to come by land. Thus divided, the two Carthaginian armies were separated, and one was destroyed by the combined actions of the Roman generals. Also in preface Mahan took up the challenge of a self-styled reformer of naval historiography and method, for he chided naval historians for troubling themselves so little regarding the connection between their own particular or special topic and general history. He objected to naval historians acting as mere chroniclers, and he put the blame more squarely on the English than the French, the latter's genius and training making them more careful in their inquiries into causation and relationships. Last of all in his prefatory

⁶ Alfred Thayer Mahan, *The Influence of Sea Power Upon History, 1660-1783* (Boston and London, 1890). All quotations of Mahan's 1660-1783 book are from my paperback edition, published in New York by Hill and Wang, 1957. Inasmuch as numerous editions of this work exist, and the excerpts cited are readily found in the Preface, Introductory and First Chapter of the book I have not provided page numbers and notes for the same.

remarks Mahan stated that to his knowledge no other author had sought to evaluate "the effect of sea power upon the course of history and the prosperity of nations. As other histories deal with the wars, politics, social and economical conditions of countries, touching upon maritime matters only incidentally and generally sympathetically, so the present work aims at putting maritime interests in the foreground, without divorcing them, however, from their surroundings of cause and effect in general history, but seeking to show how they modified the latter, and were modified by them." He closed with a most cursory explanation as to why he chose the period 1660 to 1783 by stating that he intended a clear and accurate outline of successive events, adding "Writing as a naval officer in full sympathy with his profession, the author has not hesitated to digress freely on questions of naval policy, strategy, and tactics, but as a technical language has been avoided, it is hoped that these matters, simply presented, will be found of interest to the unprofessional reader."

At the outset of his Introductory, Mahan discloses his own purpose without bias. He makes his intention abundantly clear. "The history of Sea Power is largely, though by no means solely, a narrative of contests between nations, of mutual rivalries, of violence frequently culminating in war." To this he added, "The profound influence of sea commerce upon the wealth and strength of countries was clearly seen long before the true principles which governed its growth and prosperity were detected." Then, in appreciation of a mercantilist rhetoric which had long been discarded in England, he noted: "To secure to one's own people a disproportionate share of such benefits, every effort was made to exclude others, either by the peaceful legislative methods of monopoly or prohibitory regulations, or, when these failed, by direct violence. The clash of interests, the angry feelings roused by conflicting attempts thus to appropriate the larger share, if not the whole, of the advantages of commerce, and of distant unsettled commercial regions, led to wars." As to the conduct of these maritime wars, he wrote: "On the other hand, wars arising from other causes have been greatly modified in their conduct and issue by the control of the sea. Therefore the history of seapower, while embracing in its broad sweep all that tends to make a people great upon the sea or by the sea, is largely a military history; and it is in this aspect that it will be mainly, though not exclusively, regarded in the following pages."

A section of the Introductory is given over to a discussion the second Punic War and some references to English naval policy and actions in the late eighteenth century, and it is tempting for the reader to pass over easily the strategic dimension of this chapter that is so central to Mahan's historical explanation of naval science. Writing in an age when steam propulsion was fast displacing wind as a motive force, Mahan was intrigued by the similarities between galleys and steam ships, but mindful of the lessons to be learned from the history of sailing ships. The precedents were not to be more significant than the principles, he argued: "War has such principles; their existence is detected by the study of the past, which reveals them in successes and in failures, the same from age to age. Conditions and weapons change, but to cope with the one or successfully wield the others, respect must be had to these constant teachings of history in the tactics of the battlefield, or in those wider operations of war which are comprised under the name of strategy." No matter how wide the operations, the size of contending armies, and the scope of the necessary movements, the principles of war remained. The place for the necessary concentration of force, the logistics of deployment, the disposition of the enemy forces—all remained the same, though the march on foot gave way to travel in coaches and then railroads. The same was analogous in naval war, from the galley to the sailing ship to the steamer, and the scope and rapidity of naval operations were increased without necessarily changing the principles directing them. The whole plan of naval war, he stressed, depended on fulfilling the function of a navy: its true objective, the point or points of concentration, the place of supply of coal and supplies, the maintenance of communications between these depots and home base, the utility of commerce-destroying, or *guerre de course*, as a decisive or a secondary operation of war, and how this mode of war should be prosecuted, whether by scattered cruisers or control of vital centers of passage, sealanes—"All these are strategic questions, and upon all these history has a great deal to say."

He had come to his main point. In his words, "It is then particularly in the field of naval strategy that the teachings of the past have a value which is in no degree lessened. They are there useful not only as illustrative of principles, but also as precedents, owing to the comparative permanence of the conditions." The conditions of war would vary from age to age, he contended, and would do so with the change of weapons. Even so, the teachings of the school of history remain constant, and as being universal in application can be ranked as general principles. For this reason, then, the study of the sea history of the past provides instruction in the form of examples of the general principles of maritime war. The successful conduct of war was thus based on strategic principles, and tactical ones, too, that were rooted in the "essential nature of things."

Here then, in its raw simplicity, was the Mahan view that history was scientific, that is, that it had principles. Thus he who could understand the principles could develop a strategy and deploy the weapons of a naval war by certain tactics. Here then was the "influence of sea power upon history".

How had Mahan come to this conclusion that past practices could lead to the discovery of principles and that the knowledge of these could provide the clues to the waging of a successful war at sea? A few postulations are in order here.

It seems rather clear from the letters and other papers of Mahan's that have survived, that he came to this perspective by himself.[7] There were professional influences upon him, as will be explained presently, but his theory of history seems to have been his own. The personal details of his life germane to this branch of the explanation are that he was born at West Point, the son of a professor in the Academy well versed in fortifications and in the thinking of the Swiss strategist Antonie-Henri Jomini. Although the relationship of his father's appreciation of Jomini's thought to the wide acceptance that Alfred held is suggestive rather than conclusive, there can be no doubt but that the naval historian was convinced of the applicability of Jomini's principles of strategy and tactics to fleet deployments and actions at sea. Yet another significant influence on Mahan was that of Stephen B. Luce, the first President of the Naval War College, likewise a careful student of Jomini's thought. Luce's letters to Mahan during the initiatory stage of the founding of the College, and also during Mahan's assumption and preparation of his lectureship there, suggest that Luce may even have provided the theoretical model for the principles of waging a maritime war according to history. As Robert Seager II has explained, there is a great similarity between Luce's concept and Mahan's theory as put forward in his Introductory.[8] Indeed, more than Luce's suggested line of reasoning was embraced by Mahan. The first chapter of Mahan's *Influence of Sea Power Upon History*, entitled "Discussion of the Elements of Sea Power," owes not a little to a prize-winning essay written by Ensign David in 1882, as Seager suggests.[9]

To whom else was Mahan dependent for his ideas? I think we can conclude that apart from some personal experiences and predispositions, important in themselves, most of his thought was derived from historical perceptions and writings rather than from contemporary points of view. The personal aspects of Mahan at this stage of this life are illuminating. We know that he was bright, extraordinarily vain, though he tried to hide it, and personally attractive, or at least he thought so. He was unpopular and isolated at the Naval Academy because of his rigid belief in discipline. He admired the Royal Navy, and sought to emulate its discipline in the United States Navy. He was socially awkward with women, and apparently as isolated from them as he was from the men of the navy. His love of the sea was not strong, and if his biographers are to be believed, he hated ship-board life. Somehow in Stephen B. Luce he found a patron, and had he not done so he would never have been afforded the opportunity to lecture, and had he not had that opportunity it seems probable that he would not have taken to the task of becoming a first rate historian. Certainly his *The Gulf and Inland Waters*,

---

[7] See Robert Seager II and Doris D. Maguire, eds., *Letters and Papers of Alfred Thayer Mahan* (3 vols. Annapolis, 1975).

[8] Robert Seager II, *Alfred Thayer Mahan: The Man and His Letters* (Annapolis, 1977), p. 169 and elsewhere.

[9] *Ibid.*, p. 209.

published in 1883 as Volume 3 of Scribner's "The Navy in the Civil War" series, an excellent survey of the subject, shows no theoretical framework and no flash of brilliance. Written in a hurry, it was undertaken in part to take the pressure off Mahan's bank account balance.[10]

What should be noted here is that Mahan's *magnum opus* was written at a time when many persons in numerous branches of intellectual inquiry were seeking scientific explanations of human behavior. The British historian Henry Thomas Buckle was laying down the universal principles of the scientific explanation of history and convinced Luce of the operative rules of progress. Charles Darwin, who wrote the other major profoundly influential book of the late nineteenth century, *Origin of Species*, was seeking a more general theory of mutation and evolution. This was an era of extraordinary historical theorizing, as Clark Reynolds has stated in putting Mahan in context.[11] Important theories were being expounded concerning historical development and philosophical understanding, by Burkhardt, Nietzsche, Seeley and Bury. It was an age for "the cohesion of history," to use Page Smith's explanation.[12] The "Social Darwinists," as they are called, played a very strong role in the shaping of American and British political thought. The belief that England and America were bound together by means of a racial identity, and with a date with destiny, was something that Mahan shared, as did Charles Beresford and Winston Churchill to cite two English examples. Seen in this light, Mahan's anglophilia may have been more widely agreeable to the reading public than more nationalistically minded and xenophobic critics may like to believe.

Besides this, there is the fact that Mahan believed that the United States Navy suffered from a decline in professionalism, and this coupled with dramatically changing international circumstances meant, that as far as he was concerned, the American navy was not prepared for a war at sea. He was appalled by the unseaworthyness, armament and limited cruising range under steam of his last command, the *Wachusett*. On the various duties of showing the Stars and Stripes in protection of national interests in the Gulf of Panama, Commander Mahan came to realize that United States, imperial obligations were enlarging and changing in scope. More coaling stations were needed here and elsewhere. Gradually he became an imperialist, and he shared this with his distinguished contemporary, Rear Admiral Robert W. Shufeldt, whose biography in the capable hands of Frederick C. Drake has demonstrated so markedly the fact that the seaborne empire of the United States was well

---

[10] *Ibid.*, p. 135.

[11] Clark G. Reynolds, "The Thalassocratic Determinism of Captain Mahan," in Reynolds and McAndrew, *1971 Seminar*, p. 77. This work is reproduced in Clark Reynolds, *History and the Sea; Essays on Maritime Strategies* (Columbia, S.C., 1989), ch. 3. Others included in Reynolds' list are Dilthey, Spengler, Henry Adams, F.J. Turner and Charles Beard.

[12] Page Smith, *The Historians and History* (New York, 1964), p. 56; quoted, *ibid.*

advanced before the Spanish American War,[13] a fact that any student of British naval and imperial affairs would long ago have descried. To Mahan's way of thinking, the United States Navy had to ready itself for meeting its national obligations, and that necessitated the building of a state-of-the-art, highly mobile, and well gunned and armored fleet. By the time *The Influence of Sea Power Upon History* appeared, the United States government was well on the way to the sort of professional changes and fleet construction that Mahan would have applauded, and his concepts were vital in providing the intellectual fabric that government leaders could accept and promote.

Digressing for the moment on the subject of history as science, it may be observed that Mahan was not the first to view naval history through the telescope of science. His English contemporary John Laughton was first off the mark in this line of inquiry. In fact, sixteen years before the appearance of Mahan's opus, Laughton, sometime professor of history at Kings College London, a lecturer at the naval college at Greenwich, and the founder of the Navy Records Society, had delivered a lecture to the learned Royal United Services Institute in Whitehall under the heading "The Scientific Study of Naval History."[14] That paper was published in the *Journal* of that institution, where some time later it was read by Mahan, who according to his own admission had not previously thought much about the discipline of history. Yet another English contemporary who sought scientific explanations of history was Sir John Seeley, Regius Professor of Modern History at Cambridge, who on the very eve of Mahan's completion of the manuscript of his book, then in the hands of his publisher, had printed the text of a talk he had given to a military club in Aldershot entitled "War and the British Empire," that appeared in the September 1889 issue of the RUSI *Journal.*[15] Mahan was not only put into a state of terror, thinking that he had been "scooped," as it were; he must have been gratified to think that he, too, was on the scent of a compelling, significant theme. Seeley's paper was "such an epitome of the scheme of my book," Mahan confided to Luce, that he sent it to Little, Brown, his publisher, fearing a rejection on the grounds of possible duplication.[16] Little, Brown evidently concluded that Mahan was on to a good thing and proceeded apace. Laughton and Seeley were ploughing the same furough; what makes them important to the current discussion is that they were two historians interested in strategic questions who took the long view of history. Unlike Mahan who was brought to history by strategic needs and

[13] Frederick C. Drake, *The Empire of the Seas: A Biography of Rear Admiral Robert Wilson Shufeldt, USN* (Honolulu, 1984).
[14] John K. Laughton, "The Scientific Study of Naval History," *Royal United Services Institute Journal,* 1874, pp. 1-18. Despite the title, Laughton was never a formulator of rules. For a discussion of this, see Donald M. Schurman, *The Education of a Navy: The Development of British Naval Strategic Thought, 1867-1914* (Chicago, 1965), pp. 85-89.
[15] John R. Seeley, "War and the British Empire," *Journal of the Royal United Services Institution,* September 1889, pp. 488-500.

professional opportunity, Seeley and Laughton came to strategy from the historical perspective. All the same, the three had in common the fact that they were seeking an ordered explanation of human progression.

This Victorian world that had given rise to the thinking of Laughton and Seeley was vitally concerned with the history of the ancient world. The Victorians were deeply influenced by the study of Greek and Roman history, and the great civilizations of the Mediterranean in times past placed a decided stamp on the architecture of the British Isles, on the great public buildings and private clubs, and on the character of education. In these circumstances it was no wonder that the British as rulers of the waves were entirely in sympathy with the aims and objectives of the *Pax Romana*, to which the architects of the *Pax Britannica* owed much. The fight against piracy on the seas, against the seaborne slave trade, and in support of legal commerce and economic expansion on and over the seas—these constituted the holy trinity of the British *pax*. Enforcing these obligations resulted in a growing degree of imperial duty.[17] In the free trade era, in which Mahan was writing, British policy aimed at peace for the purpose of profit. Throughout much of that century empire in and of itself was much despised by British policymakers themselves, who though much imbued with the idea that they should liquidate their empire, or otherwise diminish their obligations by withdrawing their garrisons or letting their colonists live in happier harmony with their neighbours, never actually adopted an anti-colonial mind, and never put in place a system of liquidating the red spots on the map of the world. Rather the reverse, for defending the ocean routes of the world for strategic advantage or trade protection required augmenting the number of bases overseas—Aden, the Falklands, and Esquimalt being but three added to the nineteenth century, though not always exclusively for naval or strategic purposes. This was an era of gunboat diplomacy, when the mere display of the White Ensign on some distant coastline where British interests were in need of succor was sufficient to make the point that Britannia ruled the waves, and could wave the rules if circumstances warranted.

Yet the imperial obligations of playing the role of amphibious policeman was not only confined to the British. The French and Americans were similarly involved, and Mahan knew this.

It was on his gunboat duties where he was learning that peace had to be won by force. He yearned for home, more specifically the society of New York, and of his family. He saw sea life as a mode of exile, and yet he was able to continue his endless politicking as well from the quarterdeck as from the hearth. Once he learned from Luce that he was to be assigned to the Naval War College, he took up the reading of history with a passion, and out of

---

[17] Barry M. Gough, "*Pax Britannica*: Peace, Force and World Power," *The Round Table*, April 1990, pp. 167-88.

necessity. He was in Lima, Peru, in November 1884, fetched up in the English Club, where he read the celebrated work of the Berlin historian and archaeologist Theodor Mommsen, *The History of Rome* (1854-56). In reading Roman history Mahan was struck by the non-recognition of sea power's vital influence upon Hannibal's career.[18] As he explained to a publisher some years later, "The incident is to myself interesting because I attribute any success not to any breadth or thoroughness of historical knowledge but a certain aptitude to seize upon salient features of an era—salient either by action or non-action, by presence or absence." Here is a frank and sober reminder; in Lima Mahan undertook what we would now call a "quick study" on historical fact and perhaps on interpretation.

He grasped the single insight that so revolutionized the study of naval history, and he held that that insight came from within. It was, as he put it, "the suggestion that control of the sea was an historical factor which had never been systematically appreciated and expanded. For me . . . the light dawned first on my inner consciousness; I owed it to no other man."[19] But Mommsen had pointed the way. His debt to Mommsen he acknowledges in several letters, and fleetingly in his Introductory, but is otherwise conspicuously missing from his book. Once back in New York, enroute to Newport, he attacked the holdings of the Astor Library and the New York Lyceum, working up his two sets of lectures. He worked first on his "Fleet Battle Tactics," and then on those that became his book *The Influence of Sea Power Upon History*. Probably the first was the easiest, and in any event a bread-and-butter proposition so to speak, necessary as it was to instruct students in this particular, specific branch of naval science. Harder it was to master the English, Dutch and French texts (the Spanish sources are absent) that were to form the basis for his *Influence*. He read, or re-read Jomini's *Critical and Military History of the Campaign of the Revolution from 1792 to 1801* (1820) and his *Summary of the Art of War* (1836). He read, too, La Peyrouse Bonfils' *History of the French Navy* and Henri Martin's *Popular History of France*. He read a number of other contemporary strategists. The footnotes of his masterpiece, as noted by diligent, even envious English critics, were all too sparing: they tell us all too little about the sources he used. Even so, we can note his obligation to the French tactician Morogues who a century and a quarter before Mahan on the enduring principles of naval war wrote: "Naval tactics are based upon conditions the chief causes of which, namely the arms, may change; which in turn causes necessarily a change in the construction of ships, in the manner of handling them, and so finally in the disposition and handling of fleets."[20]

---

[18] Mahan to Roy B. Marston, "Captain Mahan and Our Navy," *The Sphere*, 17 (June 11, 1905), p. 250. He put it this way in his autobiography: "It suddenly struck me, whether by some chance phrase of the author I do not know, how different things might have been should Hannibal have invaded Italy by sea." *From Sail to Steam* (New York 1907), p. 277.

[19] Seager, *Mahan*, p. 145.

[20] Mahan, *Influence*, Introductory.

Doubtless Mahan had all the details of the battle of Navarino at his fingertips, and those of the naval battles of the Crimea and Lissa as well. He was fully familiar with the naval actions of the Civil War, and he had read widely the works of Sir John Barrow, many of them biographies of Howe, Rodney, Jervis and Nelson. His reading in tactics provided the historical examples upon which his principles rested; in addition, his reading in tactics helped sharpen his perspectives in the writing of his own analysis of history. He knew that the object of navies was to bring a concentration of firepower to bear against the enemy in superior degree, and this concept, derived essentially from Jomini, he applied to his two sets of lectures.

Gradually his massive notes were beginning to take on the center of gravity that is so desperately needed in original research, where a real thesis, original and magisterial, is to be the outcome. At this juncture on 22 January 1886 he wrote to Luce,

> Now I believe myself to have a good working knowledge of most, of all the important, naval campaigns of the years 1660-1815, and the tactics of the various battles. Of course the question thrusts itself forward: *under all the changed conditions of naval warfare of what use is the knowledge of these bygone days?* Here I am frankly still a little at sea how to point my moral . . . For instance strategy, as distinguished from tactics, will have plenty of illustration; the advantages and disadvantages of the possession of sea power and its effects upon specific campaigns must always possess useful lessons. Ships will no longer tack nor wear; but they must turn round sometimes; and I fancy that some thought expended upon the difficulties and confusion that may be thrown into an enemy's line or other order by forcing them to a change of order in action will have some fruit in the consideration of naval tactics in action; and I believe that knowledge of the great battles between sailing fleets will help in the solution of the problem. There will too always remain the great naval lessons . . . of the preponderance gained by activity, promptness, watchfulness, care, foresight and attention to details . . . I think [these are] most true relatively to an army, land force. The admiral will not, nearly as far, make or mar as the general. By February 1st I expect to begin with Jomini, etc. and, having naval conditions constantly before my mind, I shall hope to detect analogies.[21]

His reading of past naval history with the general theory of war went hand in hand. To Luce he wrote again on 22 January 1886:

> With regard to my own course of lectures my ideas have not yet attained the precision which I would like to throw into any reply to you. In a general way they are these: I think to begin with a general consideration of the sea, its uses to mankind and to nations, the effect which the control of it or the reverse has [had] upon their peaceful development and upon their military strength. This will naturally lead to . . . a consideration of the sources of Sea Power, whether commercial or military, depending upon the position of the particular country - the character of its coast, its harbors, the character and pursuits of its people, its possession of military posts in various parts of the world, its colonies, etc. - its resources, in the length and breadth of the word. After such a general statement of the various elements of the problem, illustrated of course by specific examples - the path would be cleared for naval history. There are a good many phases of naval history.

---

[21] Quoted in Seager, *Mahan*, pp. 169-70. My italics.

I have been led, and I think upon the whole happily led, to take up that period succeeding the peace of Westphalia, 1648, when the nations of Europe began clearly to enter on and occupy their modern positions, struggling for existence and preponderance. I have carefully followed up this period both in respect of naval history and the general struggles of Europe; for it has seemed to me . . . that the attempt to violently separate the naval history from that context will be something like . . . Hamlet with all but the part of Hamlet left out. I have nearly finished, within a week's work, this general consideration down to 1783. . . . Whether I can accomplish anything more, in the matter of naval history of other epochs, this year, I cannot say . . . I am working to my full capacity - have to feel that that is less than it was. . . . I would like this letter, however, to be confidential - in case any of my thunder should turn out *real* thunder.[22]

Once completed, Mahan's *Influence of Sea Power Upon History, 1660-1783* constituted a deliberate attempt to define the principles of sea power in an age of technological transition. This work set forth three considerations on which maritime dominance could rest: instruments of war (including bases), seaborne commerce, and colonies. These three, what we might call the three inter-circling rings, gave Britain pre-eminence, argued Mahan. Not only did Britain possess weapons of war, including overseas bases and a controlling geographical position athwart the portals of the European continent, she also possessed the near monopoly of the carrying trades of the ocean and a host of colonies overseas from which to draw resources, material, supplies, food, and manpower. National prosperity, founded upon a program of mercantile regulation and support, also gave Britain her greatness. From this, Britain possessed a theory or rationale of naval strategy and defense. Without a profitable seaborne carrying trade, without colonies, and without trained seamen and ships, Britain was powerless. Thus, by extension of the argument, any nation aspiring to greatness must maintain the instruments of war, the means of its overseas trade, and the mechanisms of colonial influence.

The fallacies of Mahan's theoretical perspective are three in number. Firstly, Mahan believed that a concentration of battle units was essential for the nation-state, and that concentration, and that concentration only, could win a sea war. In itself, coastal defense was of minimal value. Moreover, cruiser warfare - that is, discursive naval action such as the raiding of enemy ports or the sinking of merchant ships far away from the likely main center of battle - did not really count for much. The big blow, the decisive battle - that was the key. Secondly, as regards the value of seaborne commerce, Mahan believed that the merchant marine formed a certain shield of defensive power, an auxiliary force behind which a people in time of difficulty could gather strength. The merchant marine as a reserve force may have utility in a sea war, but as a backbone of naval power it was readily understood by the British in the mercantilist age, though rejected in the nineteenth century by Nelson's successors with no real loss to British naval preeminence.

---

[22] *Ibid.*, pp. 174–75.

After all, navies are artificial creations of states. They do not grow from the ports or the fishing folk of great lakes and sea waters. As the third consideration, colonies, here Mahan was weakest. He assumed that Britain was great because of her colonies, colonies won at the expense of Spain, Holland and France. In fact, Britain was great because of the succus of her Acts of Trade and Navigation, a policy that coupled defense with opulence; a nation does not have to possess colonies to have naval power and greatness and can have instead many forms of informal control equally as valuable as formal possession. Mahan led European states into a trap. Not only did Mahan influence governments to build battleships and establish bases, but he induced them to annex territories overseas that would afford them new keys of control as the routes of oceanic commerce or warship passage.

However, on purely strategic considerations, Mahan deserves a more sustained investigation. He argued that the past demonstrated that sooner or later command at sea - that is, acquisition and control of the ocean's communications - could only be obtained by a great battle or a series of battles ending in a decisive and clearly established outcome. Naval strategy, Mahan wrote, was based on some immutable, fundamental truths derived from historical example. Only by scientific development and technological innovation, he reasoned, would the immutable strategic laws be modified though not fundamentally altered. In consequence, readers of his work and listeners to his lectures were led to believe that the great battle at sea was the principal thing and all others were ancillary thereunto. They were also convinced that cruiser warfare and technological innovation - torpedoes, mines, cruiser warfare, submarines, submarine communications - were all of secondary merit.

In many of these things Mahan was not alone, either in America or England. More and more we are beginning to realize that even the greatest of intellectual evangelists do not stand in isolation, and that many of the great achievements of thought are derivative. This does not detract from the genius of the person; rather it heightens their conceptualization of the matter before them. In the United States, Ensign David, Stephen Luce, and Robert Shufeldt shared Mahan's concept. In England, Admiral Philip Colomb, whose *Naval Warfare* was published almost concurrently with Mahan's 1890 book, endeavored to derive rules of naval warfare from the examples, and made an important contribution to the development of "blue water" naval thought. His work has come back into print after many years.[23] Laughton and Seeley, already mentioned, were bringing popular attention to the role of force in human affairs, and they were the precursors of vitally important concepts of naval strategy as given in the writings of Sir Julian Corbett, Sir Herbert

[23] See my Introduction to the new edition of Vice Admiral P.H. Colomb, *Naval Warfare: Its Ruling Principles and Practice Historically Treated* (Annapolis, 1990: new printing of the 3rd edition, 1899).

Richmond and the Thursfields, father and son.[24] In short, Mahan was part of a larger process. Just as he accelerated the naval armaments race so, too, did he give added fuel to the historical profession.

However, his greatest success lay in moving politicians to action. Mahan awakened political heads of various nations to the reality of naval warfare by great ships. He also, after nearly a century of gunboat influence, restored to pre-eminence the vitality and utility of the great fleet and the strategy and tactics of using the fleet to obtain command of the sea, by means of which a war could be won. He was misguided in believing that colonies were a necessary foundation of a great nation and fleet. Similarly he convinced many of the necessity of a merchant navy ancillary to a fighting navy. Lastly, he generated a "big ship" mentality and a belief in the necessity of a concentration of force which was strategically acceptable in one way, for such a force was necessary, but then in another, denied the principle of sea war which he had in fact described in his books: *viz.*, that in a sea war, discursive action will occur: the weaker power will employ cruiser warfare, or commerce raiding, against its more powerful adversary and will do so rather than risk engagement with the units of the enemy. And again, Mahan failed to appreciate fully the central role of convoys in a protracted war and the profound effect that submarines, torpedoes and mines would play in a future naval war. In any case, it does not affect his authority on matters as they were in his own era. In short, Mahan deserves to be evaluated in the context of the times in which he was writing which were those of profound technological change during which the principles of maritime strategy were changing.

It may also be observed that Mahan, though confessing an attraction to the economic realities of naval power, tended to ignore them almost completely. Even though environmental circumstances shaded the nature of his thinking he was not geopolitically oriented in a way that would give his concepts breadth and depth. He had not read much English history before embarking on his historical enterprise; otherwise he would have realized that the famous acts of navigation and trade were phased out in the early nineteenth century as part of the free trade movement. To contrast Mahan to Sir Halford Mackinder, as has so often been done, by Paul Kennedy and Chester Starr to cite a couple of recent examples,[25] is fair in the sense of contemporary strategic analysis. But maritime dominance vs. continental dominance has always seemed such a shallow discussion to me, for strategy is much more complicated than that, as history shows. I am all too uncomfortable with the

---

[24] Other notable historian-commentators were Cyprian Bridge and Reginald Custance.
[25] For instance, Paul Kennedy, "Mahan *versus* Mackinder, Two Interpretations of British Sea Power," in his *Strategy and Diplomacy, 1870-1945* (London, 1983), ch. 3. Chester Starr, *The Influence of Sea Power on Ancient History* (New York, 1989), pp. 83-84.

thallasocratic view of history or any other monocausal explanation of human progression.[26]

The study of Mahan's *Influence of Sea Power Upon History, 1660-1783* - and of the larger corpus of his writings - is of enduring value. This is so not because he was right, for he was not always so, and it is useful because he was sometimes wrong.[27] He is the touchstone. He enlarges our world. He is a prism through which we view the changing colors of a much larger spectrum than he could ever perceive from his limited vantage point in the late 1880s and after. He was aware of the need for highly educated, disciplined, and strategically-oriented naval officers. He was mindful, too, of the momentous changes that were occurring in naval technology, in weapons and propulsion especially. He was mindful, moreover, of the growing role that the United States was making playing in world affairs, and he became an imperialist. He was of course part of a much larger conversion of humanity in that personal change, for who was not among the informed individuals of the late nineteenth and early twentieth century an imperialist in one sort or another?

This brings us to a number of matters that need further exploration. Mahan was a publicist of naval matters, and the world had never seen one who was so effective in that realm. Not the first naval historian, he was the first to conceptualize the role of sea power in the human affairs of his time, rescuing from the forgotten historical record the relevant details of how victory at sea was arrived at and what benefits devolved to the victor at sea. It was in the popularization of these affairs that war became more certain, so Sir John Seeley attested, arguing as he did that as the public became more aware of the possibilities of arms so, too, did they more demand their use.[28]

Besides this theme for future examination is another. Nations in the era of Mahan's glory were concerned with their rise and fall, an enduring state of affairs, if the reception accorded Paul Kennedy's 1988 work is indicative. Mahan, it seems, wrote his book of essays for his students at the Naval War College, but he also had the wider world in mind when he added his Preface, his Introductory and his first chapter, that on the Elements of Sea Power. It was this popularization that was the key, as he himself knew. Those of us who toil in the archives have much to learn from Mahan in this regard. We have to broadcast our larger findings, and to reach out to a much larger audience than our students and our fellow scholars. The success accorded

---

[26] Great modern naval theorists employing historical examples can be counted on the fingers of one hand, in my opinion. They are Mahan, Colomb, Corbett, Wegener and Reynolds (on the latter, see sources given in n. 11 above).

[27] Gough, "Maritime Strategy," pp. 55-57.

[28] Seeley, *op. cit.* On the theme of popular politics and the use of naval force, see the discussions of "Navalism" in the British and international contexts in, respectively, Arthur J. Marder, *Anatomy of British Sea Power: A History of British Naval Policy in the Pre-Dreadnought Era, 1880-1905* (New York, 1940), and W.J. Langer, *The Diplomacy of Imperialism, 1890-1902* (2nd ed., New York, 1965), ch. 13. Incidentally, I do not subscribe to Seeley's argument that the availability of arms necessarily invites their use. The largest standing armies in history, 1945-1989, did not engage in war in Europe.

Mahan and Kennedy were naturally derivative of their abilities to see the larger issues of their subjects.[29] Not all scholars are able to do this, and few have the power to grow wings and take to the skies in a larger view of an enlarging world lying below them. But Mahan challenges us to do that, and for that reason alone, besides his many other contributions, we are in his debt.

---

[29] Paul Kennedy, *The Rise and Fall of the Great Powers: Economic Change and Military Conflict from 1500 to 2000* (London, 1988). See also his *The Rise and Fall of British Naval Mastery* (2nd ed., London, 1983).

It was as commander of the USS *Wachusett* stationed off the west coast of South America that Mahan received the call from Stephen B. Luce to join the faculty of the Naval War College in 1884. He accepted the invitation, but missed the first College course in the summer of 1885.

Chapter 3

Mahan, Tactics and Principles of Strategy

Captain Wayne P. Hughes, Jr., U.S. Navy (Ret.)

I hope you have noticed that my title is asymmetrical. We cannot discuss Alfred Thayer Mahan's tactical principles, because he neither sought nor found them. Some of what I have to say is along lines that this is regrettable. The title also serves as the apology of a speaker who is not an historian, here delivering a paper to the eminent historians of naval affairs. I do have three points I hope are worthy of your attention. They may even be jarring, so I will work up to them carefully.

After he became celebrated, Mahan felt free to express himself about tactics and naval combat, but he never regarded himself as a tactician nor believed that his expertise lay there. Still, Mahan's reputation must live with an analytical but artificial distinction between tactics and strategy that he helped foster. In rereading Colomb's *Naval Warfare* for the Naval Institute Press's new series, Classics of Sea Power, I was struck by the fact that in it there was a refreshing absence of differentiation between policy, strategy, operations, tactics, and technology. With Colomb all were a seamless blend. Mahan, who had well defined and distinguished strategy and tactics, could not help but be swept back into the world of tactics, and (remember that at the beginning of this century the characteristics of warships were regarded by all tacticians as their domain) the technology that was creating a tactical revolution.

Here is an example of Mahan's vulnerability. In June, 1906 at the height of his international reputation, he ventured to write an article for the Naval Institute *Proceedings* with lessons learned from the Battle of Tsushima, called "Reflections, Historical and Other, Suggested by the Battle of the Japanese Sea." These were wholly tactical with a heavy emphasis on the design of future warships. He concluded in favor of (1) armament and armor over speed (about which I will say more later), (2) a main battery of mixed calibers, and (3) numbers over size of capital ships. In the next issue of the *Proceedings* appeared a scathing rejoinder. It was a mere Lieutenant Commander taking on a Captain of great renown, but the Lieutenant Commander's name was William S. Sims, and he was then President Theodore Roosevelt's own Inspector of Target Practice. As his title, "The Inherent Tactical Qualities of the All-Big-Gun, One-Caliber Battleship of High Speed, Large Displacement and Gunpower," made clear he would, Sims attacked Mahan on all three points. Mahan had the misfortune of facing the Navy's *ex officio* gunnery expert, who was also an advocate of the "high mix" school of the day: when it came to battleships, nothing was too good for the Boys in Blue. Sims intended to destroy Mahan's case, which was along lines similar to Soviet Admiral Gorshkov's more recent expression, the best is enemy of good enough. HMS *Dreadnought* was then under construction amidst great debate, as were other all big gun prototypes for the navies of the United States and Japan. The advocates were not going to accept any contrary views even from a world-famous maritime strategist.

Sims' attack led from his strength. "Captain Mahan is greatly in error in saying that if we determine the number of shots fired by each caliber we may assume a 'probability of a proportionate number of hits.' [He] draws his conclusions from the 'volume of fire' of different calibers instead of the volume of hitting or 'rapidity of hitting,' which is the only true standard of efficiency." Sims goes on to exploit his authority as the Navy's gunnery expert to contend that at effective battle range the "danger space" (hitting area) of 12-inch gun will be almost twice that of a 6-inch gun, because of the lower trajectory of the larger projectile.[1]

Mahan had the misfortune of having written before many reports of the battle were in. Specifically, in the same June issue of the *Proceedings* appeared a detailed narrative of it by an American observer, Lieutenant R. D. White, which Sims drew from with devestating effect. Mahan, who had lost touch with current technology and who was in any case overreaching in his use of history to draw his lessons, did not have the facts to rebut Sims. Somewhere in the *Proceedings* I have seen a generous acquiescence to Sims by Mahan but at the moment cannot find it.

But Sims was disingenuous in places. To further undergird the point above, he wrote that Mahan "also assumed that the Japanese rapidity of 6-inch fire was about four times as great as that of the 12-inch fire, when as a matter of fact, it was probably not much more than twice as great . . . we know 12-inch guns can fire two shots a minute and that 6-inch controlled firing is at a rate of four shots per minute." In contrast, another giant of navy fire control, Bradley A. Fiske, had written only a year earlier, ". . . the energy of projectiles thrown by a big gun is about equal to the aggregate energies

---

[1] Lieutenant Commander William S. Sims, "The Inherent Tactical Qualities of All-Big-Gun, One-Caliber Battleships of High Speed, Large Displacement and Gunpower," U.S. Naval Institute *Proceedings*, (Sept. 1906), p. 1346.

of the projectiles thrown by smaller guns of equal aggregate weight, and the smaller guns can be fired more often. A 12-inch gun, for instance, weighs about as much as eight 6-inch guns [note the parallel choice of caliber for comparison with Sims] and a 12-inch projectile has about as much energy as eight 6-inch projectiles; but a 6-inch gun can fire projectiles about eight times as often, so that in a minute 6-inch guns can fire projectiles having eight times as much energy as an equal weight of 12-inch guns. *They also expend eight times as much ammunition* [the emphasis is Fiske's]."[2]

Now, Fiske was of course describing *schematically*—he was a brilliant mathematical modeler—but his expertise stands in stark contrast with Sims'. For one thing, it is dubious that a 12″ gun of the day could be fired twice a minute. Since Fiske was the technical expert who made possible the ambitions of Sims for centralized fire control and continuous aim fire, Sims either was or ought to have been aware of Fiske's position. The technical debate was crucial in the final decision to adopt the all big gun ship. Fiske himself soon was converted, doubtless influenced by his last, underlined, statement. But Mahan was not well enough informed tactically and technologically to deal with gunnery issues. We will see that his views were hardier vis-a-vis Sims when it came to the issue of speed.

When one compartmentalizes strategy and tactics he is led into a chicken or egg problem as regards which is paramount. This leads to the first point I have to make to a body who may regard strategy as both the more interesting and preeminent. It is a commonplace, true as far as it goes, that strategy must direct operations and choose the scenes of action, else battle becomes purposeless and a thing unto itself. It is also true that when the goal is the establishment of future force requirements to execute a desirable military strategy, a top down approach is always impeccable.

But pause a minute and listen to Clausewitz. I have quoted him at length elsewhere[3] lest someone suspect that I am using him out of the whole context of *On War*. "The latter [strategic planning] therefore, can never be considered *as something* independent," wrote Clausewitz, "it can only become valid when one has reason to be confident of tactical success . . . it is useful to emphasize that all strategic planning rests on tactical success alone, and that—whether the solution is arrived at in battle or not—this is in all cases the actual fundamental basis for the decision."[4] Tactics determine the efficacy of forces; it is the correlation of two forces that reveals what strategy is supportable; and it is a supportable military strategy that limits national aims and ambitions. Here is a little example.

---

2 Commander Bradley A. Fiske, "American Naval Policy," U.S. Naval Institute *Proceedings*, (Jan. 1905), pp. 24-25.
3 W.P. Hughes, Jr., *Fleet Tactics: Theory and Practice* (Annapolis: Naval Institute Press, 1986), p. 219; and Hughes, "Naval Tactics and Their Influence on Strategy," *Naval War College Review*, (Jan-Feb 1986), p. 2.
4 Carl von Clausewitz, *On War*, trans. by Howard and Paret,

Both Mahan and Corbett knew the British Admiralty regarded one three-decker as the equal of two two-deckers. With that calculus the Admiralty strove to blockade with firepower equivalent to that of the French ships in a port. Equivalence sufficed because of the Royal Navy's ship-for-ship superiority in combat potential.[5] Tactical success without strategy is a meandering river; strategy without tactical success is a dream that becomes a nightmare.

As for the second element of the strategist's proposition, that strategy guides future requirements, it is equally true that the capabilities of existing forces must govern present planning, in peace and war. This seems a point to make at present, when a drawdown of national capability is under way. It is too easy to slash away at the United States Navy without realigning the strategy and deployments that the lower force levels can support.

I do not want to make much of this except to note that strategy and tactics are bound together. Mahan was continually drawn into questions of tactics and technology, and in practice no one thought much of the distinction. One of my favorite quotations from Mahan is "The true speed of war is not headlong precipitancy, but the unremitting energy which wastes no time." The intimacy of the bond between strategy and tactics leaps at us when we see the rest of the passage. "The great end of a war fleet . . . is not to chase, nor to fly, but to control the seas . . . Not speed, but power of offensive action, is the dominant factor in war . . . . Force does not exist for mobility, but mobility for force. It is of no use to get there first unless, when the enemy in turn arrives, you also have the most men, the greater force."[6] The speed of the battle fleet was much at issue then. Sims and many other officers notwithstanding, there was a serious tradeoff between armament, armor, and speed. Mahan was forcefully for guns and armor, and ultimately that was what the U. S. Navy chose: the slowest battle line of the world's navies, right up to World War II, and a disposition away from the fast battleships and battlecruisers of Great Britain and Japan. This is not the place to develop who was right and why, but if asked I will argue that Mahan and the U. S. Navy have the better case.

The second and far more serious mischief Mahan created is traceable directly to the book we are honoring here today. Everyone will recognize the passage: "from time to time the structure of tactics has to be wholly torn down, but the foundations of strategy so far remain, as though laid upon a rock." Mahan believed the principles of strategy were easier to discern than those of tactics, because the latter "using as its instruments the weapons made

[5] Presumably the Admiralty's basis was purely empirical. The argument can also be made mathematically. A three-decker will be computed to be worth slightly more than two two-deckers. For its firepower a frigate did not count at all; but frigates were vital as scouts. See Hughes, *Fleet Tactics*, p. 43.
[6] A.T. Mahan, *Lessons of the War With Spain*, (Boston, 1899), pp. 82-84.

by man, shares in the change and progress of the race."[7] As far as I know (I am tentative only because Mahan was so prolific) the only tactical principle he enunciated was in support of concentration. Concentration of force, either strategic or tactical, may or may not be the most important principle of war but either way it the most obvious and least exciting, the sort of thing that school boys find out the first time two gang up on one. It can also be expressed in a corruption of an old aphorism, which may be rephrased for military purposes, "Never pick on somebody your own size." I thought of this when I heard some people say we were behaving like bullies when we went into Grenada a few years back.

Whatever you may think of Mahan's circumscribed view of the robustness only of strategic principles, I can tell you that I was a faithful disciple until 1982, and there were generations of naval officers who subscribed to it. But Mahan was wrong. As I have written elsewhere:

> Tactics change, but that does not preclude the search for tactical principles, and if there are strategic principles, that does not mean that strategies do not change. Strategies as well as tactics are influenced by "weapons made by man." We may forgive Mahan for not foreseeing how weapons of the future would influence strategy, but there was evidence of change even as he wrote. All the strategic effects of blockading were modified by the transition from sail to steam. Sailing ships that stayed on station for months were being replaced by ships that lacked endurance and depended on coaling stations, the competition for which itself had a profound influence on strategy.[8]

The very term for an intercontinental ballistic missile, "a strategic weapon," and the Polaris and Trident strategic submarines which carry them, belie that strategic concepts are etched in stone. Mahan said the scales fell from his eyes when he speculated as to the consequences if Hannibal had attacked Rome from the sea. We need only to give Hannibal the means to deliver one Hiroshima-sized atomic bomb to see all the strategy of Carthage and Rome overturned.

A case study of Mahan's faith in his tenet of strategic constancy is the way he deals with blockade. In it is all the false dichotomy of strategy and tactics. In 1895 Mahan was asked by the Royal United Services Institute whether new technology had so altered tactics that a blockade would no longer be effective. It was clear that steam, steel, mines, and torpedoes were affecting the way ships would fight. Mahan clung to his faith in historical precedent and strategic principles and reaffirmed the blockade as a tool of strategy. Later, after assimilating the lessons of the Russo-Japanese and Spanish-American Wars,

---

[7] A.T. Mahan, *The Influence of Sea Power Upon History, 1660-1783*, (Boston, 1890), p. 88. Mahan did not reject tactical principles entirely, but he said they were transitory. See his Introduction, pages 7-11. One gets the impression that Mahan was making a concession to the large body of opinion among naval officers that believed technology affected naval warfare to the extent that study of history had no value; that he was willing to concede on tactics to make his case for strategy.

[8] Hughes, *Fleet Tactics*, pp. 140-141.

he repeated his stand in *Naval Strategy*.[9] Mahan referred to two cases. The first was offensive and interdiction of trade; it was illustrated by the North's blockade of the South in the Civil War. The second was defensive; it was illustrated by the Royal Navy's containment of French and Spanish fleets in the Napoleonic wars. Mahan largely set aside the former and concentrated on the latter, and it is here as well as anywhere that we observe Mahan's focus on command of the sea and fleet actions: the object of blockade was a fleet. With that perspective, he showed that distant blockade was nothing new. Nelson, he pointed out, was happy to stand back because he *wanted* his enemy to come out.

Mahan stressed that a blockade was not an absolute thing. With a defensive blockade the question was "Does this impose upon him such risks as to give a considerable chance of either stopping or crippling him? And not only is this chance in your favor to be considered at the immediate locality, but also as to its deterrent effect upon the enemy."[10] Mahan had a fine sense of scouting. Success is, he said, "a matter of look-out, instituted and sustained, and of inter-communications between vessels of the blockading force . . . this is the crux of the matter." Mahan concluded, ". . . the old question and the new alike is not 'Can the enemy be prevented from coming out' but 'If he does, can touch with him be gained and preserved?' Steam, in my opinion, has simply widened the question, not changed its nature. I believe that provision can be made which will give [blockade] a high probability of success, but I do not believe in certainties in war."[11]

The above is Mahan at his best. We find him adapting his vast reservoir of history and extending it to the present. Indeed, he had flawlessly anticipated the Royal Navy's constraint of the German High Seas fleet from out of Scapa Flow in World War I. We must concede to him that execution is a matter of tactical detail, whether with sail or steam. But the events of World War I also illustrate the limits of Mahan's perspective, and it was very much a shortcoming of strategic vision. Blockade of the High Seas Fleet was necessary but not sufficient. There was to be the rest of the German Navy, what Sir Julian Corbett called "the cruisers" now manifested as U-boats, that would threaten the lifeblood of Britain. Offensive, not defensive, blockade would eventually hold the key to the war at sea. We may even say that the blockaders became themselves the blockaded, once we adopt Mahan's own relaxation of the distance from the ports at which it is imposed.

Though Corbett expressed his role of cruisers with clarity in how they played for and against the interdiction of trade, he himself did not foresee the efficacy of the U-boat and the scale of merchant shipping protection it

[9] A.T. Mahan, *Naval Strategy*, (Boston, 1911), p. 2 ff.
[10] A.T. Mahan, "Blockade in Relation to Naval Strategy," U.S. Naval Institute *Proceedings*, (Nov. 1895), p. 862.
[11] *Op. cit.*, p. 866

would require. Nevertheless, Corbett best established the business of navies. He did so very much against the preponderant attitude of naval officers who embraced Mahan and his words, "the proper main objective of the navy is the enemy's navy."[12] Whatever provisos Mahan applied, his followers too eagerly accepted the big battle as the be-all of a fleet. Corbett starts with "The object of naval warfare must always be directly or indirectly either to secure the command of the sea or to prevent the enemy from securing it."[13] Already Corbett confronts Mahan who disparaged *guerre de course*, or any other form of sea denial as a proper role of a fleet. But Corbett's opening salvo is merely warming his Mahan-oriented readers to the subject. He reaches the kernel of his position four pages later with: "Command of the sea, therefore, means nothing but the control of maritime communications, whether for commercial or military purposes." Lest the reader fail to appreciate the sharp distinction between operations on land and sea, as at least one recent writer has done,[14] Corbett follows immediately with "The object of naval warfare is the control of communications, and not, as in land warfare, the conquest of territory. The difference is fundamental . . . [Communications ashore] refers to the communications of the army alone, and not to the wider communications which are part of the life of the nation."[15] By passing too quickly from the denial of movement of goods and services (offensive blockade) to the containment of the enemy fleet (defensive blockade), Mahan helped make his case that the strategy of blockade was as robust as ever, but begged the equally important question of blockade of communications and commerce.

And more: here are the delicious words of a great Russian leader, Admiral S. O. Makarov, on the subject:

> Up to the present this [command of the sea] has been understood to mean that the fleet commanding the sea openly plies upon it and the beaten antagonist does not dare to leave his ports. Would this be so today? Instructions bearing on the subject counsel the victor to avoid night attack from the torpedo-boats of his antagonist . . . If the matter were represented to a stranger he would be astonished. He would probably ask whether he properly understood that a victorious fleet should protect itself from the remnant of a vanquished enemy.[16]

---

[12] Mahan, *Naval Strategy*, p. 199.

[13] Julian S. Corbett, *Some Principles of Maritime Strategy*, (Annapolis, 1988), p. 91. Originally published London, 1911.

[14] Thomas R. Pollack, "The Historical Elements of Mahanian Doctrine," in Chapter 5, *Military Strategy: Theory and Application*, (Carlisle, Pa.: Army War College). Reprinted from *Naval War College Review*, (July–August 1982), pp. 44–49. Pollack attempts to show that "Mahan's genius may not be in his theories of naval strategy but rather in his insight into the similarities between the principles of warfare ashore [adapted from Jomini] and that at sea. He redefined, rather than initiated, strategy in terms of naval warfare." The burden of proof on Pollack is a heavy one, especially for five pages. Soviet military science is the most stubborn in clinging to universal laws of war.

[15] Corbett, p. 94.

[16] Vice Admiral S.O. Makarov, *Discussions of Questions in Naval Tactics*, trans. Lt. J.B. Bernadou, (Washington: ONI, 1898), p. 26. Reprinted in Classics of Sea Power Series, (Annapolis: Naval Institute Press, 1990), with an introduction by Robert Bathurst.

Mahan was blind to the extent that mines, torpedo boats, submarines, in due course land based aircraft, and in the present day land launched missiles, would add new constraints on the ability of a modern fleet to assert sea control against an inferior enemy who wished to dispute it. We have two modern examples of nations whose navies were utterly swept from the seas that still created the greatest difficulties for their opponents. One is Japan off Okinawa in 1945, whose Kamikazes destroyed ships of the U. S. Navy at the rate of one a day. The other is Argentina, which though isolated from the Falklands by sea, posed a frightening threat of air, missile, and even submarine attack (with an effective order of battle of one submarine!) throughout the war.

Now I turn to a matter of taste or preference and offer it for your consideration. Thus far I have asserted that there probably are as many durable principles of tactics as of strategy. But I prefer to refer to *constants* instead of principles, so that I may draw a distinction between them and *trends*, the things wrought by "the change and progress of the race." I am glad to have an opportunity to express this point of view to historians, however tenuous is the connection with Alfred Thayer Mahan and his penchant for principles, because there is much in it for you to ponder.

Before getting to the underappreciated significance of trends, it is well first to distinguish their companion, constants, from principles. A principle is a guide to action. A constant is an assertion about unchanging truth. I must be careful here. The dictionary definitions of principle are sufficiently encompassing that the user may make about what he wishes of them: rule, code, law, doctrine, assumption, guide, fundamental, comprehensive, a law or fact of nature, are all terms one finds associated with a principle. I think Mahan himself thought of principles as what may more precisely be termed constants. The six great properties or factors he labeled elements of sea power in Chapter One of *The Influence of Sea Power* are descriptive, not prescriptive. One thing is clear: whether the element is a principle or a constant, whether it is prescriptive or descriptive, Mahan's interest is with immutability.

Now, the usual principles of war have no such ambiguity. They are prescriptive: they say "do this to succeed." In contrast a constant says "this is so, now apply the knowledge wisely." A principle from the Army's FM 100-5 is "Direct every military operation towards a clearly defined, decisive, and attainable objective."[17] A tactical constant, taken from *Fleet Tactics: Theory and Practice* and chosen because it is attention-getting and perhaps a bit of a surprise, reads thus: "The pace at which control of a fleet can be exercised has not changed much through history. Planning, doctrine, and training as well as combat experience help reduce the possibility of a commander and his fleet being overwhelmed by the tempo of battle."[18]

---

[17] Department of the Army, *Operations FM 100-5*, (May 1986), p. 173.
[18] Hughes, *Fleet Tactics*, p. 199.

There was a time—I think it is passing now—when students of military history sought principles of war. We know Mahan *espoused* them, as did his inspiration, Jomini. Corbett for navies and Fuller for armies were supreme in organizing and structuring the lessons of history, with as much emphasis on constants as principles. Historians *qua* historians eschew the function of structuring, but few resist drawing lessons, and in fact we all know that an historian without premises will describe chaos, a *pot pouri*, or something worse.

Since that is so, I want to urge on you my perspective. It is that the establishment of trends is every bit as worth your while as the establishment of principles or constants. At the tactical level, which is the one I have studied, trends are probably more important. Obviously Mahan thought so: "tactics . . . shares in the change and progress of the race." But then he ignored the implication, which was to study the changes. Here are some examples of trends, taken from *Fleet Tactics*:[19]

- Speed in the platform has become subordinate to speed of weapon delivery. Speed of delivery is governed by scouting and command and control processes as well as the sheer velocity of weapons.

- Scouting systems have had to race to keep up with weapon range . . . The effects of air, surface, and subsurface scouts are increasingly interrelated because more new weapons cross the boundaries of the three domains.

- Tactical commanders have had to devote more of their attention to scouting and less to delivery of firepower.

The importance of establishing trends has to do with helping military men avoid fighting the last war. Their dilemma is this. The experience of the older generation, who are the leaders directing preparations for the next one, is going to be dated. Presently the dating is since 1945, if we are talking about a war which threatens the national jugular vein. Subsequent experience with the likes of Korea, Vietnam, Grenada, Lebanon, and the Persian Gulf, colors their thinking. Insofar as the *combat* in those small wars and big crises is concerned, the difference between them and World War II is the difference between penny ante poker and a game for table stakes. Consider this. Admiral Kelso's standard of performance for his strike aircraft in the attacks against Libya was a no-loss criterion: not one prisoner to be marched around Tripoli. In Korea and Vietnam losses of 2% per sortie were thought to be serious, 5% unsustainable. But in the five big force-on-force carrier duels in the Pacific during World War II (Coral Sea, Midway, Eastern Solomons, Santa Cruz Islands, and Philippine Sea) the average aircraft losses *per battle* were 40% for the Americans and 60% for the Japanese. We don't think that way anymore, but if there are enough chips in the pot we will see such losses again.

---

[19] *Op. Cit.*, pp. 196 and 198.

Happily because of the turmoil taking place in the Soviet Union, little wars are now more likely to continue, to be at the core of relevance. Nevertheless, we are as dated in understanding the nature of real naval combat as were the tacticians who struggled to sort out the effects of new technology—steam, rifled guns, armor and steel hulls, fire control and electricity—during the period from the end of the Napoleonic Wars to the beginning of World War I, a period when there were very few data from combat at sea. To most military men the study of history is restricted to study of the last war. If they have time or inclination to probe history at all, it is usually as much for inspiration as for analysis. Small wonder that we officers are accused of preparing to fight the last war.

If historians are going to help military men to fight in the future, then a search for constants, or principles as Mahan called them, is not enough: it is necessary, but not sufficient. To see from the last war to the next, however dimly, the key is the study of *trends*. In order to see trends, one must grasp the sweep of history, and know what transpired looking back from the last war to the next-to-last, to the next-to-next-to-last. Few men in uniform have time to do that and fewer still believe the rewards are worth the time. But it is very important. When I wrote *Fleet Tactics* and saw that trends were at the heart of understanding, I had to incorporate some naval history; there was no evading it. Not very much—only four chapters—but nothing I did was more valuable in gaining perspective about naval tactics in the future. I commend to you that trends are the neglected aspect of military history. I have never seen a military historian make that point, unless it is Trevor Dupuy.

There is one last self-appointed duty to perform, and it is a pleasant one. Seeing now that the study of history at the tactical level is for more than entertainment, we should all want to know how good were Alfred Thayer Mahan's descriptions of naval tactics. Does Mahan help us discern the trends when we look for them? Well, not directly, because at the tactical level that was never his object, but the raw material is all there. Now, I cannot critique his research nor would you want me to try. But I can talk about his insight into naval operations, battle tactics, and naval leadership, and it is a great strength. I think he is at his best in his first book, *The Gulf and Inland Waters*, before he became captivated by strategic constants. Strange to say, clear narrative that holds the reader's attention, engagement after engagement, is not easy to write. For example, the renowned Civil War historian, Bruce Catton, fails. With him your mind wanders. Catton has so many personal anecdotes of the everyday man—it is like the fetish of modern journalism and its face-to-face interviews—that one loses sight of the battle. I know Catton wants to put us there, to smell the gunpowder and fear, but that won't do for my stated purpose. A military historian who does both is John Keegan, not in *The Price of Admiralty* because the sea is not Keegan's realm, but in *The*

Face of Battle. Keegan has the knack of giving you the forest and the trees: both the tactical and the personal truth of combat.

Put Catton aside and compare Mahan with two of the best writers on the Civil War, Douglas Southall Freeman in, say, *Lee's Lieutenants*, and U. S. Grant in his *Memoirs*. About that war I think Mahan had their clarity and insight. To another standard, he also had great influence among the naval historians of later secondary works, like Carrol S. Alden, Allan F. Westcott, William O. Stevens, Fletcher Pratt and E. B. Potter. Mahan is lucid, objective and searching. Those who are only acquainted with his ponderous and pedantic style of later years should be treated to a sample:

> It was the daily custom for one of the gunboats to tow down a mortar-boat and place it just above Craighead's, remaining near by during the twenty-four hours as guard. The mortar threw its shells across the point into Pillow, and as the fire was harassing to the enemy, the River Defence Fleet, which was now ready for action, determined to make a dash at her. Between 4 and 5 A. M. on the morning of the 10th of May [1862], the day after [Flag Officer] Foote's departure, the *Cincinnati* placed *Mortar No. 16*, Acting-Master Gregory, in the usual position, and then made fast herself to a great drift-pile on the same side, with her head up stream; both ends of her lines being kept on board, to be easily slipped if necessary. The mortar opened fire at five. At six the eight Confederate rams left their moorings behind the fort and steamed up, the black smoke from their tall smoke-stacks being seen by the fleet above as they moved rapidly up river. At 6.30 they came in sight of the vessels at Plum Point. As soon as they were seen by the *Cincinnati* she slipped her lines, steamed out into the river, and then rounded to with her head down stream, presenting her bow-guns, and opening at once upon the enemy. The latter approached gallantly but irregularly, the lack of the habit of acting in concert making itself felt, while the fire of the *Cincinnati* momentarily checked and, to a certain extent, scattered them. The leading vessel, the *General Bragg*, was much in advance of her consorts. She advanced swiftly along the Arkansas shore, passing close by the mortar-boat and above the *Cincinnati*; then rounding to she approached the latter at full speed on the starboard quarter, striking a powerful blow in this weak part of the gunboat. The two vessels fell alongside, the *Cincinnati* firing her broadside as they came together; then the ram swinging clear made down stream, and, although the Confederate commander claims that her tiller ropes alone were out of order, she took no further part in the fray.[20]

Sounds like the brown water naval war in Viet Nam? Not quite, but closer than any alternative you could have named in 1964. Had any of our young naval officers read it as part of their shift in thinking from blue water operations to the land-locked guerrilla war they were about to face? Not very likely.

Mahan moves here and carries you along. His description of the intricate Vicksburg campaign is vivid and (as far as I can tell) the source of many later writers' descriptions. It wants only an appreciation of how much Grant's operations depended on the Mississippi—how essential the rivers were to everything he accomplished then and before, at Fort Henry and Fort

20 A.T. Mahan, *The Gulf and Inland Waters*, (New York, 1883), pp. 43-44.

Donelson, and how Grant could be light on his feet because the river craft were his logistics tail; and even that may be inferred. I had no idea until I read *The Gulf and Inland Waters* how swiftly the Union Navy swept on up or down a river, wreaking havoc, once a strong point was breeched. A mere three days after Fort Henry fell three Union gunboats had penetrated up the Tennessee River all the way to Florence, in northern Alabama, destroying bridges, riverboats, and goods along the shore. It would be thus again and again. The mobility and logistic might of ships at sea is well known; they were just as remarkable on rivers.

It seems to me the book that Mahan published seven years later and that we honor today, *The Influence of Sea Power Upon History*, is also cogent, and must have been harder to research. I do not say that Mahan was a better, nor more accurate narrator of naval operations than Colomb or Corbett. And they all were flowery and lacked crispness, for this was the Victorian age in all its ostentation. His words are like a many-gabled mansion, bright with frills, "All tarted up," as grandmother would say. But I like Mahan's elegance in small doses, and he knows seamanship, and he paints a picture full of truth, heroic enough but also critical.

I have said four things, and in doing so offered three pieces of advice. The first is to correct the impression that strategy is somehow "more important." Strategy is constrained by the capacity to win battles; means must determine ends, just as much as ends govern means. My advice is to think of them as two sides of a single coin, and if you are enthralled by strategy, remember to look at the backside of the coin.

The second is that there are principles, or constants, and there are trends, or changes in warfare. This is true of both strategy and tactics, and for that matter of policy, logistics, and campaigning (or operational art). My advice is to forget forever the common interpretation of Mahan that he preached merely a search for principles of strategy. The uses and lessons of history run much deeper, and are in any case as likely to have tactical as strategic consequences.

The third is a theorem deriving from the first two. It is that discerning trends is the special way history can help keep from fighting the last war. Since tactics are as important in the long run as strategy, and since both constants and trends of tactics will be manifest to an acute observer, it is important to look for both. My advice to military historians is to help military men, who seldom know history well enough establish the tactical and technological trends of the past in order to see the implications for the future.

Fourth and last, I am pleased to help honor Alfred Thayer Mahan. He still enriches our knowledge of naval battles and maritime operations, their ships, their tactics, and their leaders. That is as important now as is the great influence he once had in the citadels of power in bygone days.

Chapter 4

Mahan: Then and Now

Rear Admiral J. C. Wylie, U.S. Navy (Ret.)

If we are going to look at Mahan's work, his perception and analysis of sea power as it was a hundred years ago, and then look at what it means today, the first thing to be done is to get a sensing of what that world was like in 1890. There are several aspects of that world which are pertinent to our discussion.

And here I should half-apologize, because I am going to list half a dozen of these without the grace of transitional connecting paragraphs. I am going to jump from one to the next rather abruptly to save time.

For one, in 1890 it was a Euro-centered and Euro-dominated world. The United States, while intellectually and socially a part of this, was on the outer edges of it. The world of western Europe was the center and all else somehow a lesser fringe.

For a second, within the United States, its interests were largely, though not entirely, focussed on the enormous westward continental expansion that followed the Civil War. Along the Atlantic coast there was a surge of maritime commercialism, the European trade and the China trade. And I doubt that many people noticed that this American maritime commerce was largely a free ride on the coat-tails of the Pax Britannica, the near dominant British world-wide naval hegemony. This was not altruism. Britain, for instance, found it convenient to support the American Monroe Doctrine because that held in check French or Spanish exploitation of the Americas.

A third aspect of relevance toward the end of the nineteenth century was that the first phase of the Industrial Revolution was approaching maturity. The development of steam power was beginning to transform industry and provide electricity as well as both land and maritime propulsion. A new phase of industry, commerce and finance had taken root.

Fourth, the great intellectual achievements of the nineteenth century were found in the concepts of Charles Darwin. These not only signalled the basis of an alternate to the Biblical origins of the world, but, more importantly, they opened up a more perceptive study of all the natural and social sciences.

At this time, the physical sciences were still plugging along quietly in the wake of Sir Isaac Newton.

Fifth, the second great age of exploration had penetrated the inner lands of the continents of Asia, Africa, and the Amazon basin of South America.

Sixth, this land exploration led to an enthusiastic adoption and expansion of colonialism by the leading nations of Europe. Britain (which already had a good head start), France, to a lesser extent Germany and Belgium, all assembled their own overseas empires in Africa, the Middle East, Southeast Asia, and the Pacific Islands.

And for one more illustrative aspect of the nineteenth century I am going to describe a state of mind. In the early years of the nineteenth century immediately following the generation of Napoleonic Wars, there had arisen an interest in how to manage great land wars on the continent of Europe. Clausewitz, Jomini, and several lesser men had put their minds to this problem. But by the end of this century, with the whole world opened up, with colonialism as the wave of the future, and with the great unifying force of the world's interconnecting maritime communication system open to everyone's view, the time was ripe for a new concept.

Mahan supplied it: the concept that sea power and national greatness were closely intertwined. Mahan's great contribution was that he found and illustrated a quite impressive correlation between national power and maritime power.

Toward the close of the nineteenth century, with the industrial revolution an established fact, with the expansion of world trade, with the opening of the non-European continents (particularly Africa), and with the general acceptance of the concept of colonialism, the whole world had become a single coherent strategic entity. It was an exciting prospect. This was when Mahan's timely new expositions on the role of maritime power in history came along to fill a need in the ordering of men's patterns of thought.

The basic vision, the insight, that successfully brought the whole subject into public view and attention, belongs to Mahan. He had the insight; the time was ripe; and because of this, to Mahan belongs the credit.

And what was the effect of this at the time?

Others, in this gathering, are discussing what it meant in Germany and Japan. So I limit my short comment to the effect of Mahan in the United States and Britain.

In our own country, two men were early and strongly influenced. Theodore Roosevelt, from the time he was Police Commissioner in New York through his Presidency, continuously received stimulus from Mahan in their sometimes heated exchanges. The elder Henry Cabot Lodge, first in the House of Representatives and then in the Senate, was for three decades a disciple and supporter of Mahan. These two men, between them, set much of the course of United States policy during the productive years of their lives.

Rear Admiral J.C. Wylie delivering the after dinner talk, "Mahan: Then and Now" at the Viking Hotel during the Mahan Centennial Conference.

In Britain, Mahan was perhaps even more widely recognized than in the United States through the governing establishment. But at the same time these British, in some strange way, accepted Mahan's work as well-earned praise for past performance without realizing that a good track record does not itself win races. While recognizing that Mahan (and shortly after him Corbett, with his perhaps more graceful prose) had perceived a principal basis of the growth and prosperity of the British Empire, they did not identify and alter the radical reversal of traditional policy built into General Wilson's army staff agreements with the French before the 1914 war. The British committed their troops to the heart of the coming bloody, continental, Clausewitzian, war.

The great maritime tradition that had been built starting with the Armada and through the Napoleonic wars had been an oral tradition. During the century of peace of the Pax Britannica this oral tradition had lapsed. The thoughts of such men as Anson and the two great Pitts and Barham ashore, and the intuitive deep understandings of that magnificent string of fighting sailors at sea, Drake and Hawke and Collingwood and Saumarez and the incomparable Nelson, those understandings had been forgotten. Their memories were bright and the pub signs were beyond counting, but their lore had been lost. These men must all have squirmed in their graves at this essentially irrevocable reversal of the British maritime policy of centuries.

Sadly leaving behind us this incredibly costly aberration in British thinking before World War I, let us look at Mahan's sea power in the middle years of this twentieth century. Let us look at sea power as it was exploited by the United States, not as a policy but as a basis for policy from which to project and exploit other elements of national strength: military, political, economic, financial, and psychological power.

Militarily, and in this case, in close cooperation with Britain, sea power made it possible for the western allies to furnish the arms that kept the Soviets fighting and to re-enter and win the European portion of World War II after they had literally been driven off the continent, much as sea power had eventually made it possible to dethrone Napoleon a century and a half earlier.

Politically, sea power made possible the critical political victories in Italy and Greece and Turkey in the first few years after World War II even though the United States was five thousand miles away and Soviet Communism was just across the borders. Through sea power, we were closer, for all practical purposes, to the scenes of action than was the Soviet Union.

Economically, sea power is even more subtle. A major corporation, some decades ago, built a large mill on the Delaware River to process Venezuelan ore. Behind that action was the firm and probably unrecognized assumption of sea power and maritime access to that overseas ore. That same general assumption prevails today, and, I might add, a lot of other nations are taking a welcome free ride on it.

Financially, the Marshall Plan and the hundreds of grants, loans, and economic and military subsidies all around the world during and after World War II all had maritime power as their firm but tacit policy basis.

And psychologically, recall that the missiles and warheads were pulled out of Cuba thirty years ago.

In looking carefully, if all too briefly, at this mid-century exploitation of several of our national strengths overseas, there emerges a rather special aspect of sea power that is all too little recognized.

I have just noted five of the areas in which, during the mid-century years, sea power played a critical role, in which sea power was quietly, at times almost sub-liminally, involved in the extensions overseas of five areas of national strength. I mentioned the military, the political, the economic, the financial, and the psychological strengths of the United States.

Of these five, and there are others, only one was involved with actual combat with war itself. Only the projection of military power normally involves fighting.

Now let us put this special aspect of sea power in perspective. Armies and navies and air forces, while they are all basically instruments of governmental force, are not the same kind of force. They can not be equated by mere acknowledgement of the technical differences that they operate in the different media of land, sea, and air. The difference is both profound and much more subtle than is generally recognized. And here I hasten to interject that "different" does not mean "better" or "worse". I am neither criticizing nor denigrating armies and air forces. When I say that navies are different I mean just that and only that. "Different" means different characteristics and capabilities and limitations as direct or indirect instruments of national strength.

Of these three major kinds of armed forces, only navies can have benign as well as an effective general employment in times of relative peace because, basically, they operate in the relatively neutral medium of the world's ocean waterways. Navies do not normally intrude upon the sovereignties of other and sometimes sensitive nations around the world.

It is difficult to imagine a friendly visit of a regiment of troops, or even a platoon, to an Asian or an African nation. It is difficult to imagine a flight of bombers or fighter planes paying friendly and even casual calls on other nations around the world.

I am not talking about the special cases, which by the way, may soon diminish, in which U.S, troops and aircraft are stationed, by agreement and often by request, in places such as NATO nations or Japan or Panama. I am talking about the normal and almost casual intermittent maritime presence of naval forces wherever in the world that presence may be mutually appropriate.

This almost indefinable quality of "maritime presence"—subtle, benign, ubiquitous presence—actual or potential presence—is the great asset of sea power in times of peace and even in times of one or another variety of tension. This quality of actual or even potential maritime presence anywhere around the world is the quality that sets navies apart from armies and air forces in employments short of war. This world-wide and benign ubiquity, this subtle evidence of naval and thus of national strength is what makes viable the other and normally benign elements of national strength when extended overseas.

A navy has a peacetime as well as a wartime employable usefulness to the nation. This usefulness is that it provides a basis for other national policies which call for the extension overseas of other and benign elements of our national strength.

I think we can trace much of this mid-century exploitation of sea power as evolving from the initial brilliant and perceptive vision of Mahan. He has exercised enormous influence on the thoughts and actions of other men.

But the post-World War II situation is now essentially behind us.

On the other side of this bi-polar world, the presumption of economic historical determinism, the intellectually insupportable and practically unworkable rationale of the communism of Marx and Lenin, and the subsequent total arrogance of Stalin, are all collapsing. They are foundering under the irresistible weight today of a two-hundred-year-old idea first, as far as I know, set forth in the Declaration of Independence—those five imperishable words ". . . . the consent of the governed . . . ."

As for the free world today, a hundred years after Mahan published his most famous book, let us look back at the half dozen representative (but not random) illustrations of the nature of the world in 1890 with which this discussion opened.

1. It is no longer a world centered on western Europe. Nothing less than a world-wide comprehension will now serve the strategist.

2. The United States has moved from an isolated internal focus on itself to a world wide accommodation of its interests, its responsibilities, and its involvements.

3. The Industrial Revolution has been overtaken by several aspects of the techno-electronic revolution. Perhaps the two most important are the world wide communication revolution (which has enormous social and political as well as military implications), and the vast and still embryonic information-management revolution (which has equally vast implications in almost every walk of life).

4. Darwin and the revolution in the natural and social sciences has been balanced by Einstein's ideas and the resulting incredible explosion of knowledge in the physical sciences, an explosion of knowledge which ranges from the macro-physics of Stephen Hawking through the many aspects of

space travel and nuclear energy and even floppy discs to the mini-micro-bio-physics of the men who are altering genes.

5.   The earth is now known. The frontiers of exploration are now in the laboratories and in space and the universe.

6.   Colonialism, that driving force of the late nineteenth century, has now become a universal sin. The concept of colonialism, the assumed natural dominance of one people over another, has been rejected in favor of the new assumption of equality of all mankind. This new assumption of equality may, in turn, be the spark behind that most powerful political force in the world today: the concept of nationalism. Thus colonialism has been succeeded by nationalism.

In sum, every characteristic that I cited to describe the nature of the world of Mahan in 1890 has been upset or superceded. Not one of those six 1890 aspects is valid today.

Without taking the time to explain, even had I the skills and the knowledge, I posit that the world at this closing of the twentieth century is in the midst of the greatest combined moral and social and intellectual and political and techno-scientific revolution in all history, greater even than that of the combined Renaissance and Reformation which brought the European world out of the Dark and Middle Ages in the fifteenth and sixteenth centuries. These are turbulent and exciting times. Practically nothing is the same as it was a hundred years ago.

So, where does that leave Mahan's notions of sea power today?

Since the moral, intellectual, social, political, economic, military, financial, and technological criteria of the late nineteenth century have all changed so radically as to be largely irrelevant, it seems to me that the only way to appraise sea power then and now is to start with abstractions. Only in the abstract can we connect 1890 and 1990.

In non-specific terms, what is strategy? What is its aim? How might the aim be achieved? And what is the role of sea power in that process as it applies to the United States?

And here again, as I did earlier, I should half-apologize. For the sake of the brevity appropriate to after-dinner comment, I am going to offer a series of theorems without the proof that should accompany them. I am willing to argue them later and privately if any of you should find that appropriate.

The first theorem is that a strategy is a plan for doing something to achieve some known aim.

The second is that the aim of strategy is some measure of control over some other individual or group. This control may be direct or indirect. It may be partial or complete. It may be subtle or obvious. It may be immediate or slow. But, whatever may be its characteristics, it should be sufficient to induce or to force its target into some status or position or action or attitude acceptable to the strategist.

Then a third theorem is that this desired measure of control may be achieved by manipulation of a pressure point, a center of gravity, a leverage which will control or sway or influence the situation to the advantage of the strategist.

Please note that everything I have said about strategy in these last few paragraphs pertains to any strategy or plan for doing something. It applies to a domestic political strategy. It applies to a strategy for peddling breakfast food. It applies to the strategy of a game of poker. It is not limited to national or military strategy.

So we now narrow the focus of the discussion to national strategy, which includes, but by no means is limited to, military strategy.

National strategy comes into play when one nation wants another to adopt a course acceptable to the strategist. This requires some degree of control, of influence, some kind of leverage, social, political, economic, military, or whatever may be appropriate.

The connecting link between Mahan's sea power of 1890, the sea power of the middle years of this century, and sea power today at the end of the twentieth century is the inherent capability, then and now, in peace or in war, to extend some kind of control or influence, some kind of leverage, from the sea on to the land.

As it did in Mahan's writings a century ago, as it did for the United States in the middle years of this century, one nearly universal vehicle for this leverage, for extension of control today may be found in sea power, not as a policy in itself, but as a *basis* for policy. Exploitation of this capability to extend some measure of control, more often a degree of influence, from the world's great interconnecting maritime communication system, from the sea on to the land, is the great asset of sea power then and today. A kind and degree of control that may be direct or subtle, immediate or slow, forceful or benign, the variations are infinite—some measure of control or influence extended from the sea on to the land.

This worldwide and normally quite benign ubiquity is the great and unique asset of sea power.

As long as the United States chooses to continue as the leader of the free world, sea power is the absolutely vital *basis* for United States policy, in peace or war, anywhere in the world. Without sea power as its tacit, but no less real, *basis*, no policy in the world wide interests of the United States would be fully viable. Such a policy would have little substance.

No matter what course is adopted by Nato, if it continues to involve any United States military support, the United States policy must have sea power as its basis. Whether it means maintenance of troops in Europe, or it means promised help from this side of the ocean in event of need, the U.S. policy *vis a vis* Nato must be predicated on sea power as its basis.

Argue as you will our policy toward Israel, as long as it contains some kind of assurance, implicit or tacit, of Israel's survival as a nation, it must be based on sea power.

Argue as you may be inclined the continued access of the free world to Middle-Eastern petroleum, any United States policy short of willingness to surrender that access must be based on sea power.

Argue the commercial or political access of the United States toward the Pacific rim, from Korea to Singapore to Melbourne, any way you choose, any U.S. policy short of surrender of that access must be based on sea power.

Argue the United States financial or economic support of any portion of the third world, in Asia or Africa or Latin America, any positive policy must be based on sea power.

As long as the United States chooses to continue as leader of the free world, then the moral, social, political, economic, military, technological, financial and psychological influences of the United States—and I have deliberately been repeating these many elements of our national strength almost to the point of boredom in order to drive home the fact that all of them together make up the composite whole of our national strength—as long as the United States chooses to continue as leader of the free World, then this composite amalgam of all elements of national policies must have sea power as their basis for policy. That policy basis is the capacity inherent in sea power to extend some measure of control, more often a control better described as influence, from the sea on to the land.

Sea power in this decade ahead is not a policy to be debated in isolation or by itself. Sea power, this essentially benign, ubiquitous, worldwide maritime presence, is the indispensable *basis* for the many different aspects of our American foreign policies all around the world.

Mahan's sea power has grown to be immeasurably more important, not only to the United States but to the entire free world, immeasurably more important in 1990 than it was in 1890.

Captain William McCarty Little, well-known in College history as the "Attendant Spirit" and "Father of Naval War Gaming," was associated with the school for nearly 30 years, from its founding in 1884 until his death in 1915, almost half of the time as a volunteer. McCarty Little drew some of the diagrams used in Mahan's first sea power book, and with the founding father, Rear Admiral Stephen B. Luce, urged the reticent Mahan along the path toward publication of his naval history lectures in 1890.

It was through the efforts of James Soley, lecturer on international law at the fledgling Naval War College, 1885-1888, that a publisher was found for Mahan's first sea power books. Soley introduced Mahan to one of the principals in Little, Brown & Company of Boston.

Portrait of William McCarty Little (left) by Tony Sarro and James Soley (right) by George K. Sottung. Naval War College Museum.

PART II: THE INFLUENCE

岸艦隊ヲ指揮セルストアー、でームス、ソーでレッニ下ス特

「本覆ノ當ニ防ムヘキ所タリ刻下ノ計ヲ為ス者ハ近

國ヲ利セスル者アラバ之ヲ閣下ニ陳述シテ取捨ヲ煩ハサ

書ヲ遣リテ見ニ「今國家危急ノ秋ニ当リ高モ美

ノ意ナキカ如シ是ヲ以テシャールヴィスハ胖ノ海軍大臣ニ

二出シ「明カニシテ愛蘭ノ如キハ仏後々之ヲ襲ハント欲スル

其右水常ノ窮極境ニ陥リタルヲ仏政府之ヲ救フノ挙

扮シ拿破崙ハ強ニ之ヲ失ハサランコヲ欲セリ今ヤ仏人ノ西代

弦ニ地中海ニ在リテハ仏人ハ既ニ援及モルヲ三ニ脚ノ地ヲ

A page from the manuscript of an unpublished translation by Lieutenant Commander S. Maki, IJN, made about 1920 of chapter 11, "The Atlantic 1796—The Brest Blockade—The French Expedition against Ireland" from *The Influence of Sea Power Upon the French Revolution and Empire.* (Naval Historical Collection, Naval War College, Ms. Item 88)

Chapter 5

Japan and Mahan

Roger Dingman

In May 1890, just a few months short of his fiftieth birthday, Alfred Thayer Mahan published the book that gained him a place in history. *The Influence of Sea Power upon History* made its author famous, gave him a second career, and cast its shadow over the subsequent development of navies around the world. During the century since its publication the influence of *The Influence* has been analyzed and debated extensively by historians, strategists, and naval officers in the English-speaking world. In 1990, we know a great deal about Mahan's impact upon the navies of the two nations that most concerned him: America and Britain.

Once one leaves the Anglo-American world, however, it becomes quite clear that we know relatively little about the impact of Mahan and his writings. If one looks far to the west, across the Pacific to Japan, the question of Mahan and his influence upon naval developments becomes quite murky. That assertion might seem, on its face to be counter-factual. Mahan himself said that more of his works were translated in his lifetime into Japanese than into any other language. His *Influence* came out in a new Japanese translation only eight years ago, and a Japanese language biography of the admiral has just been published. Moreover, scholars here and in Japan have not been loath to suggest that Mahan cast a long shadow across the Pacific. Fifteen years ago two leading American and Japanese historians agreed that Mahan's ghost propelled the United States and Imperial Japanese navies toward Pearl Harbor. Only two years ago, the most recent analyst of Mahan's influence in the United States asserted that the Imperial Japanese Navy (IJN) had pursued Mahan's strategic doctrine "in purer form" than any other navy.[1]

---

[1] Alfred Thayer Mahan, *From Sail to Steam Recollections of Naval Life* (New York: Harper & Brothers, 1907; New York: Da Capo Press ed., 1968), p. 3; John B. Hattendorf and Lynn C. Hattendorf, comp., *A Bibliography of the Workds of Alfred Thayer Mahan*, (Newport, R.I.: Naval War College Press, 1986), entry A2 translation n; Tanimitsu Tarō, *Koko nō teitoku Arufuredo T. Mahan* (The Noble Admiral Alfred T. Mahan) (Tokyo: Hakuto shōbo, 1990); Asada Sadao, "The Japanese Navy and the United States" in *Pearl Harbor as History*, Dorothy Borg and Shumpei Okamoto, eds., (New York: Columbia University Press, 1973), p. 259; Richard W. Turk, *The Ambiguous Relationship: Theodore Roosevelt and Alfred Thayer Mahan* (Westport, Connecticut: Greenwood Press, 1987), p. 4.

I am skeptical of these claims about Mahan's influence across the Pacific for several reasons. They are, in the first place, little more than claims, unsupported by any substantial body of evidence. They reflect the superannuated notion that the flow of "influence" across the Pacific was unidirectional – from America to Japan. They also presume a singularity about Mahan and his ideas that contradicts the multi-faceted character of both.

Consequently, this essay addresses one central question: To what extent did Alfred Thayer Mahan have an impact upon Japan and its navy? In developing an answer to that puzzle, I will focus on but three of the many roles Mahan played with regard to Japan. I will leave in the background his role as arms-merchant in the late 1860's, when he witnessed the delivery to Japan of the former Conferederate ram *Stonewall*, the vessel that sealed the fate of the shogun's navy and, paradoxically, helped make its defeated commander one of the founding fathers of the IJN.[2] In that role, the young lieutenant was but an executor of the policies of others, not a force for change in his own right. Nor will what follows analyze Mahan's role as historian, for I have found no evidence of his significance in that capacity on the far side of the Pacific. Instead, I will focus on Mahan as publicist for building a great navy, as naval thinker, and as the "god of seapower."

Mahan played the first two of those roles, simultaneously, in life; the third was his only in death. In this essay I will, for the sake of analytical clarity, consider each separately. But in fact three fundamental questions about Mahan's "career" in Japan recur in a way that provides unity to the inquiry that follows. First, how did the Japanese come to know Mahan and his writings? Secondly, how did they make use of him? And, finally, what impact, if any, did he have upon Japan's naval policies?

II. NAVAL PUBLICIST

Mahan first became a potential force for change in Japan in his role as publicist for the building of a great navy. Kaneko Kentarō brought Mahan, figuratively, to Japan. Kaneko, who as a youth had gone to America with the Iwakura Mission, stayed on to obtain a Harvard bachelor's degree, and eventually accompanied his patron, Prince Itō, on a tour of Europe, was one of the great importers of foreign ideas into mid-Meiji Japan. In 1890 he went to the United States and there, in all probability, was introduced to *The Influence of Sea Power Upon History* by his old Cambridge friend and its most famous reviewer, Theodore Roosevelt. Kaneko read the book with great enthusiasm. It brought to him something akin to a burst of Zen enlightenment. When he reached home, he translated its first, seminal chapter and gave a

---

[2] Mahan, *From Sail to Steam*, pp. 251-252; Mark R. Peattie, *Nan'yō: The Rise and Fall of the Japanese in Micronesia 1885-1945* (Honolulu: University of Hawaii Press, 1988), p. 5.

copy to the Navy Minister. In that form, Mahan appeared in *The New Seapower Magazine*, the journal of the Imperial Japanese Naval Officers Association.[3]

Kaneko brought Mahan's *Influence* to a navy and a nation that were poised, for yet another time in the barely two decades since the restoration of the Meiji emperor in 1868, on the brink of great changes. The Japanese navy in 1890 was a healthy adolescent. Pieced together as a distinct force from domain (han) and shogunal naval forces eighteen years earlier, it consisted of nearly sixty ships of which twenty-five could be considered modern warships. Some 1400 officers and ten thousand men manned this force, which was divided into two elements, one to defend the Japan Sea coast, the other to operate in the Pacific. The largest of its ships were modern cruisers, all of which were built abroad. The ships of this navy, British and American built, were like their captains, men trained in Holland, England, and Germany, an amalgam of foreign influences.[4]

This navy's leaders were strong and shrewd - but politically weak. Its two key figures were losers. Admiral Enomoto Takeaki had commanded the shogunal navy defeated by the Emperor Meiji's champions. Admiral Saigō Tsugumichi was in charge of the ill-fated 1874 expedition to Taiwan. Although both men were "rehabilitated" and rose to prominence as effective bureaucrats in what was essentially a government of oligarchs, the navy remained distinctly subordinate in power and influence to the army. It had no independent general staff until 1893. Indeed, barely ten days after Mahan's *Influence* was published, Marshal Yamagata Aritomo, the prime minister, removed both Enomoto and Saigō from the cabinet.[5]

Much like an adolescent, this navy had many visions of what it wanted to be. It wanted, in the first instance, to be big. In 1888, Navy Minister Saigō argued that a fleet appropriate for "an independent nation" should consist of eight armored battleships, eight armored cruisers, sixteen first class and thirty two cruisers, and a variety of smaller craft which, in total, added up to a force more than twice the size of the existing navy. The Imperial Navy also wanted to be on the cutting edge of technological innovation; two of its steel cruisers were considered the most powerful in the world. The Japanese Navy also wanted to be very much like the Royal Navy. Indeed, by putting

[3] Takenobu Y., ed., *The Japan Year Book, 1915* (Tokyo: Japan Year Book Office, 1915), p. 157; Obata Kyugorō, *An Interpretation of the Life of Viscount Shibusawa* (Tokyo: Tokyo Printing Company, 1937), p. 79; Hamada Kenji, *Prince Itō* (Tokyo: Sanseido, 1936), p. 84; Turk, p. 16; Kaneko Kentarō, Preface to Alfred T. Mahan, *Taiheiyō kaiken ron* [On the Command of the Pacific] (Tokyo: Senryu do, 1899; Asada Sadao, ed. and transl., *Arufredo T. Mahan*, Volume 8 of *Amerika kotenbunkō* [Classics in American Culture] (Tokyo: Kenkyū sha, 1977), p. 8.
[4] Peter G. Cornwall, "The Meiji Navy," Unpublished University of Michigan Ph.D. dissertation, 1970, pp. 42-52; Toyama Saburō, *Nihon kaigun shi* [A History of the Japanese Navy] (Tokyo: Kyoiku sha, 1980), p. 20; Stephen Howarth, *The Fighting Ships of the Rising Sun: The Drama of the Imperial Japanese Navy 1895-1945* (New York: Atheneum, 1983), pp. 15-16; Peattie, *Nan'yō*, pp. 5-6.
[5] Nagasaka Kaneo, *Denki dai nippon shi dai jusan kān kaigun hen* [A Biographical History of Great Japan: Volume 13: The Navy] (Tokyo: Shinzan kaku, 1936), pp. 33-41, 61-82; Tokinotani Masaru, ed., *Nihon kindai shi jiten* [Historical Dictionary of Modern Japan] (Tokyo: Tōyō'keizai shimpo sha, 1958), p. 682.

its naval academy in the hands of a team of British instructors who required mastery of English as well as naval science, the IJN made clear its desire to be an international gentleman of sorts.[6]

Precisely what that meant was not, as yet, very clear. Navy leaders spoke of protecting the nation's long coastline and counted the number of European and Chinese warships in East Asian waters. But they had no designated hypothetical enemy. The army wanted a force to guarantee safe transport of troops to the Asian mainland; and diplomats needed ships to back up their efforts to "open" Korea. Admiral Enomoto, however, thought the navy's future lay to the south and east, rather than to the west. He used it to annex Iwo Jima and to stimulate interest in further expansion, by trade and emigration, into the Pacific islands. In 1890, he sent the IJN training ship *Tsukuba* to Hawaii for the first time.[7]

This navy served a state that was experiencing dramatic political, economic, and diplomatic changes. Japan was about to embark upon an experiment in constitutional government. In 1890 the nation held its first elections. They ushered in a decade and more of debate and tension between advocates of party government in the Diet (legislature) and the men of 1868 who had become the oligarchs of Japanese politics. These political changes meant that the navy had to appeal for funds for its growth to a broader, less homogeneous audience.[8]

Economically, that would not in and of itself be difficult. During the years that Mahan was drafting his *Influence*, Japan's GNP grew by twenty-five percent; in the decade between the book's publication and the end the century, it would more than double. In 1890, the navy's budget was barely one percent - precisely the magic number for today's Japanese defense budget - of the GNP. Moreover, the Meiji oligarchs, and their parliamentary adversaries, were prudent managers of the national accounts. Government expenditures exceeded revenues in only six of the 23 years since the Restoration. In eight of the ten years remaining in the nineteenth century, they preserved that relationship.[9]

But much like the navy, the Meiji state as yet seemed unsure of the role it should play on the stage of world politics. Its foreign policy aimed, in the short term, at ending the vestiges of extraterritoriality imposed upon the shogun's Japan by Commodore Perry and his successors. But in the longer term, Japan appeared to be torn between contradictory visions of what its

---

[6] Kaigun shō hen, *Yāmamoto to Gombei to kaigun* [Yamamoto Gombei and the Navy] (Tokyo: Hara shobo, 1966), pp. 302-304; Howarth, p. 15; Cornwall, pp. 85-86.

[7] Kaigun sho, *Yāmamoto*, p. 306; Peattie, p. 7.

[8] Kenneth B. Pyle, *The New Generation in Meiji Japan: Problems of Cultural Identity, 1889-1895* (Stanford, California: Stanford University Press, 1969), pp. 144-145.

[9] B.R. Mitchell, ed., *International Historical Statistics: Africa and Asia* (New York: New York University Press, 1982), pp. 660, 728; Kaigun shō, *Yamamoto*, p. 401; Boei cho Bōei kenshūjo senshi shitsu, ed., *Senshi sōsho kaigun gunsenbi (1) Shōwa jūroku nen jūichigatsu made* [War History Series: Naval Armaments 1: To November 1941] (Tokyo: Asagumo shimbun sha, 1969), Appendix chart 5.

foreign policy should be after that - torn, indeed, between conflicting views of what economic growth and political modernity would mean internationally. Most Japanese thought their empire must expand; the question was - in which direction and by what means? Indeed, competing visions of continental and maritime empires - the latter a concept central to Mahan's *Influence* - had already appeared. The critical, and by 1890 as yet unresolved issue, before the Japanese people was how naval force might be used to assure the security, prosperity, and continued growth of their empire.[10]

Kaneko thought Mahan offered guidance in answering that question. As he later recalled, the *Influence* provided "an opportunity to resolve questions that had haunted me for a very long time." He acted, joining the Oriental Association and the Japanese Colonial Society, groups made up of politicians, officials, businessmen, and educators who advocated the creation, in one way or another, of a stronger, more independent, and greater Japan. But at least in the short term, Mahan had little impact on the navy, the cabinet, or the Diet. In September 1890 the admirals sought funds for a scaled down version of their fleet construction program, emphasizing the need for two 9500 ton battleships to match growing British and Chinese naval strength. But the cabinet pleaded poverty, and the government sought only two cruisers and a destroyer from the Diet. A year later, the admirals tried but failed to commit the government to a long-term building program centered on four battleships and four armored cruisers. Not until 1893, after demonstrating its power by completely rejecting the cabinet's previous year's proposed budget, did the Diet approve construction of two battleships, one cruiser, and one gunboat.[11]

The Sino-Japanese War of 1894-1895, however, changed the politics of naval expansion. The IJN's success in the Battle of the Yalu fueled a wave of patriotism. The foreign ministry's compromises in the Treaty of Shimonoseki and intervention by France, Russia, and Germany that deprived Japan of control of the Liaotung Peninsula triggered an explosion of xenophobic nationalism. The war, moreover, left Japan a proto-maritime empire, with new territory in Taiwan, new influence in Korea, and the prospect of commercial, if not territorial, growth in Manchuria. From 1895 onwards, far more citizens and legislators were ready to believe that a strong navy was essential to the prosperity and survival of the Japanese Empire.[12]

---

[10] Akira Iriye, *Pacific Estrangement: Japanese and American Expansion, 1897-1911* (Cambridge, Massachusetts: Harvard University Press, 1972), pp. 21-25. For a different view, which argues that Imperial Japan was from first to last a continental empire, see Clark G. Reynolds, "The Continental Strategy of Imperial Japan," *U.S. Naval Institute Proceedings*, 109 (August 1983), pp. 65-67.
[11] Kaneko, Preface to *Taiheiyo kaikēn ron*; Alfred T. Mahan, *Kaijō kenroyoku shi ron* (Tokyo: Toho kyokai, 1896), volume 2, appendix: An explanation of the establishment of the Oriental Association; Iriye, p. 40; Kaigun sho, *Yamamoto*, pp. 309-337, Bōei cho, *Kaigun gunsenbi 1* appendix: chart 5; Iwanami shoten henshu bu, *Kindai nihon sōgō nempyō* (General Historical Tables for Moder Japan) (Tokyo: Iwanami shoten, 1968), p. 134.
[12] Iriye, pp. 45-47; Pyle, pp. 179-183.

The IJN did grow dramatically over the next eight years. In 1894, it went to war against China with an assemblage of ships numerically inferior to those of its prospective foe. In 1904, Japan challenged Russia with a force whose nucleus was six battleships and six armored cruisers, enough to give it a slight numerical and definite technological edge over the enemy's Far Eastern fleet. In the interim, the Japanese navy experienced what a Philadelphia shipbuilder called a "cyclone" of growth: its manpower nearly doubled; the number of its ships rose almost 30%; and its total tonnage jumped nearly 300%. The average naval budget in this pre-Russo-Japanese War period was almost seven times the annual average of those during the five pre-Sino-Japanese War years. And yet the cost of the navy as a percentage of GNP was more than halved.[13]

The Imperial Navy, however, had to fight for funds in a political environment that was much more turbulent than that of the pre-Sino-Japanese War years. Its leadership was stable; only five men served as Navy Minister between the publication of Mahan's *Influence* in 1890 and his death nearly twenty-five years later. Cabinets were more fractious and fragile, as oligarchs and proto-party leaders jockeyed for power. Only three cabinets governed between 1890 and 1896; but twice as many were formed during the next eight years. Departing from usual practice during that same period, the government in four different years, spent more than it took in. The year of the first deficit, it should be noted, was 1897 - when the naval budget climbed to an all-time high, topping out at more than seven times what it had been in 1890.[14]

In this kind of environment, those who championed building a great navy appear to have found Mahan useful. He was, of course, by the latter half of the 1890's a much more authoritative figure than he had been earlier. The captain was the Paul Kennedy of the decade - a man who metamorphosed from struggling scholar into celebrity of world-wide renown. Queen Victoria and Kaiser Wilhelm had received Mahan and reportedly had read his book. The *Influence*, by the end of the decade had run through fifteen English language editions and been translated into five languages. By 1897, the flow of articles from his pen was thought important enough to warrant re-publication as *The Interest of America in Sea Power*. Mahan had also been called back from retirement to become a *persona* in Washington, the city which by decade's end was the capital of the newest, great power.[15]

[13] Toyama Saburō, *Nihon kaigun shi* [A History of the Japanese Navy] (Tokyo: Kyoiku sha, 1980), pp. 68, 91; Cornwall, pp. 45-46, 52; Kaigun shō, *Tamamoto Gombei*, p. 401, Boei cho, *Kaigun gunsenbi 1*, appendix, chart 5; B.R. Mitchell, comp., *International Historical Statistics, Africa and Asia* (New York: New York University Press, 1982), pp. 660, 728.

[14] Tokinotani, *Kindai nihon shi jiten*, pp. 682-685; Mitchell, *Africa and Asia*, p. 660; Boei cho, *Kaigun gunsenbi 1*, appendix, chart 5.

[15] Robert Seager, II, *Alfred Thayer Mahan: The Man and His Letters* (Annapolis: Naval Institute Press, 1977), pp. 279-281, 348-352, 354-429, *passim*; William E. Livezey, *Mahan on Sea Power* (Norman: University of Oklahoma Press, 1947), p. 67; Hattendorf and Hattendorf, entries A2 a-q, A2 Trans a-j.

In July 1895 Navy Minister Saigō Tsugumichi used Mahan-like language in proposing to the cabinet a 75-ship building program, of which four were to be first class battleships. He argued that the naval engagements of the war against China proved the need for an effective fleet rather than simply a particular number of ships. His rationale for building such a fleet was, in essence, Mahan's: the Imperial Navy must be able "to exercise control of the sea". The power of that phrase was not great enough to overcome the cabinet's caution and Saigō's colleagues divided the building program into two phases, the first of which was presented to the Diet in December 1895, the second a year later. That prudence paid off, for early in 1896 the legislators, for the first time, committed themselves to fund a long-term, naval expansion program.[16]

With that preliminary victory in hand, first the Naval Officers' Association, and then the Oriental Association, swung into action with a complete translation of Mahan's *Influence*. In April 1897, he learned that the latter group had presented copies of the book to the emperor and crown prince. The book was used as a text at the military and naval academies, and, the Imperial Household Agency had purchased three hundred copies for placement in every middle and high school in the empire. Two years later, having returned to America to claim an honorary degree from Harvard, now Baron Kaneko was, once again, taken with Mahan's latest work. He brought it home for translation and distribution by the Oriental Association under an intriguing new title. What was originally *The Interest of America in Sea Power* became *On the Command of the Pacific*.[17]

That metamorphosis suggests an important point about how and why Japanese naval expansionists found Mahan as naval publicist useful to their cause. He was not so much the propounder of specific doctrines as the reaffirming expositor of ideas they already held. His *Influence* was not received as gospel, but it was taken out of mothballs and refurbished, so to speak, when it became politically prudent to do so. Baron Kaneko and those like him did not see Mahan as a provider of insight into immediate American policies; if they had, more than a year would not have passed between the publication and translation of his *America's Interest*.

Instead, Baron Kaneko and Japanese naval expansionists found in Mahan more general arguments about the relationship between seapower and national power that suited their immediate political needs. *The Influence of Sea Power Upon History* was presented to naval officers and ordinary citizens as a reminder that principles - ideas that could be discerned from the study of the past - and not technology or politics alone must guide the development

16 Kaigun shō, *Yamamoto Gombei*, pp. 246-260; *Kindai nihon sōgō nempyō*, p. 146.
17 Secretary, Oriental Association to Mahan, April 1, 1897, box 3, Alfred T. Mahan papers, Library of Congress; Kaneko Kentarō, *Yubei kenbun roku* [A Record of Things Heard and Seen on a Journey to America] (Tokyo: Hachiya shoten, 1900), Preface; Kaneko preface to *Taiheiyō kaiken ron*.

of the fleet. Mahan provided, as Kaneko argued in his introduction to *America's Interest*, evidence that the Americans had awakened from their illusions about the need for a great navy. If Japan was to retain its position as the greatest maritime nation in the Pacific, its citizens ought to read what Mahan had written. For after all, one of his essays in this second volume to appear in Japanese culminated in the classic defense for spending money on arms in peacetime: "A navy . . . is, in the last analysis, a political factor of the utmost importance in international affairs, one more often deterrent than irritant."[18]

To suggest that Mahan the publicist of seapower was a tool of potentially great value to Japanese naval expansionists, however, is not to argue that he was in any sense the *cause* of their actions. The IJN's leaders had outlined the kind of fleet they wanted before his *Influence* appeared. While they invoked his ideas and used his language in the wake of the Sino-Japanese War to justify fleet expansion, it was that conflict - and the prospect of another with Imperial Russia - that provided the much more basic sense of threat that yielded affirmative Diet votes for a bigger navy. At no point between 1890 and the outbreak of the Russo-Japanese War was Mahan presented as spokesman or prophet for a hypothetical foe. He was, at most, a tool which others employed to serve their own ends.

III. NAVAL THINKER

If Mahan as publicist was a useful tool for Japanese naval expansionists, can it also be said that Mahan as naval thinker became a force for intellectual change within the IJN?

The short answers to that question are quite clear. In 1974, Stephen Pelz suggested that Mahan was a kind of intellectual godfather to the IJN's two most important early twentieth century strategists, Akiyama Saneyuki and Satō Tetsutarō. Through them the concept of a battleship fleet whose purpose was to seize and maintain command of the sea became the dominant element in Japanese naval thought. Mahan also provided the enemies of arms control, Admiral Katō Kanji foremost among them, with the intellectual ammunition which they used in the early 1930's to destroy the Washington naval arms limitation system. Thus Mahan slew the lesser dragon of *guerre de course* in the Pacific precisely as he slaughtered its more terrible French counterpart in the Atlantic and Mediterranean.[19]

Such short answers leave open at least three questions which must be resolved if Mahan's impact upon the IJN is to be properly understood. First,

---

[18] Ibid; Suikosha introduction to Mahan, *Kaijō kenryoku shi ron*, pp. 1-12; Alfred T. Mahan, *The Interest of America in Seapower, Present and Future* (Boston: Little, Brown, & Co., 1898 ed.), pp. 171-172.
[19] Stephen Pelz, *Race to Pearl Harbor* (Cambridge: Harvard University Press, 1974), pp. 25-27; Kenneth Hagan, "The Influence of Mahan on History: A Centennial Reassessment," speech at American Military Institute luncheon, Organization of American Historians Annual Meeting, Washington, D.C., March 23, 1990.

what was the character of that navy's leadership at the beginning of the century, and how intellectually open was it? Second, how did Japanese naval leaders come to know Mahan and to what extent did they consider him useful to their purposes? And thirdly, what impact, if any, from Mahan is to be found in their writings on strategy?

The leadership of the IJN during Mahan's lifetime was small, savvy, and most certainly open to ideas from outside Japan. There were, until the turn of the century, only three admirals, five navy ministers, and, in the seven years of its existence, two chiefs of the naval staff. Some of these men enjoyed what seem by today's standards remarkably long tenure in office. Itō Sukeyuki commanded the naval staff for a decade, from 1895 to 1905. Yamamoto Gombei would be chief of the powerful naval affairs bureau, navy vice minister and minister, or prime minister from 1895 until 1914. Moreover, each generation of the inner leadership corps saw to it that the next was exposed to foreign ideas as it had been either indirectly through higher education or directly through assignments overseas.[20]

One measure of this openness was the 1886 decision to establish a higher naval college, one not implemented until November 1888 when Captain John Ingles, RN, arrived to take charge of its instructional program. Over the next six years, he made it a good professional school, one which emphasized engineering and mathematics, to which were added other specialized scientific courses. Following an interruption occasioned by the Sino-Japanese War, the college curriculum in 1897 was modified to take account of recent developments in Europe. The president, Captain (later Admiral) Sakamoto Toshiatsu, introduced a course modeled on that taught at the French Naval War College. For the first time, a handful of students would concentrate on strategy and tactics, naval administration, and leadership rather than more technical subjects. Even so, this course ran for a mere six months, while those in engineering and related specialties kept students for two years.[21]

1897 also brought a decided change to the IJN's other institutional window on the outside world, the overseas resident observer system. From its beginning in 1873 through 1896, this program sent 106 men to study in nine countries; nearly a third of them left Japan after the publication of Mahan's *Influence*. All but six officers concentrated on engineering or technological subjects. In 1897, and again in 1900, five officers were sent to the United States, Britain, France, Germany, and Russia for two year terms to study such subjects as strategy, naval administration, and national defense policy. Three years later, another group of five went to Europe and the United States to study those subjects as well as international law and naval building programs. From

[20] Tokinotani, *Kindai Nihon shi jiten*, pp. 682–686; Toyoda Jō, *Kaigun gunreibu* [The Naval General Staff] (Tokyo: Kodansha, 1987), pp. 85–86.
[21] Sanematsu Yuzuru, *Kaigun daigaku kyōiku* [Education at the Naval War College] (Tokyo: Kojin sha, 1985), pp. 48–49, 54–55.

this group came the senior strategists at the Imperial Japanese Naval War College, two of its presidents, a chief of the naval staff, and the two senior, uniformed delegates to both the Washington and the First London Naval Arms Limitation Conferences. Collectively these men represented the "brains" of the IJN over the next three decades.[22]

How did these leaders of the future come into contact with Alfred Thayer Mahan? Some, if not all, knew him through the translated *Influence*. Others learned of his writings at the Naval War College, as Captain Ingles attested. None met Mahan until the autumn of 1897, when Akiyama Saneyuki, a twenty-nine year old lieutenant who had graduated from the Naval Academy barely ninety days after Mahan's *Influence* was published, came to his New York City home. Akiyama presented himself to Mahan as a would-be student of strategy, but in fact, as he had indicated at a farewell party with his cohort of overseas students, he was as interested in military and naval psychology as in strategy more narrowly defined.[23]

In this first meeting with Mahan, he behaved more like an intelligence officer than a would-be student of strategy. Although he had already been given a negative reply by the State Department, he asked Mahan whether foreign students might attend the War College at Newport. The captain recalled that a Dane and a German who had previously sought to attend had been rejected, and then quickly added that there were matters of national security under consideration there that could not be divulged to foreigners. Akiyama then got some advice on what to read from Mahan - who started with Jomini. The captain also offered to provide an introduction to the Naval Library in Washington where the young lieutenant could peruse books on strategy. In time, before his two year stay in America ended, Akiyama did get to Newport where he heard Captain Charles Stockton's lectures on international law.[24]

Before that occurred, however, the Imperial Navy made a second attempt to come to know Mahan and profit from his works. Nearly two years later, in March 1899, one of the three Japanese midshipmen Mahan had come to know and welcomed into his home while teaching Gunnery at Annapolis twenty-two years earlier, suggested to his superior in the Naval Affairs Bureau that his former instructor be invited to teach strategy at the Imperial Japanese Naval War College. The proposal worked its way up the bureaucratic ladder in Tokyo and emerged as an order to the Japanese naval attache in Washington to search out and engage a veteran of the Newport faculty who would be willing to come for a three year term. Salary would

[22] Suekuni Masao and Koike Iichi, comp., *Kaigun shi jiten*, [Dictionary of Naval History] (Tokyo: Kokusho kankō kai, 1985), pp. 189-191; *Denki dai nihon shi* 13: 117-131, 178-183.
[23] Seager, p. 659; Shimada Kinji, *Amerika ni okeru Akiyama Saneyuki* [Akiyama Saneyuki in America] (Tokyo: Asahi shimbun sha, 1975), 1: 42-44.
[24] Shimada, 1:45-46; 182; Sanematsu, pp. 160-161. Two Swedes had attended the U.S. Naval War College in 1893, but U.S. policy changed by 1897 when the college was considering war plans.

depend upon rank, and that listed for the first name on the list, Mahan's, was twelve thousand yen per year, or approximately six thousand dollars. This was a sum slightly less than twice his captain's retirement pay, but roughly equal to his average annual earnings during the last twenty years of his life. But before the attaché could open negotiations with Mahan and the authorities at Newport, the captain was appointed to the American delegation to The Hague Peace Conference of 1899.[25]

That occasion gave the Japanese - not just Akiyama, but also his fellow overseas observers, including the then acting president of the Imperial Naval War College, Captain Sakamoto Toshiatsu - the chance to see Mahan over an extended period of time. Most probably, they liked what they saw. The captain's definition of his mission - to keep American civilians from proposing or saying anything foolish or harmful to the necessary growth of the navy - coincided precisely with their own objective. For Japanese and American naval representatives alike, the journey to The Hague was a damage control mission.[26]

In another sense, however, it provided Captain Sakamoto, Akiyama, Satō Tetsutarō and their fellow overseas observers with an opportunity to assess the state of naval thought in the West. Their contact with distinguished naval personalities and the various schools of naval thought which they represented appears to have produced the conclusion that Mahan was but one of several important naval thinkers in the West, and not necessarily the pre-eminent one. Several facts point to this conclusion. First, Akiyama and his colleagues talked as much about French Foreign Minister Leon Bourgeois, Captain "Jackie" Fisher, and the Russian tactician, Admiral Stepan O. Makarov as about Mahan. Then, too, neither the Japanese naval attaché in Washington nor Naval War College President Sakamoto followed up on the idea of inviting Mahan or another Newport personality to Tokyo. It was also true that Satō Tetsutarō, after leaving The Hague, went to England to study national defense policy; it would be 1901 before he turned his gaze to Mahan's America.[27]

It can not be said that the Japanese were sufficiently impressed by Mahan as to rush, upon their return home, his remaining works into print. His *The Influence of Sea Power on the French Revolution and Empire*, published in English in 1892, did not appear in Japanese until 1900. Mahan's *Nelson*, which struck Akiyama as more valuable for its insights into the psychology of leadership than for anything it said about naval tactics or strategy, was not published

[25] Shimada, 2:222-224; Mahan's student was later Vice Admiral Serata Tasuka, for whose Japanese biography Mahan later wrote a preface. Seager pp. 331, 628; Cornwall, pp. 201-204.
[26] Shimada, 2:217-222; Seager, 410-411; James Brown Scott, comp., *The Proceedings of the Hague Peace Conferences Transcripts of the Official Texts The Conference of 1899* (New York: Oxford University Press, 1920), 1:267-368, 375.
[27] Shimada, p. 222; Suekuni and Koike, 191; Makarov had published his major work, *Discourses on Questions of Naval Tactics* in 1897. See *The Great Soviet Encyclopedia* 15:339.

in translation until 1906, nine years after it came out. Neither Mahan's geopolitical musings in *The Problem of Asia* (1900) nor his attempted summation of basic principles in *Naval Strategy* (1911) became available to Japanese readers during his lifetime.[28]

In short, it would appear that Mahan, at the turn of the century, was known to and respected by the most important leaders of the Imperial Japanese Navy and its educational elite. However, his influence upon their thinking about naval strategy, whether through his *Influence* or his other writings, was far from exclusive. Mahan's was but one of many foreign voices to which the most ambitious and intelligent IJN officers felt they must listen.

What impact did the American have upon the two Japanese strategists, Akiyama Saneyuki and Satō Tetsutarō, most often described in the West as his followers? The evidence currently in hand suggests that Mahan's "influence" upon both men was less than has previously been thought. Although Akiyama read Mahan during his sojourn in the United States, he was much more enthused and instructed by what he saw as an observer of the U.S. Navy's treatment of the Spanish fleet off Cuba. Upon returning to Japan, he continued to read Mahan's works, but he also devoured Sun Tzu, the writings of contemporary European navalists, and a treatise by one of his ancestors which stressed the need to seize the offensive in battle. Akiyama's 1903 *Lectures on Naval Tactics* also reflected his collaboration in war-gaming with Lieutenant Hirose Takeo, who brought back Admiral Makarov's tactical ideas from Imperial Russia. In 1912, a year after Mahan's *Naval Strategy* appeared, Akiyama published his *Fundamentals of Naval Strategy*. He echoed Mahan in stressing the need for the fleet to determine base needs and in insisting that fleet's ships have similar characteristics so that they might better the operate under a single command. However, Akiyama wrote more to garner support for building a Japanese fleet with eight battleships and eight cruisers as its core than to educate fellow naval officers on basic principles of naval strategy.[29]

What was true of Akiyama appears to have been even more so for Satō Tetsutarō. Admiral Yamamoto Gombei sent him first to England in the belief that Britain, as an island empire, had more wisdom pertinent for Imperial Japan than any other nation. Satō spent less than a third of his period of overseas study in the United States. The book he produced after returning to Japan as an instructor at the Imperial Naval War College, *On the Defense of the Empire* (1902), differed substantially in structure, content, and purpose

---

[28] Hattendorf and Hattendorf, entries A4 trans c; A6 trans b; A18 trans c.

[29] Sanematsu, pp. 161-165; *Kaigun gunsenbi 1*, pp. 108, 126-129; for a fuller appreciation of Akiyama's role in the development of naval thought in Japan, see Mark Peattie, "Akiyama Saneyuki and the Emergence of Modern Japanese Naval Doctrine," *U.S. Naval Institute Proceedings* 103 (January 1977), pp. 60-69. Peattie puts to rest the World War II notion that Japanese naval officers were uninterested in and incapable of abstract thought, a notion put forward by Alexander Kiralfy, "Japanese Naval Strategy," in Edward Mead Earle, ed., *Makers of Modern Strategy* (Princeton: Princeton University Press, 1943), p. 461.

from any of Mahan's writings. Only two of its twenty chapters dealt with the "lessons" of history and three focused on Japan's "national essence". Sato drew upon the ideas of Mahan and European naval thinkers, but he organized them so as to instruct the Japanese public in the fundamentals of naval balance of power politics rather than strategy. The original version of his work, copies of which were presented to the emperor, sounded a clarion call for more naval construction to maintain that balance. In 1908, after Tsushima, when a revised, retitled, and enlarged version appeared as *The History of Imperial Defense*, his aim was to promote the building of a great navy that looked more to its own experience than to American or British ideas for strategic insight.[30]

In short, when Akiyama's and Sato's writings are considered in the context of the Imperial Navy's efforts to keep abreast of developments in naval thought in the West, it appears that the two men were more than mere transmitters of Mahan's ideas to Japan. They may have drawn inspiration from him; but both looked to other authorities, both ancient and modern, in writing their books. Akiyama and Sato were also nationalists, men who set out to create Japan's own tactics and strategy. Moreover, as participants in both the Sino-Japanese and Russo-Japanese Wars, they turned more to their own empire's recent history than to the more distant past as Mahan had. Finally and most importantly, a comparative analysis of their writings suggests that they, much more than he, were men whose pens were mobilized more to support specific building programs than to elucidate general principles. In that sense, neither should be dubbed "the Mahan of Japan."[31]

IV: "THE GOD OF SEAPOWER"

In a traditional Japanese family, when someone dies the remains are cremated, a funeral is held, and a tombstone bearing his posthumous Buddhist name is placed in the cemetery. A small tablet bearing that name is also placed on the "Buddha shelf" or miniature altar in the family home. There the tablet remains as a reminder of the deceased's contribution to and influences upon the family. After Alfred Thayer Mahan's death in December 1914, the Japanese treated him very much as if he were a family member whose tablet occupied a position of honor on the "Buddha shelf". On five occasions someone in that family chose to pick up that tablet, read the name inscribed upon it, and reflect on the meaning, for Japan, of what Mahan had written.

[30] *Kaigun gunsenbi 1*, pp. 119-125; Suekuni and Koike, p. 191; Satō Tetsutarō, *Teikoku kokubo ron* [The Defense of the Empire] (Tokyo: Suikosha, 1902); *Teikoku kokubō shi ron* [The History of Imperial Defense] (Tokyo: Suikosha, 1908). Second and third editions of the latter were published in 1910 and 1912, respectively. In 1913, Satō put his fundamental ideas forward in their most politically usable form, a pamphlet entitled *A Study of National Defense*. I am indebted to Mark Peattie for this point. His "Satō Tesutarō and the Contradictions of Modern Japanese Naval Strategy", co-authored with David Evans, will appear in the Fall 1990 issue of *Naval History*.

[31] Toyama Misao, ed., *Rikukaigun shōkan jiji soran (Kaigun hen)* [An Overview of Army and Navy Officer Personnel - The Navy] (Tokyo: Kyoiku shobo, 1981), pp. 55, 65; Iriye, p. 146.

To recall those occasions is, in a sense, to consider how Mahan over the more than three quarters of a century since his death, became for Japan's navies, a kind of "god of seapower".

Eighteen years after his death, Mahan reappeared in Japan in a translation of his least successful book, *Naval Strategy*. By 1932 the Japanese Empire and the Imperial Japanese Navy were quite different from what they had been in 1911, when Mahan's book first appeared. Japan's informal empire was, thanks to the Kwantung Army's actions in Manchuria, on the verge of becoming a formal, if not formidable, continental sphere. The IJN was the third largest navy in the world with ships technologically equal or superior to those of the other two. Once again, the nation and the navy, much as they had been forty years earlier, had reached a turning point in their relationship to one another. This time the navy, and its arch-rival the Imperial Japanese Army, gained the upper hand over civilian legislators. Yet victory, if it be defined as security, eluded empire and fleet alike. Both perceived themselves to be under siege, from the Anglo-American seapowers who would not recognize Japan's predominance in East Asia and from Soviet communism, whose agents and soldiers menaced the empire's possessions on the Asian mainland.[32]

In these circumstances, the Naval Staff sponsored the translation and publication of two editions of Mahan's *Naval Strategy*. Both stressed his most basic message: seapower was an essential element of national power. The first edition admonished its intended readers - general staff officers, Naval War College instructors, and their students in its elite staff officer preparatory course (nearly twice as many annually as in Mahan's day) to study diligently the relationship between international politics and the rights and interests of the nation state. Mahan was particularly valuable for that purpose because he elucidatated so thoroughly the relationship between U.S. naval strategy, the American national character, and geographic position. His navalism, readers were advised, ranked with the Monroe Doctrine and the Open Door policy as a fundamental principle of American national policy.[33]

The second edition, which appeared barely six months after Secretary of State Henry L. Stimson pilloried Japan for its actions in Manchuria and China, was intended for a wider audience. Its preface ominously suggested that what in the past had been mere theories about a war between Japan and the United States had become pressing and very real problems of naval strategy. The informed citizen ought to read Mahan so as to better understand the elements

---

[32] Pelz, p. 28; W.G. Beasley, *Japanese Imperialism 1894-1945* (Oxford: The Clarendon Press, 1987), pp. 175-197.

[33] Alfred Thayer Mahan, *Kaigun senryaku* [Naval Strategy], Ozaki Shūzei, transl. (Tokyo: Kaigun gunreibu, 1932), translator's introduction. This edition, published in April 1932, is not listed in Hattendorf and Hattendorf. One clue as to the uses to which the Naval Staff put this edition can be found in the fact that the National Diet Library copy of the book came from the personal library of the diplomat, publicist, and later (1948) Prime Minister, Ashida Hitoshi.

of American grand strategy underlying the particulars of Washington's naval policies. By implication, the preface echoed Satō Tetsutarō's message in *New Approaches to National Defense*, published two years earlier: the need for more, and bigger, naval weapons.[34]

A decade later, when an abridged version of this translation was published in Tokyo, Japan and America, the USN and the IJN were locked in a struggle for mastery of the Pacific. Both navies were training hundreds of thousands of officers and men to fight the greatest sea battles in history. Who could be more useful for that purpose than "the god of seapower?" Just as Margaret Sprout revived Mahan and made him useful in inculcating officer candidates (through the NROTC and OCS programs) with basic principles of seapower, so, too, in Japan Mahan served to educate ensigns to be. That he was available in shortened form in language they could understand made him all the more useful in trying to teach these young men how to use surface ships, aircraft, and submarines to defend the empire.[35]

Thirty-five years later, Alfred Thayer Mahan reappeared in Japan for a third time. By the late 1970's, Imperial Japan and the IJN had long since vanished. In their places a new Japan with a new navy, the Maritime Self Defense Force, had arisen. The former was at last territorially whole, save for two tiny islands held by the Soviet Union; and its vibrant economy made it the envy of Asia and of its most important trading partner, the United States. The Maritime Self Defense Force, not unlike the Meiji Navy of the 1890's, was a healthy twenty-three year old, bursting with visions of what it might do in the future, albeit this time in collaboration rather than competition, with the United States Navy.[36]

In 1977, it was a scholar, not a sailor, who detected sufficient contemporary relevance in Mahan to publish a new translation of portions of his *Influence* and several of his articles. Asada Sadao, a Yale Ph.D. who had studied with that most patriotic of American diplomatic historians, Samuel Flagg Bemis, made Mahan accessible to post-World War II generations unable to comprehend the archaic Chinese characters and Sinicized style in which Mahan's writings had originally appeared. He de-mythologized the admiral, introducing him as a representative of 19th and early 20th Century American culture and reviewing the debate over the quality of his work as history and the extent of its influence on policy. Asada argued forcefully that one must read Mahan in order to understand how and why the United States had become

[34] Alfred Thayer Mahan, *Beikoku kaigun senryaku* [American Naval Strategy], Ozaki Shūzei, transl., (Tokyo: Chikura shobo, 1932), preface. This edition is listed as A18 trans c. in Hattendorf and Hattendorf; Satō Tesutarō, *Kokubō shinron*, especially chapters 6, 8, and 17; *Kaigun gunsenbi 1*, pp. 679–682.

[35] *Kaigun senryaku*, Ozaki Shūzei, transl., (Tokyo: Koa Nihon sha, 1942), listed as A 18 Trans. e in Hattendorf and Hattendorf; Margaret Sprout, "Mahan: Evangelist of Seapower," in Earle, ed., *Makers of Modern Strategy*, pp. 415–445; Asada, *Arufredo T. Mahan*, p. 9.

[36] *Japan Times, The Defense of Japan, 1981* (Tokyo: The Japan Times, 1981), pp. 167, 347; Japan, Statistics Bureau, Prime Minister's Office, *Statistical Handbook of Japan 1980* (Tokyo: Statistics Bureau, Prime Minister's Office, 1980), pp. 28, 79.

the predominant power in the Pacific. His comments echoed, with a significant difference, the pre-Pearl Harbor arguments as to Mahan's importance: Now the admiral's writings might provide insight into the policies, not of an enemy, but of Japan's most important ally.[37]

The following year, Toyama Saburō republished and provided a fresh introduction to Mahan's *Naval Strategy*. Doing so came naturally to the then professor of naval history at the Japan Defense Academy, for first as a midshipman at Etajima and then as an instructor there during the Pacific War, he had struggled to comprehend the American's ideas. Now he made the case for Mahan's relevance to Japanese naval professionals explicit: Mahan had discovered principles which constituted the foundations of naval strategy. They were no less fundamental to Japan in devising a policy of maritime defense at the end of the eighth decade of the century than they had been to America at its beginning. Defense Academy cadets and senior staff officers ought to read *Naval Strategy* so as to better comprehend the principle of "concentration of forces." Mahan's arguments about the relationship between bases and fleets would also provide insight into the two superpowers' actions in and around Japan. Most importantly, Toyama argued, by studying Mahan naval officers could improve their ability to use history in trying to resolve contemporary and future problems.[38]

Four years later, in 1982, retired Admiral Kitamura Kenichi brought out the most recent translation of Mahan's *Influence of Seapower Upon History*. That must certainly have eased the burden of fledgling staff officers at the Naval War College, who were required to write one of six major essays on a classic Western naval or military strategist. But Kitamura, not unlike the prewar Naval General Staff translator of Mahan's *Naval Strategy*, probably had a wider audience in mind. He summed up the admiral's contemporary relevance by recalling what had occurred a few years earlier when he met Chief of Naval Operations James L. Holloway, III. When the American asked him what he thought Soviet strategy was, Kitamura replied that Admiral Gorkachov seemed high on Mahan. Admiral Holloway heartily agreed. The Japanese admiral noted the differences between the geopolitics of the world which Mahan described in his most famous book and the strategic situation of the late Twentieth Century. But he clinched his case for Mahan's contemporary relevance by arguing that the Soviet threat showed increasing signs of being maritime in the sense in which the American admiral had written.[39]

---

[37] Asada, pp. 8-13; Asada's translations included 13 articles, the first of which was the introduction to Mahan's *Influence*.
[38] Toyama Saburō, introduction to Mahan, *Naval Strategy* (Tokyo: Hara Shobo, 1978), pp. 1-14, publication data page. This edition reprints the 1932 Naval Staff translation.
[39] Kitamura Ken'ichi, translator's introduction to Mahan, *The Influence of Sea Power Upon History* (Tokyo: Hara Shobo, 1982), pp. 1-16, publication data page, listed as A2 Trans n in Hattendorf and Hattendorf; April 24, 1990 telephone interview with Captain James E. Auer, USN (Ret), the first U.S. Navy student at the Japanese Maritime Self Defense Force Staff College, 1977.

With that argument, Kitamura brought the argument for Mahan's relevance around full circle. Once again, Japan must turn to "the god of seapower" in order to understand and deal with its most formidable enemy.

V: CONCLUSION

One searches the pages of recent histories of the Imperial Japanese Navy in vain for any mention of Alfred Thayer Mahan.[40] That his name does not appear raises, again, the question with which this essay began: What impact did Mahan have upon Japan and its navy? Was "the god of seapower," nothing more than a very distant, scarcely visible, and not terribly important deity after all?

I think not.

Mahan, in each of his roles in Japan, did not cause things to happen. But he did aid men who already knew what must be done achieve their goals. Kaneko Kentarō found in Mahan the naval publicist arguments with which to champion maintaining a great navy to advance the interests of a growing empire. Akiyama Saneyuki and Satō Tetsutarō - and their superiors who sent them abroad to take soundings on naval thought - found in Mahan the naval thinker ideas which, when mixed with those of others and their own, yielded arguments for building a fleet to defend that empire. And Mahan in death did provide a reminder that Japan as a maritime empire needed a navy to protect its interests, whether in conflict or collaboration with the United States.

In each of these roles, however, Mahan was being used by, not serving as instructor to, the Japanese. That fact suggests to me a larger truth about the importance of Alfred Thayer Mahan's "career" in Japan. In his *Influence*, Mahan sought, like the Nineteenth Century man of principle he was, to elucidate basic principles which should serve as guides for future action. He, like virtually every other military and naval thinker of his time, wanted to simplify and reduce complex realities so as to prescribe conduct.[41] Implicit in that approach to strategy-making was the notion that man, with the "correct" ideas, could manage, if not command, his future.

On one level, the Japanese might be said to have reversed that ideal relationship between ideas and action. They, much like the military leaders of late imperial Germany and the Third Reich as Michael Geyer has explained them to us, let ideas, Mahan's ideas, become the servants of organization, the tools for acquisition of new technologies, the means to preconceived ends.

---

[40] For examples of such histories, see Nomura Minoru, *Rekishi no naka no Nihon kaigun* [The Japanese Navy in History] (Tokyo: Hara shobo, 1980) and Toyama Saburō, *Nihon kaigun shi* [A History of the Japanese Navy] (Tokyo: Kyoiku sha, 1980).
[41] John Shy, "Jomini" in Peter Paret, ed., *Makers of Modern Strategy from Machiavelli to the Nuclear Age* (Princeton: Princeton University Press, 1986), p. 179.

In that respect, the turn-of-the-century Japanese figures upon whom I have focused attention, might be seen as harbingers of a grim future. They might even be said to have anticipated the thought of former Army Chief of Staff Creighton Abrams, who was recently reported to have said that the theoretical constructs of strategy were just so much gas - that budgets, politicians, and the sheer force of events, not ideas, determine outcomes.[42]

On another, deeper level, however, the story of Mahan in Japan might be read so as to yield a less dismaying conclusion. For the Japanese who used Mahan did try, however imperfectly, to make ideas work for themselves and their nation. They did attempt, by using Mahan and his works, to let ideas make a difference. Perhaps on this centenary observance of the publication of *The Influence of Sea Power upon History*, we should let their efforts remind us of our responsibility to do the same.

ACKNOWLEDGEMENTS

I wish to acknowledge with particular thanks two persons without whose timely assistance this essay could not have been written: Ms. Barbara Donnelly of the U.S. Naval War College Library, and Mrs. Emiko Moffet, East Asian Section, Hoover Institution Library.

Throughout this essay, Japanese names are cited in the normal order, that is surname followed by personal name.

---

[42] Michael Geyer, "German Strategy in the Age of Machine Warfare, 1914-1945," in ibid., pp. 527-597; Harry Summers quotes General Creighton Abrams in *Los Angeles Times*, April 20, 1990.

Chapter 6

The Influence of A.T. Mahan
Upon German Sea Power

Holger H. Herwig

In May 1890, when Little, Brown at Boston published at four dollars a heavy tome entitled *The Influence of Sea Power Upon History, 1660-1783*, it could hardly have anticipated its success: the book eventually went through fifty editions, and was translated into six major languages. Its author, an obscure captain on the staff of the Naval War College, likewise could hardly have known that he was about to launch a remarkable career as naval historian and propagandist: Alfred Thayer Mahan went on to write more than twenty books, 160 journal articles and 100 newspaper articles, many of which were translated into a wide variety of languages, including Chinese, Dutch, French, Italian, Japanese, Korean, Russian, Spanish, and Swedish.[1]

Mahan's *Influence of Sea Power* appeared at a propitious time in German history. Two months earlier, the young Kaiser Wilhelm II had brusquely "dropped" the "pilot," Chancellor Otto von Bismarck, in order, as the monarch put it, to become sole "Officer of the Watch of the Ship of State."[2] The half-English Kaiser was bedazzled by Britain's maritime greatness, and Mahan's book convinced him of the need to expand overseas, to raise Germany to the status of a global (rather than continental) power on the basis of a symmetrical fleet whose locus of power was the battleship. In 1894, Wilhelm II "devoured" Mahan's *Influence of Sea Power*, richly annotated his copy of the book, and recommended that German naval officers commit it to memory. The following year, he took great delight

---

[1] See John B. Hattendorf and Lynn C. Hattendorf, eds., *A Bibliography of the Works of Alfred Thayer Mahan*, Historical Monograph Series No. 7 (Newport: Naval War College Press, 1986); and John B. Hattendorf, ed., *Register of the Alfred Thayer Mahan Papers*, Manuscript Register Series No. 15 (Newport: Naval Historical Collection 1987).
[2] See Holger H. Herwig, *"Luxury" Fleet: The Imperial German Navy 1888-1918* (London and Atlantic Highlands, NJ: Ashfield Press, 1987), pp. 17 ff.

in receiving the American captain on board the Royal Yacht at Cowes.[3] More realistically than memorizing Mahan, Wilhelm II was instrumental in persuading the editors of the semi-official naval journal *Marine-Rundschau* to commission Vice Admiral Karl Batsch to translate Mahan's opus: it was published in 1986 as *Der Einfluss der Seemacht auf die Geschichte 1660-1783* by the military publishers E.S. Mittler und Sohn at Berlin.

Alfred von Tirpitz (ennobled 1900) was appointed State Secretary of the Navy Office in June 1897, and he immediately secured publication of a second edition of *Der Einfluss der Seemacht* in 1898. Most of Germany's future admirals, from Assmann to Wegener, at some point in their earlier careers read, annotated, and commented upon Mahan's great book. Indeed, Mahan rapidly became a familiar figure in German naval circles. In order to popularize the idea of sea power generally and to secure passage of two navy bills in 1898 and 1900 specifically, Tirpitz secured translation also of Mahan's *The Influence of Sea Power Upon the French Revolution and Empire, 1793-1812*. It appeared in two volumes in 1898-99 and, as Mahan by now was a best seller, both volumes were offered to the public at less cost than the captain's first book.[4] Mahan's 1897 discourse upon *The Interest of America in Sea Power, Present and Future* also appeared in German translation—with a commercial publisher this time, and with the more explicit title of "The White Race and Sea Power."[5] Finally, the editors of the *Marine-Rundschau* were sufficiently impressed with Mahan's articles on the "Lessons of the War With Spain" in *The Times* of London that they procured a four-part translation in 1899. Perhaps of interest in understanding how much of Mahan the Germans took to heart is the fact that Tirpitz did not opt to translate the American's forays either into international relations or into naval strategy and military operations.[6]

Both Mahan and Tirpitz realized that the public had first to be made aware of the need for a battle fleet. In the United States, Mahan was instrumental in founding the Navy League. In Germany, Tirpitz raised the art of public opinion manipulation to new heights. A special News Bureau within the Imperial Navy Office as well as the two semi-official journals *Marine-*

---

[3] William E. Livezey, *Mahan on Sea Power* (Norman: University of Oklahoma Press, 1981), pp. 67, 73. Richard von Kühlmann, *Erinnerungen* (Heidelberg: Lambert Schneider, 1948, pp. 130, 291-92, recollected that "the best heads" in the Foreign Office studied Mahan's work "exactly word for word." After his stint as State Secretary of the Foreign Office, Kühlmann concluded: "Wilhelm's entire maritime *Weltanschauung* was built upon Mahan. Mahan's ideas about the supremacy of a battle fleet based upon capital ships set the stamp upon the third German emperor's reign and decisively influenced Germany's political fate for a very long time." See also Andrew D. White, *Autobiography* (London: Macmillan, 1905), v. 2, p. 224.

[4] *Der Einfluss der Seemacht auf die Geschichte. Zweiter Band 1783-1812, Die Zeit der Französischen Revolution und des Kaiserreiches* (Berlin: E. S. Mittler, 1898-00), 2 vols.

[5] *Die Weisse Rasse und die Seeherrschaft* (Vienna and Leipzig: M. Braunschweig, 1909).

[6] *Retrospect and Prospect: Studied in International Relations, Naval and Political* (Boston: Little, Brown, 1902), and *Naval Strategy Compared and Contrasted with the Principles and Practice of Military Operations on Land* (Boston: Little, Brown, 1911). The latter, however, was translated into Chinese, French, Japanese, Korean, and Spanish.

Rundschau and *Nauticus* brought the Mahanian message to the remotest corners of the Reich. Pastors and so-called "fleet professors" vied with one another to spread the gospel of "navalism." And a German Navy League, boasting one million members by 1914, produced *Die Flotte*, a glib publication with a circulation of 750,000, in order to provide grass-roots support for Tirpitz's naval program.[7]

Mahan, for his part, had been too preoccupied with the Royal Navy to take much note of developments in Germany. While still a young man, Mahan had completed grammar courses in German at Columbia College in 1855 and 1856, but his keen interest in German naval policy unsurprisingly came only with the onset of the Anglo-German naval race. By 1911, German naval expansion had impressed Mahan sufficiently to revise "as tenable no longer" his earlier view that "European politics are scarcely to be considered as part of the Naval War College course."[8]

In fact, Mahan took his case to the public. In April 1909, he lectured Americans concerning "Germany's Naval Ambition" in *Collier's Weekly*. In June and July 1910, he turned to *The Daily Mail* in London in order to explain to Britons "The International Significance of German Naval Developments." On 24 May 1912, Mahan warned his fellow countrymen through *The New York Times* that the Monroe Doctrine was now at "Germany's Mercy." By the eve of the First World War, Mahan had become highly alarmist about the unchecked growth of German sea power; in August 1914, he used both *The New York Evening Post* and *The New York Times* to lay down a challenge that "England Must Fight Germany." Two days after his death, the *New York American*, on 3 December 1914, published Mahan's posthumous appeal to the nation, "Mahan Foresees Peril to U.S. if Germany Wins."[9]

The gist of all these writings was that "the growth of Germany in industrial, commercial, and naval power" constituted "the distinctive feature of the change" in European relations since the turn of the century. The "power of the German Navy" was now also "a matter of prime importance to the United States." In Europe alone, the Royal Navy of Great Britain possessed the "power to control Germany."[10]

The enthusiastic reception of Mahan in Germany, then, rested mainly upon the American's overall advocacy of sea power, rather than upon the specific historical "lessons" that he had drawn from his study of Britain in the age of sail. Indeed, anyone who reads *The Influence of Sea Power Upon History* will

---

[7] The most exhaustive study of what Tirpitz called "spiritual message" is by Wilhelm Deist, *Flottenpolitik und Flottenpropaganda: Das Nachrichtenbureau des Reichsmarineamtes 1897-1914* (Stuttgart: Deutsche Verlags-Anstalt, 1976), esp. pp. 71 ff.

[8] Mahan, *Naval Strategy*, p. 103.

[9] Many of these articles have been reprinted in Charles C. Taylor, *The Life of Admiral Mahan* (New York: Doran, 1920), pp. 293-94, 325-26, 308-45; and Robert Seager II and Doris D. Maguire, eds., *Letters and Papers of Alfred Thayer Mahan* (Annapolis: Naval Institute Press, 1975), v. 3, pp. 457-59, 550-51, 698-700.

[10] Mahan, *Naval Strategy*, pp. 108-110.

admit that it is heavy going. For the most part, the book consists of a rather plodding chronology of British sail from the Second Dutch War to the Surrender at Yorktown. One really has to mine the book for the few nuggets that it contains. The Germans, in fact, could have been content to translate merely the first chapter dealing with the hallowed six "Elements of Sea Power," for Mahan's enunciation of the basis upon which Britannia had built its maritime dominance was what mattered to Wilhelm and to Tirpitz.

It is not surprising, therefore, that Mahan's opus was immediately put to practical political use by Tirpitz. Fully one-fourth of the 8,000 copies extant were distributed in support of the First Navy Bill in 1898. Copies were soon placed on board every warship in the Imperial Navy. Tirpitz next appealed to the Prussian minister of culture, the chief of the General Staff, and the war ministers of the four federal armies (Prussia, Saxony, Bavaria, and Wurttemberg) to do all within their power to popularize Mahan's work in military installations and in public schools. In addition, Tirpitz called upon every state secretary in the Reich government, all four state premiers (in Berlin, Dresden, Munich, and Stuttgart), the Senates of the Hanseatic cities, and the rectors of all universities to spread the gospel according to Mahan; order lists for *Der Einfluss der Seemacht* accompanied the admiral's appeal.

This almost slavish devotion to Mahan served several purposes. First, and most obvious, Mahan's ideas lent credence and gave impetus to the fleet propaganda already being generated by Tirpitz's Navy Office. Second, the manner in which emperor and admiral endorsed and supported Mahan's writings tended to give them quasi-official character. This, in turn, led to the third feature: having elevated Mahan's writings to semi-official status, Tirpitz used them to discipline his officers. As early as June 1897, Tirpitz had an imperial decree issued prohibiting public discussion of the basic tenets of German naval developments—and these, of course, were purely Mahanian. In short, deviation from the philosophy of sea power as laid down by Mahan became cause for censure or even dismissal in the German navy.[11]

Unfortunately, Tirpitz never offered his own critical discussion of Mahan's ideas. Instead, he was content to exploit Mahan for the task of creating a German battle fleet second only to that of Britain. After the first World War, Tirpitz rather pompously declared in his memoirs that he had "empirically developed" his own naval plans "in the small exercise area before the Kiel Bay" while Mahan had "simultaneously developed them theoretically from history" at Newport.[12] Put differently, Mahan the prophet rather than Mahan the historian best served German needs.

By the late 1930s, Erich Raeder no longer felt the need to enunciate his own theory of sea power according to Mahan, for the American's writings

---

[11] See Deist, *Flottenpolitik und Flottenpropaganda*, p. 89, Two celebrated early victims of this decree were Vice Admiral Victor Valois and Captain Curt Baron von Maltzahn.

[12] Alfred von Tirpitz, *Erinnerungen* (Leipzig: K. F. Koehler, 1919), p. 47.

by then had become an article of faith with most *Seeoffiziere*. Raeder's main task, in fact, was to sell the doctrine of sea power to the Austrian Adolf Hitler. Hence, in lieu of Tirpitz and Raeder's intellectual analysis of *The Influence of Sea Power upon History*, it remains to be seen to what degree the German naval buildup both at the turn of the century and in the 1930s corresponded to Mahan's maxims.

First and foremost, it must be stressed that Mahan, Tirpitz, and (to a lesser degree) Raeder developed not merely naval strategies but rather philosophies of sea power that encompassed national elements of culture, politics, economics, and military-military-naval doctrine. All three sailors sought to change their respective nation's strategic culture. They perceived the hierarchy of Great Powers to be constantly in a state of flux. To stand still meant decline. Sea empires rose and fell. Especially Mahan and Tirpitz unabashedly extended the crude doctrines of social Darwinism to the field of international competition. And whereas Mahan in time developed an overtly anti-German posture, Tirpitz (and later Raeder) came to view the Anglo-Saxon Atlantic world as the Reich's natural nemesis.

National greatness could be achieved only through sea power, which for these sailors revolved around symmetrical battle fleets whose center of gravity were powerful battleships. Concentration of the main fleet and decisive battle on the world's oceans alone led to "command of the sea" and the full blossoming of "sea power" to include not only its naval but also its commercial component. In short, control of what Mahan termed "the great throughways of the world's traffic" through strategic "stations along the road," that is, naval bases, led to Great Power status.

To be sure, along the way, international conflict was unavoidable. Maritime commerce was intensely competitive, and would of necessity lead to expansion and possibly to war. As Tirpitz put it in February 1896: "If we intend to go out into the world and strengthen ourselves commercially by means of the sea . . . we shall come across interests everywhere that are either already established or to be developed for the future. This means conflict of interests." Yet, this could not be avoided. Mahan had suggested that a strategy of offensive sea control was the only means of survival in a world of inevitable commercial struggle. Tirpitz, in his rather opaque manner, likewise argued that "sea power alone comprehends the many-sidedness of world policy."[13]

Tirpitz's famous "Service Memorandum IX" of 16 June 1804 became the blueprint for German "navalism" for the next forty years. It is purely

---

[13] Tirpitz to General Albrecht von Stosch, 13 February 1896, Cited in Tirpitz, *Erinnerungen*, p. 55. See also Holger H. Herwig, "The Failure of German Sea Power, 1914-1945: Mahan, Tirpitz, and Raeder Reconsidered," *The International History Review*, February 1988, pp. 68-105. In 1894 Tirpitz couched the rationale for German sea power in purely Mahanian terms: "Does one really think that worldwide industry is possible without world trade, and world trade without world power? But world power is inconceivable without a strong fleet." Cited in Deist, *Flottenpolitik und Flottenpropaganda*, p. 35.

Mahanian. "A state which has sea interests," Tirpitz stated, "must be able to represent them and to make its power felt beyond territorial waters." A high seas fleet alone could guarantee Germany a secure role in "world trade, world industry, and to a certain degree high-seas fisheries, world transportation, and colonies." Such a fleet, as Mahan had already enunciated, would require one-third numerical superiority over any potential adversary. "The natural deployment for a fleet," Tirpirz argued, "is the strategic offensive." Sole aim of the latter was "to come to battle as soon as possible." History had shown that "squadron war" was "the most effective type of fleet offensive" and "its major decision lies in battle."[14] In short, the objective of war at sea was to sink the hostile fleet, thereby securing one's own coast and commerce, rendering the enemy impotent, and his shores vulnerable to blockade—in a word, absolute sea denial.

In time, Tirpitz's views would rigidify into the dogma of the decisive battle (*Entscheidungsschlacht*) to be fought in the waters "between Helgoland and the Thames." Such a naval Armageddon would bestow "command of the sea" upon the victor. For Tirpitz, as for so many others of his generation, life was reduced to a simplistic either-or situation: either "decisive battle on the high sea" or "inactivity, that is, moral self-destruction."[15] Sea power was thus viewed as absolute, rather than as provisional or proportional. Doctrinal and organizational rigidity became the dominant feature of Tirpitz's hermetic naval thought.

Admiral Erich Raeder adopted unquestioningly most of the Mahan-Tirpitz philosophy of sea power. One year after Adolf Hitler's appointment as German chancellor, Raeder announced what was to become the credo of the *Kriegsmarine*: "The scale of a nation's world status is identical with the scale of its sea power."[16] Again, the ideal weapon with which to attain sea power was the symmetrical battle fleet centered around battleships. And whereas the imperial Navy during the First World War had laid down plans for 50,000-ton capital ships, Raeder by 1937 had his staff draw up blueprints for 100,000-ton behemoths.[17]

Raeder proved to be a good salesman. While Hitler generally failed to appreciate sea power and specifically denigrated the Imperial Navy as a

---

[14] Bundesarchiv-Militärarchiv (hereafter BA-MA), Freiburg, West Germany, Nachlaß Tirpitz, N 253, v. 34. Taktische und Strategische Denkschriften des Oberkommandos der Marine Nr. IX. Allgemeine Erfahrungen aus den Manövern der Herbstübungsflotte, 48 pp.

[15] Loc. cit. Also, BA-MA, Nachlaß Tirpitz, N 253, v. 4, A-B 4-5. Tirpitz's notes for an imperial audience, 15 June 1897, Many of the basic documents pertaining to the "Tirpitz Plan" have been published by Volker R. Berghahn and Wilhelm Deist, eds., *Rüstung im Zeichen der Wilhelminischen Weltpolitik, Grundlegende Dokumente 1890-1914* (Düsseldorf: Droste, 1988).

[16] Cited in Wilhelm Deist, "Die Aufrüstung der Wehrmacht," in *Das Deutsche Reich und der Zweite Weltkrieg* (Stuttgart: Deutsche Verlags-Anstalt, 1979), v. 1, p. 454.

[17] Bernd Stegemann, "Hitlers 'Stufenplan' und die Marine," in *Historische Studien zu Politik, Verfassung und Gesellschaft, Festschrift für Richard Dietrich zum 65. Geburtstag* (Bern and Frankfurt: H. Lang, 1976), pp. 308-311.

"parade piece" whose role in the Great War had been insignificant, Raeder by 1934 had convinced Hitler that even a land war was "impossible" without sea power capable of guaranteeing ore shipments from Scandinavia.[18] That same year, Raeder demanded that the Third Reich build a surface fleet one-third the size of England's; later he raised the desired ration to thirty-five percent and then to fifty percent of British surface tonnage.[19] Therewith, Tirpitz's magical formula of two German to every three British capital ships was almost within sight.

By February 1937, Raeder had become so bold as to lecture Hitler and leading party members in the role of sea power in modern German history. The Imperial Navy's strategic defensive of 1914-1918 had cost the Reich the war; Raeder vowed never to repeat it. Like Mahan and Tirpitz before him, Raeder defined sea power as *"command of the maritime lanes of communication."* The strategic offensive alone guaranteed success: the *Kriegsmarine* would be able to fulfill its assigned role in any future war only through "the most powerful initiative, deploying even the highest war craft, on the broad high seas."[20] Raeder's famous "Z-Plan" of January 1939 became a final attestation of Mahanian and Tirpitzean logic with its pronounced emphasis upon battleships, battle-cruisers, and heavy cruisers within the overarching notion of the symmetrical battle fleet.[21]

Cruiser warfare, the *guerre de course* of the French admiral Théophile Aube's *Jeune Ecole*, was fought as heresy by Mahan, Tirpitz, and Raeder alike. The American never tired of lecturing his readers that "the enemy's ships and fleets are the true object to be assailed on all occasions," and deemed cruiser warfare "unsubstantial and evanescent in itself," wholly incompatible with "command of the sea," a "dangerous delusion . . . presented in the fascinating garb of cheapness."[22]

Tirpitz could not have put it more bluntly. Already in the "Service Memorandum Nr. IX" of 1894 he had asserted that cruiser warfare would always "be fought under the most unfavorable circumstances" and "at places where hostile squadrons rule the sea." But above all, cruiser warfare by its very nature renounced "the strongest means which naval war offers," namely, "the struggle for control of the seas." The latter could come about only "through battle"; cruiser warfare thus remained "the last and only means

---

[18] Raeder's discussion with Hitler, 2 November 1934, cited in Michael Salewski, *Die deutsche Seekriegsleitung 1935-1945* (Frankfurt, Bernard & Graefe, 1970), v. 1, pp. 15-16.

[19] Salewski, *Seekriegsleitung* v. 1, pp. 8, 13; and Deist, "Aufrüstung der Wehrmacht," pp. 453-54.

[20] BA-MA, RM 8, v. 1491, pp. 55-76. "Grundsätzliche Gedanken der Seekriegsführung. Vortrag Ob. d. M. gehalten am 3. February 1937." The document was almost seventy pages long.

[21] See Deist, "Aufrüstung der Wehrmacht," p. 471; and Gerhard Bidlingmaier, "Die strategischen und operativen über legungen der Marine 1932-1942," *Wehrwissenschaftliche Rundschau*, June 1963, p. 317.

[22] Mahan, *The Influence of Sea Power upon History 1660-1783* (New York: Hill and Wang, 1957), pp. 116, 288, 481.

of the vanquished or originally impotent sea power."[23] Tirpitz simplistically equated sea power with battleship strength.

Erich Raeder likewise dismissed cruiser warfare as being incompatible with sea power. Already in the 1920s, during his brief stint as naval historian, Raeder had introduced his two volumes of the official German history of the war at sea dealing with "Cruiser Warfare in Foreign Waters" by parroting Mahan (without acknowledgment): *guerre de course*, Raeder asserted, constituted but a "dangerous delusion . . . presented in the fascinating garb of cheapness."[24]

Lest the impression be given that Tirpitz and Raeder were the only two German admirals who unabashedly trumpeted such Mahanian assertions, note should be taken that both Admiral Reinhard Scheer, commander of the German High Seas Fleet from 1916 to 1918, and Captain Magnus von Levetzow, his chief of staff, fully endorsed the heavy emphasis upon battleships and the centrality of battle. While Scheer was quite prepared to endorse unrestricted submarine after the Battle of Jutland as the only available means of overcoming Britain's numerical superiority in warships and its advantageous maritime-geographical position, he nevertheless remained wedded to the Mahanian philosophy of sea power. In January 1917, he tersely reminded his staff that the U-boat was but a temporary expedient on the ultimate road back to Mahan and Tirpitz: "The peace we seek to bring about with submarines must become the second birthday of the German High Sea Fleet."[25] Nearly twenty years later, Admiral Raeder's official naval historian, Vice Admiral Kurt Assmann, summarized his chief's aversion to underwater craft in similar terms: "A U-boat power is not a sea power."[26]

Levetzow, for his part, even after the First World War could not shed a pathological obsession with the notion of centrality of battle. "The victorious naval battle," he lectured the exiled Kaiser Wilhelm II at Doorn, "is thus always *correct* and never wrong strategy—*where* at sea it will be fought against the enemy's force is really immaterial." A victorious battle, in all cases, automatically constituted sea power.[27]

While Mahan, like Carl von Clausewitz before him, has been denounced by his critics as a mere Mahdi of (battleship) mass, a careful reading of *The Influence of Sea Power* would suggest that a certain degree of subtlety and complexity of thought permeated Mahan's writings. Indeed, while the American had argued that it sufficed for a first-rate naval power "only to

[23] BA-MA, Nachlaß Tirpitz, N 253, v. 34, "Dienstschrift Nr. IX."See also Tirpitz, *Erinnerungen*, p. 80.
[24] Erich Raeder, ed., *Der Kreuzerkrieg in den ausserheimischen Gewässern* (Berlin: E. S. Mittler, 1922), v. 1, pp. 3-6.
[25] BA-MA, RM 5, v. 922. "U-Bootskrieg 1916-18," memorandum of 31 January 1917
[26] Cited in D. C. Watt, "Anglo-German Alliance Negotiations on the Eve of the Second World War," *Journal of the Royal United Service Institution*, February to November 1958, p. 384.
[27] See Wolfgang Wegener, *The Naval Strategy of the World War*, ed. by Holger H. Herwig (Annapolis: Naval Institute Press, 1989), p. xl.

be able to meet the strongest" foe "on favorable terms," he had carefully added that it could do so only if it were "sure that the others will not join in destroying a factor in the political equilibrium."[28] In other words, Mahan was alive to the principle of interaction and declined to view maritime struggle in isolation from grand political developments.

Tirpitz would seize upon Mahan's caveat and over time develop a highly important component of his naval-political blueprint: the "alliance value" (*Bündnisfähigkeit*) of a battle fleet. As early as 1894, in his "Service Memorandum Nr. IX," the German had argued that a potential battle fleet would constitute a political power lever against neutral states. "Only an offensive fleet," he had written, "encompasses a desirable alliance value." In other words, a German High Seas Fleet need be sufficient numerically not only to deter "perfidious Albion," but also to rally other, lesser naval powers to the German banner.[29] In the process, Tirpitz was able to jettison Mahan's recommendation that an attacking fleet possess one-third superiority; rather, it need be only sufficiently strong both to deter attack and to attract additional naval allies.

Forty years later, Admiral Erich Raeder resurrected this theme of the potential "alliance value" of a second German High Seas Fleet—but in a slightly different form that Tirpitz. During his first official briefing of Chancellor Hitler in April 1933, Raeder cleverly suggested that a battle fleet might serve as a highly desirable complement to the Führer's program of continental expansion. In fact, the admiral summed up this first meeting with the National Socialist chancellor with the simple optimistic phrase "alliance value."[30] One year later, in March 1934, Raeder candidly suggested to the British naval attaché in Berlin that "one squadron of heavy ships" might be a "political plus" in Britain's struggle against the American rival.[31] In other words, the German admiral was quite prepared to dangle the potential "alliance value" of a squadron of German capital ships before the British in hopes that they, in return, would allow Hitler a "free hand" on the Continent. Put differently, a powerful German battle fleet would serve as a deterrent against possible hostile English interference in German affairs on the Continent; in the case of a "benevolent" Britain, it could offer the decisive edge in future Great Power conflagrations. In both cases, the German fleet would demonstrate anew its "alliance value."

[28] Mahan, *Influence of Sea Power*, p. 139.
[29] BA-MA, Nachlaß Tirpitz, N 253, v. 34, "Dienstschrift Nr. IX;" Tirpitz, *Erinnerungen*, p. 106; Alfred von Tirpitz, *Politische Dokumente. Der Aufbau der deutschen Weltmacht* (Stuttgart and Berlin: J. G. Cotta, 1924), pp. 108; Herwig, "*Luxury*" *Fleet*, pp. 35 ff.
[30] Deist, "Die Aufrüstung der Wehrmacht," p. 452; Wilhelm Deist, *The Wehrmacht and German Rearmament* (London and Basingstoke: Macmillan, 1981), p. 72; Holger H. Herwig, "Prelude to *Weltblitzkrieg*: Germany's Naval Policy Towards the United States of America, 1939-1941," *Journal of Modern History*, December 1971, pp. 649-68.
[31] Michael Salewski, "Marineleitung und politische Führung 1931-1935," *Militärgeschichtliche Mitteilungen*, Fall 1971, p. 131.

British naval supremacy was a theme central to the naval philosophies of Mahan, Tirpitz, and Raeder. For the American, the Royal Navy was a force to be studied and emulated as well as a potential ally in global power politics. For Tirpitz and Raeder, it was the most likely major adversary, the focal point of their threat assessments.

Surely, no one today will argue that the Tirpitz plan was not first and foremost directed against "perfidious Albion." As early as 1899, the admiral had confided to the Saxon government that "for political reasons" he could not simply inform the Reichstag that "naval expansion is aimed primarily against England." Likewise, Tirpitz argued that the ultimate size and deployment of the battle fleet revolved around thoughts "which really cannot be written down." By 1914, however, he was willing to concede: "We must have a fleet equal in strength to that of England."[32]

Raeder, for his part, initially also sought to disguise the anti-English nature of German naval expansion. Until 1937, he clung desperately to what Michael Salewski has termed the "tabu" of refusing to consider any future war against England. Over and over again, Raeder sought (and received) Hitler's assurance that Germany would never again become involved in a war with England, Italy or Japan.

But how realistic was this "tabu"? Any careful reading of Mahan would have revealed clearly that England, by tradition and historical necessity, had never allowed any one power to dominate the Continent. Raeder probably knew this in his heart of hearts. Already in the 1920s, in connection with his work on German cruiser warfare during the Great War, Raeder had come to the conclusion: "The case of war with England must always be taken as the basis for German strategic studies."[33] In 1928, Raeder had confided to Admiral von Levetzow that Hitler ought to avoid the topics of England and sea power for he understood neither. And finally, in June 1934, Raeder openly counseled Hitler that "the fleet eventually would again have to be built against England."[34]

In all fairness, it should also be noted that Tirpitz and Raeder readily adopted Mahan's shortcomings and oversights. Joint service operations or joint service strategic planning were foreign to Mahan, as they were to his German admirers. Tirpitz steadfastly refused to coordinate his maritime strategy with the Reich's allies at Vienna and Rome, his budgetary strategy with the chancellor and other Reich agencies, and his operational planning with the Prussian General Staff and the War Ministry. Raeder, in turn, likewise declined to coordinate his fiscal planning with other service agencies,

---

[32] See Herwig, "*Luxury*" *Fleet*, p. 37.

[33] Erich Raeder, ed., Cruiser Warfare in Foreign Waters (Berlin: n. p., 1929), v. 1, p. 9.

[34] Michael Salewski, "Die deutsche Kriegsmarine zwischen Landesverteidigung and Seemachtambitionen," in *Die Deutsche Marine. Historisches Selbstverständnis und Standortbestimmung* (Herford and Bonn: E. S. Mittler, 1983), p. 77; Salewski, *Seekriegsleitung*, v. 1, p. 14.

or his operational designs with either army or air force. And when in 1940 he developed the one German strategic alternative to the invasion of the Soviet Union, his celebrated Mediterranean program, it was done in isolation and without reference either to the *Wehrmacht*, the *Luftwaffe*, or to the regional and vital partners at Rome, Vichy, and Madrid.[35] And while concepts such as the balance of power, alliances, and coalition warfare are not to be found in the index of *The Influence of Sea Power*, neither were they in the working vocabulary either of Tirpitz or of Raeder.

Since the German navy failed in both world wars to achieve its political objective—namely, to supplant Great Britain as the dominant naval power in the Atlantic theater—it is only fair to ask whether this was due in part to basic flaws inherent in Mahan's naval philosophy. By and large, I would argue that the problem lay instead in a persistent German misreading (or ignoring) of Mahan.

In the first place, neither Tirpitz nor Raeder fully appreciated Mahan's vital precondition for sea power: "ready access to the ocean by one or two outlets." Maritime geography, as Mahan had stated repeatedly, dictated that Germany could reach the "great common" only through the English Channel or through the Scotland-Norway passage. Great Britain, Mahan wrote, "lies to Germany as Ireland does to Great Britain," flanking both German "routes to the Atlantic."[36] Neither Tirpitz nor Raeder proved willing to address squarely Germany's disadvantageous maritime-geographical location astride the "dead" North Sea.

Secondly, Tirpitz and Raeder chose to ignore Mahan's warning that no nation concurrently could be both a great land power and a great sea power. Limited material and manpower resources militated against powerful deployment on land as well as at sea. History had provided a prime example for Mahan of such a nation in the case of France under Louis XIV. "A false policy of continental extension swallowed up the resources of the country."[37] Moreover, island nations enjoyed an inherent advantage in naval competition due to their secure geographic location: "History has conclusively demonstrated the inability of a state with even a single continental frontier to compete in naval development with one that is insular, although of smaller population and resources."[38] Imperial Germany would by 1910 deplete its Treasury by military and naval expenditures, while Raeder's "Z-Plan" of January 1939 would suffer from acute lack of raw materials, labor, and construction yards.

---

[35] See especially Gerhard Schreiber, *Revisionismus und Weltmachtstreben: Marineführung und deutsch-italienische Beziehungen 1919-1944* (Stuttgart: Deutsche Verlags-Anstalt, 1978).
[36] Mahan, *Influence of Sea Power*, p. 286; Mahan, *Retrospect and Prospect*, p. 166.
[37] Mahan, *Influence of Sea Power*, p. 65.
[38] Mahan, *Retrospect and Prospect*, p. 169.

Thirdly, Tirpitz as well as Raeder sought to finesse Mahan's critical emphasis upon superior fleet size. The American had stressed that a fleet "of size and quality adequate to the proposed operations" was absolutely necessary. A fleet of inferior strength, on the other hand, "could be used offensively only by great care, and through meeting the enemy in detail."[39] Shibboleths, such as the "alliance of value" or the deterrent function of the German battle fleet, in the end, served well neither Tirpitz nor Raeder—much less, Germany.

At the political level, both Tirpitz and Raeder ignored Mahan's emphasis upon British national character as well as character of government. Even a cursory reading of Mahan would have shown both German admirals that throughout modern history, Britain had rallied to meet all continental challenges—from Louis XIV to Napoleon, and from Wilhelm II to Adolf Hitler. As Winston S. Churchill once put it, what was in the nature of a "luxury" to Germany—namely, sea power—was a vital prerequisite to England's survival. What remained of Mahan, then, was the dogged obsession with concentrated battleship fleets designed to press the offensive vigorously.

Finally, neither Tirpitz nor Raeder found strategic insight in Mahan—for the simple reason that they concentrated almost exclusively upon the American's naval philosophy, while ignoring his rich literature scattered throughout a plethora of popular and service journals dealing with maritime strategy.[40] As a result, German admirals overall suffered from what Herbert Rosinski, a former teacher at the German Naval Staff College, termed "atrophy of strategic thought."[41] Admiral von Tirpitz's pathetic question of May 1914 to the Fleet chief, Admiral Friedrich von Ingenohl, "What will you do if they [the British] do not come?,"[42] as well as Admiral Raeder's crushing conclusion of 3 September 1939, that the *Kriegsmarine* could only "die gallantly" in the war, which had come again five years too early,[43] speaks volumes for Rosinski's observation.

To be sure, a number of German naval officers had quickly grasped Mahan's notions concerning maritime-geographical position and access to the great oceanic arteries of global communication. Around 1908-09, two successive Chiefs of the Admiralty Staff, Vice Admiral Friedrich von Baudissin and Admiral Max von Fischel, had warned Tirpitz that only by attacking England could Germany hope to become a first-rate sea power and extend its naval

---

[39] Mahan, *Influence of Sea Power*, p. 460.

[40] For example, *Atlantic Monthly, Century Magazine, Collier's Weekly, Engineering Magazine, Forum, Harper's Independent, Leslie's Weekly, McClure's, North American Review, Scientific American, Scribner's,* and *World's Work.*

[41] Herbet Rosinski, "German Theories of Sea Warfare," *Brassey's Naval Annual 1940,* p. 90. This article, as well as several others by Rosinski, has been reprinted in B. Mitchell Simpson III, ed., *The Development of Naval Thought: Essays by Herbert Rosinski* (Newport: Naval War College Press, 1977).

[42] Cited in Albert Hopman, *Des Logbuch eines deutschen Seeoffiziers* (Berlin: A. Scherl, 1924), p. 393.

[43] BA-MA, PG 32023, Case 103, Kriegstagebuch Seekriegsleitung. I Abteilung, Teil A, p. 43. See also Gerhard Wagner, ed., *Lagevorträge des Oberbefehlshabers der Kriegsmarine vor Hitler 1939-1945* (Munich: J. F. Lehmanns, 1972), pp. 19-21.

reach beyond the North Sea. As Fischel had succinctly put it: "We are fighting for access to the ocean, whose entrances on that side of the North Sea are in England's hands. We are therefore basically the attacker, who is disputing the enemy's possessions."[44] Tirpitz chose not to respond. Instead, he redoubled his efforts to deny the Admiralty Staff influence over his maritime plan.

In 1915, and again in 1929, Wolfgang Wegener most sagaciously critiqued the Tirpitz plan. An avid reader of Mahan, Wegener brutally lectured both Tirpitz and Raeder that destruction of the hostile fleet was "to a certain degree" only an "incidental goal" in war at sea—*unless* it were followed by secure control of the maritime arteries of trade and communication. The German navy's "one-sided" concentration on "the battle" between Helgoland the Thames, Wegener stated, had precluded insight into naval strategy and engendered an obsession with the operational art of war. Echoing Mahan, Wegener further ventured that England's superior geographical situation astride the two exits to the North Sea as well as its crushing fleet superiority effectively blocked the unfolding of Germany's naval ambitions. Depicting the North Sea as a "dead sea," Wegener argued that "the door to the Atlantic" could be kicked open only through territorial expansion in the West (France) and the North (Norway) as well as by a larger, faster, more powerful High Seas Fleet. Like Tirpitz before him, Raeder tolerated no criticism: Wegener became the *bête noire* of the Kriegsmarine, and was singled out by Raeder for personal vilification.[45]

In conclusion, both Tirpitz and Raeder undertook inadequate analyses of Mahan's naval philosophy. Both failed to grasp the deeper meaning of Mahan's analysis of British sea power and national character. Inferior geographical position, inadequate fleet size, and "atrophy of strategic thought" in the end bedeviled both German admirals. Tirpitz as well as Raeder basically failed to confront the clear-cut alternative of both 1914 and 1939: either to build a battle fleet one-third superior to England's in order to challenge "perfidious Albion" for control of the Atlantic "great common," or, from the outset, to acquiesce in Britain's naval supremacy and to concentrate fully on the Reich's pivotal position of semi-hegemony in the heart of Europe, wedged in between two potentially hostile land powers.

It is hard to argue with Herbert Rosinski's conclusion that it was "the fundamental strategic contradiction in Tirpitz's policy that, in trying to wriggle between these two inexorable alternatives, he set himself into diametric contradiction not only to this situation, but to all the principles of naval warfare."[46] That observation pertains equally to Erich Raeder. In

---

[44] Cited in Herwig, *"Luxury" Fleet*, p. 190. See also Carl-Axel Gemzell, *Organization Conflict and Innovation: A Study of German Naval Strategic Planning, 1888-1940* (Lund: Esselte Studium, 1973), pp. 79-80.
[45] See my introduction to Wegener's *Naval Strategy of the World War*, pp. xv-lv.
[46] Rosinski, "Strategy and Propaganda in German Naval Thought," *Brassey's Naval Annual 1945*, pp. 130-131.

the final analysis, it was their incorrect reading of Mahan, rather than the American's misreading either of British sea power or of the British national interest, that accounted for the shortcomings of German "navalism" in the twentieth century.

In concluding, it should be pointed out that whether one sees Mahan as a glorified hero or as a despicable villain—and there are ample devotees of both positions—he was not as dogmatic in his views as is often presupposed. Four years after publishing *The Influence of Sea Power upon History*, Captain Mahan gave an interview to the *New York Herald* (Paris) in which he bluntly rejected the use of "pocket manuals" to set rules and standards" for instruction at the Naval War College. Likewise, he decried slavish reliance upon "the work of some one or two masters in the art" as their writings might well fail to "provoke others to search for themselves." Despite the fact that he had been reared on the works of Henri Jomini from his father's library, and had even named his dog after the Swiss hagiographer of Napoleon I, Mahan concluded the interview with an observation worthy of Carl Von Clausewitz: "War cannot be made a rule of thumb, and any attempt to make it so will result in disaster, grave in proportion to the gravity with which the issues of war are ever clothed."[47] Admirals Tirpitz and Raeder would have done well to have heeded this sage advice.

---

[47] *The New York Herald* (Paris), 7 February 1894, p. 2.

Chapter 7

140 Years of German Navies: Their Defeat and Re-Birth - From Confrontation to Co-Operation

Captain Dr. Werner Rahn, FGN

Twelve theses on the development of the German Navy in the Nineteenth and Twentieth Centuries:

1.   A Great Power with worldwide trade links, colonies abroad and free access to the seven seas, in the Nineteenth and Twentieth Centuries, required a navy as a military instrument in order to be able to assert her position in relation to other Great Powers. The concept and structure of this force was, however, dependent upon the potential threat. During the Nineteenth Century Great Britain, the dominant sea power, had an influence on the naval policy of all other Great Powers having any kind of navy. Based on the theories of Alfred T. Mahan, at the end of the Nineteenth Century, navies, in the form of a battle fleet, were increasingly regarded as an essential instrument for a Great Power wishing to represent and enforce worldwide interests.

2.   The first German Navy came into being from 1848 onwards, at a time when Germany had no answer to a Danish blockade. The Navy soon became a symbol of the armed might of the hoped-for united Reich. The idea of a fleet was seen as a political instrument and embodied demands pointed to differing tendencies: on the one hand the liberal aim of having free access to the world in order to increase trade, and on the other hand, the overt ambition of using power politics and the law of the strongest in order to create a hegemony.

3.   Owing to the German Reich's position in Central Europe, with potential enemies in both East and West, the naval buildup was for a long time overshadowed by the Army. The developments during the turn of the century showed that, because of her central position in Europe, for the young German Reich, any power policy which included a claim to rule the seas interfered with Great Britain, was bound to encounter deep mistrust on the part of this

strategically-minded sea power, a mistrust which could quickly turn out to be a deadly danger to the Reich. The German Naval Command overestimated the possibility of a German naval war against Great Britain. Due to the geographical conditions, the British were capable of achieving their strategic aims with regard to Germany without entering into a decisive battle.

4.   The buildup of the German High Seas Fleet at the beginning of the 20th century came at a time of enormous technical change in which weaponry quickly became obsolete. At almost no other time during this century did maritime weapons systems become outdated as quickly as in the decade prior to the First World War. In the maritime arms race, the Reich was unable to keep up in building capital ships, since her resources were insufficient to fulfill all the arms requirements of both Army and Navy.

5.   The outbreak and the course of the First World War showed that the German Naval Command's political and strategic concept did not work. During the July crisis of 1914 the High Seas Fleet was no deterrent. The employment of the fleet had no strategic effect on the conduct of war as a whole. Germany's one-sided and inadequate concept of submarine warfare was a large factor in the USA's entry into the war. In November 1918, due to the Navy's high-handedness, it became the starting-point for political turmoil within the Reich.

6.   During the Weimar Republic, the Navy had great difficulties in adapting to the new republican form of government. It regarded itself as an essential element of the nation's defense. However, the Navy hoped for better times, in order to build a new fleet without arms restrictions, a fleet which complied with the Naval High Command's idea of the Reich's security needs and position of power.

7.   Because not everyone accepted it, the Treaty of Versailles was incapable of supplying the basis for a lasting period of peace and security for the whole of Europe. Mutual mistrust was perpetuated. The Germans failed to draw the correct conclusions from the political and military scale of the defeat of 1918, conclusions which would have been necessary for the consolidation of the Reich both in home and foreign-policy terms. Like other parts of Germany's political and military elite, the German naval leadership did not reconcile itself to the Treaty of Versailles. However, this attitude did not mean that German policy was necessarily on a one-way route to war in 1939.

8.   After 1933, the Navy eventually became subject to Hitler's long-term ambitions for dominating the world and the seas in particular. But the Second World War broke out before his plans for a gigantic shipbuilding programme could take effect. When the war came, the Navy was totally unprepared for it. To compensate, Germany attempted to force a strategic decision by destroying the superior Anglo-Saxon maritime powers' shipping capacity (sea denial) rather than by fighting them for mastery of the Atlantic (sea control).

9. From 1940 onwards, Germany possessed a good geographical basis for naval warfare in the Atlantic, but this basis could not be fully exploited due to insufficient weaponry. The U-boat did supply an effective weapon in the fight against enemy shipping up to 1942, but, as a result of the general war situation, and the critical situation in the Mediterranean and the Eastern front, the Naval Command was forced to employ its last remaining offensive capability like a "strategic fire brigade". This led to enormous attrition, which in no way complied with the strategic concept of mass concentration in the Atlantic. The concept of the U-boat war failed in 1943 because the submarine had lost its capability of escaping from enemy surveillance and defense as the allies developed their ASW-weapons.

10. From 1943 onwards, the Navy under Grand Admiral Karl Dönitz, had an officer at the helm who was both a charismatic leader in himself, and could be seen to have close links to Hitler and Nazi ideology. Not until after Hitler's death did he change "from the almost-blind tool of criminal to the responsible soldier of the traditional Prussian school".[1] He did everything in his power to liquidate the already lost war in a proper fashion and, at the same time, to evacuate as many people as possible across the Baltic to the West. This last wartime act gave the Navy much public recognition.

11. In the course of this century, Germany has twice tried to force a strategic decision in direct-confrontation with the Anglo-Saxon naval powers by cutting the Atlantic shipping routes (SLOCs). Both attempts ended in failure. The second defeat brought with it the end of the German Reich and the dissolution of all German armed forces. The Western orientation of the Federal Republic of Germany led to the close binding of the new German armed forces into the Atlantic Alliance. This meant, for the Navy, the smallest of the armed services within the Bundeswehr (Federal Armed Forces), that for the first time in her history she was obliged merely to perform that function "which a German Navy can actually perform"[2] in close cooperation with the great maritime powers.

12. Today, the German Navy has not only a lively interest in its history, but also a special relationship to it. A clear link can be seen between the historical self-understanding of her officers and the history of their service. In the past, this link often served only to legitimize and to secure its own position. The Navy, which came into being in the mid-19th century, often had to fight for recognition and even for its existence during a relatively short history. However, there can be a danger, if historical interest is limited only to the Navy and naval warfare, too little attention may be given to the overlapping political correlations.

---

[1] Michael Salewski, *Die deutsche Seekriegs-leitung 1935-1945*, Vol. 2, Munich 1975, p. 552.
[2] Dieter Hartwig (comment) in: *Die deutsche Flotte in Spannungsfeld der Politik 1848-1985*. Ed. by Deutsches Marine Institut and Militärgeschichtliches Forschungsamt (with contributions by G. Fromm, *et al.*), Herford 1985, p. 197.

Bibliography

For further reading, see the works cited by Holger Herwig as well as the following:

1. *Guides and handbooks*:
    Bird, Keith W., *German Naval History. A Guide to the Literature*. New York, London 1985.
    Dülffer, Jost, "Die Reichs-und Kriegsmarine 1918-1939," in: *Handbuch zur deutschen Militärgeschichte 1648-1939*, hrsg. vom Militärgeschichtlichen Forschungsamt, Bd 4/ Abschnitt VIII, München 1978.
    Petter, Wolfgang: "Deutsche Flottenrustung von Wallenstein bis Tirpitz," in: *Handbuch zur deutschen Militärgeschichte 1648-1939, hrsg.* vom Militärgeschichtlichen Forschungsamt, Bd 4/Abschnitt VIII, München 1978.
2. *Series and collected essays*:
    Das Deutsche Reich und der Zweite Weltkrieg, hrsg. vom Militärgeschichtlichen Forschungsamt, Bd 1 ff., Stuttgart 1979.
    Marine und Marine politik im Kaiserlichen Deutschland 1871-1914, hrsg. vom Militärgeschichtlichen Forschungsamt durch H. Schottelius und W. Deist, 2. Aufl., Düsseldorf 1981.
    Seemacht und Geschichte. Festschrift zum 80. Geburtstag von Friedrich Ruge, hrsg. vom Deutschen Marine Institut, Bonn–Bad Godesberg 1975.
3. *Monographs*:
    Berghahn, Volker R., *Der Tirpitz-Plan. Genesis und Verfall einer innenpolitischen Krisenstrategie unter Wilhelm II.*, Düsseldorf 1971.
    Dülffer, Jost, *Weimar, Hitler und die Marine. Reichspolitik und Flottenbau 1920 bis 1939*, Düsseldorf 1973.
    Duppler, Jörg, *Der Juniorpartner. England und die Entwicklung der deutschen Marine 1848-1890*, Herford 1986.
    Duppler, Jörg, *Prinz Adalbert von Preussen. Gründer der deutschen Marine*, Herford und Bonn 1986.
    Herwig, Holger H., *Das Elitekorps des Kaisers. Die Marineoffiziere im Wilhelminischen Deutschland*, Hamburg 1977.
    Lambi, Ivo Nikolai, *The Navy and German Power Politics, 1862-1914*, Boston 1984.
    Rahn, Werner, *Reichsmarine und Landesverteidigung 1919-1928. Konzeption und Führung der Marine in der Weimarer Republik*, München 1976.
    Thomas, Charles S., *The German Navy in the Nazi Era*, Annapolis 1990.

Certificate of completion of a course in German grammar at Columbia College in 1856. Mahan completed a previous course in 1855. From the collections of the Naval Historical Collection, Naval War College. Manuscript item 104.

ESCUELA DE GUERRA NAVAL

★

INFLUENCIA
DEL

PODER NAVAL

EN LA HISTORIA

1660-1783

POR
A.T. MAHAN

SEGUNDO TOMO

Versión Castellana Para Uso Exlusivo
de la Escuela de Guerra Naval

BUENOS AIRES
1935

Title page of Spanish translation prepared for the use of the Argentine Naval War College in 1935; from the collection of the Eccles Library, Naval War College.

Chapter 8

The Character and Extent of Mahan's Influence in Latin America

Captain Guillermo J. Montenegro, Argentine Navy (Ret.)

When dealing with the historical background of Mahan's influence in Latin America, it should be taken into account that, by 1890, most Latin American countries already had significant experience related to what "Sea power" (or the lack of it) meant.

Background.

During the wars for Independence, sea power nearly played a decisive role. Episodes such as the defeat of the Spanish Squadron off Montevideo (1814), put an end to Spanish power in the River Plate area and in the South Atlantic. The seaborne invasion of the viceroyalty of Peru (1820) allowed the revolutionaries to force a decisive encounter against the Spanish at Ayacucho; and the action of Lord Cochrane's Brazilian Squadron (1823), significantly contributed to defeat Portuguese efforts to retain control of their South American colony.[1]

The significance of sea power goes beyond the wars of Independence. Spanish attempts to punish their former colonies, the "gunboat diplomacy" exercised by the Great Powers, as well as rivalries between the newly emerged nations led to several armed conflicts in which sea power was significant, if not decisive.

The following relevant examples could be mentioned:

- The Argentine-Brazilian war of 1826-1828, in which Brazil's "big navy" effectively blockaded Buenos Aires, and the Argentines could only respond by coastal actions and by resorting to the *guerre de course.*
- The Anglo-French interventions against Argentina in the 1830's and 1840's.
- The Spanish intervention in the Pacific coast of South America in the 1860's in which Chile and Peru remained on the defensive because of their inferior naval forces.
- The war between Chile and Peru in the 1870's, in which Chilean sea control proved decisive.
- Finally, even Paraguay suffered the weight of the superior Brazilian Fleet during the War of the Triple Alliance in the late 1860's.[2]

---

[1] See basically, Scheina, Robert L. *Latin America: A Naval History 1810-1987.* Annapolis, 1987. Chapter 1.
[2] *Op. cit.* Chapter 3.

This maritime heritage was interpreted in several important historical works in the late Nineteenth and early Twentieth Centuries by naval historians, such as Carranza[3] in Argentina, Meirelles da Silva[4] in Brazil, Langlois[5] in Chile and Melo[6] in Peru. Therefore, Mahan's teachings fell on fertile ground, and his influence followed several different (and in some cases interconnected paths) in addition to a direct intellectual message.

At the beginning of this century, Mahan's works were widely read and studied in Latin American naval circles. Along the years, some naval writers produced their own derivations of Mahan's theories, adapted for their own countries. A few of the early works established the basis for their own national naval thinking.

This intellectual influence was reinforced by the direct contact of Latin American naval officers with the U.S. Navy, through courses given in the United States as well as by the spreading influence of the U.S. naval missions.[7]

Particularly, in the case of Brazil, Chile and Argentina, several "waves" of Mahanian influence came by an indirect route, the examples set by the "superpower" navies of that day. This influence occurred in a period of acute rivalries between Chile and Argentina in the 1890's and between Brazil and Argentina in the first decade of the Twentieth century. All of these countries made significant efforts to create and maintain strong "battle fleets", at least equivalent to their prospective opponents. When the *Dreadnought* battleship appeared, first Brazil, then Argentina, and finally Chile joined in a regional naval race.[8]

The perceptions of the lessons of the Russo-Japanese war (1904-1905) had the effect of confirming the soundness of the concept of a strong, superior, dominant battle fleet to achieve "command of the sea".[9]

The outcome of World War I again confirmed this, taking into account the impact of the Allied blockade upon the collapse of the Central Powers, the indecisiveness of the surface raiders and the apparent containment of the submarine menace.[10]

The naval development of the Great Powers in the inter-war years, the weight of Allied sea power in World War II and the U.S.-Soviet naval rivalry after 1945, reinforced the soundness of the "strong navy" concept.

---

[3] Carranza, Angel J. *Campañas Navales de la República Argentina*, 4 Vols. Ministerio de Marina, Buenos Aires, 1914-1916.
[4] Meirelles da Silva, Theotonio. *Historia Naval Brasileira*. B.L. Garnier, Rio de Janeiro, 1884.
[5] Langlois, Luis (Commander). *Influencia del Poder Naval en la Historia de Chile desde 1810 a 1910*. Imprenta de la Armada, Valparaiso, 1911.
[6] Melo, Rosendo. *Historia de la Marina del Perú*, 3 Vols. El Auxiliar del Comercio, Lima, 1907-1915.
[7] Scheina. *op. cit.* Chapter 9.
[8] *Ibid.* Chapters 3 & 5.
[9] Montenegro, Guillermo J. (Captain, Navy). "The Influence of Naval Thought upon World War I". Unpublished essay, Buenos Aires, 1989.
[10] *Ibid.*

Finally, Mahanian inspiration was felt in the continued intervention, both intellectual and actual, of Latin American navies in the maritime affairs of their respective countries, by giving impulse to their merchant marines, harbors, shipbuilding and fishing industries, and by trying to create a "maritime mentality" in their respective populations.

Mahan and Latin American Authors.

What were the results of this multi-channeled influence?

First, what was the impact of local authors, inspired by Mahan's thought and the prevailing naval thought of the century?

Mahan's theories were known by the turn of the century. From the available data, it could be stated that the first Spanish language translation of *The Influence of Sea Power upon History* was carried out in Chile, in 1900.[11] The creation of an Argentine Naval War College in 1934 led to further editions in Spanish of *The Influence of Sea Power upon History*[12] as well as *Naval Strategy*.[13]

Moreover, the appearance of Castex's *Theories Strategiques*,[14] having a reasonable Mahanian "touch", added further impulse to the influence of classical naval thought in Latin America.[15]

Other naval literature which threw further light upon Mahan's ideas or reinforced classical naval thought were Groos' *Seekriegslehren im Lichte des Weltkrieges*;[16] Di Giambenardino's, *L'Arte della Guerra in Mare*;[17] Brodie's *A Guide to Naval Strategy*[18] and Earle's *Makers of Modern Strategy*,[19] whose chapter on Mahan is still basic reading.

These works were translated and edited by the Argentine Naval War College or the Argentine Navy Ministry, as well as Groos' and Brodie's by the Chilean Navy, and Di Giambernardino's by the Brazilian Navy,[20] and became standard classics in Latin American professional circles.

---

[11] Mahan, Alfred T. *Influencia del Poder Naval sobre la Historia*. Editorial Talleres Tipográficos de la Armada, Valparaiso, 1900; cit. by Buzeta, Oscar in *Chile Geopolítico - Presente y Futuro*. Centro de Investigaciones Socio-económicas de la Compañia de Jesús en Chile, Santiago de Chile, 1978, page 48.

[12] Mahan, Alfred T. *Influencia del Poder Naval en la Historia. 1660-1783*, 2 Vols. Escuela de Guerra Naval, Buenos Aires, 1935.

[13] Mahan, Alfred T. *Estrategia Naval*, 2 Vols. Escuela de Guerra Naval, Buenos Aires, 1935.

[14] Castex, Raoul P. *Theories Strategiques*, 5 Vols. Editions Geographiques, Maritimes et Coloniales, Paris, 1929-35.

[15] Rosinski, Herbert. *The Development of Naval Thought*. Naval War College Press, Newport, 1977. Page 33.

[16] Groos, Otto. *Seekriegslehren im Lichte des Weltkrieges*. E.S. Mittler & Sohn, Berlin, 1929.

[17] Di Giambernardino, Oscar. *L'Arte della Guerra in Mare*. Ministerio della Marina, Roma, 1937.

[18] Brodie, Bernard. *A Guide to Naval Strategy*, 3rd. ed. Princeton University Press, Princeton, 1944.

[19] Earle, Edward Mead. ed. *Makers of Modern Strategy*. Princeton University Press, Princeton, 1944.

[20] Castex, Raúl. *Teorias Estratégicas*, 5 Vols. Escuela de Guerra Naval, Buenos Aires, 1938-42; Groos, Otto. *La Doctrina de la guerra marítima segun las enseñanzas de la Guerra Mundial*. Estado Mayor General-Armada Argentina, Buenos Aires, 1935; Groos, Otto. *La Doctrina de la Guerra Marítima* Imprenta de la Armada, Valparaiso, 1939; Di Giambernardino, Oscar. *El Arte de la Guerra en el Mar*. Ministerio de Marina, Buenos Aires, 1940; Di Giambernardino, Oscar. *A Arte da Guerra no Mar*. Imprensa Naval, Rio de Janeiro, 1939; Brodie, Bernard *Una Guia en Estrategia Naval*. Escuela de Guerra Naval, Buenos Aires, 1947; Brodie, Bernard. *Guía de Estrategia Naval*. Imprenta de la Armada, Valparaiso, 1949; Earle, Edward Mead. *Creadores de la Estrategía Moderna*, 2 Vols. Escuela de Guerra Naval, Buenos Aires, 1948.

Mahan's theories were a source of inspiration for two different categories of Latin American authors.

A first group concentrated itself mainly on the naval strategy aspects of Mahan's writings and advocated the importance of sea power as a whole, *i.e.* the buildup of a strong navy, the elements of a sea power, the "fleet-in-being" concept, naval bases, interior lines, the validity of a "one power standard" for their own countries, and even the right meaning of the term sea power in their own languages; as well as the significance of own national maritime capabilities - merchant marine, shipbuilding and fishing industries, harbors, etc.- to support a sound sea power.

Among this first group, scattered along the decades of this century, one can mention authors such as Storni in Argentina,[21] Flores and Caminha in Brazil,[22] Langlois and Diaz Buzeta in Chile,[23] and Buse de la Guerra in Peru.[24]

The writers in second group, most of whom were military people, focused their efforts on the geo-political side of Mahan's ideas. When they analyzed the "classic" geo-political thinkers, they gave wide coverage to Mahan's thought, often referring to him as "the geo-politician of the sea". Some examples of writers in this group are Marini and Fraga in Argentina,[25] Flores, de Castro, Oliveira Mafra and Lima Abreu in Brazil[26] Pinochet and Buzeta in Chile[27] and Buse de la Guerra and Ramirez Canaval in Peru.[28]

It should be noted that these Latin American authors were not alone in their interpretation of Mahan as a geo-politician. Several North American scholars have stressed this same aspect in Mahan's thought.[29]

---

[21] Storni, Segundo R. (Vice-Admiral). *Intereses Argentinos en el Mar*, 2nd ed. (First published in 1916), Buenos Aires, 1952.
[22] Flores, Mario Cesar (Captain, Navy). "Poder Naval na década dos setenta". Biblioteca do Exército - Serviço de Documentaçio Geral da Marinha, Rio de Janeiro, 1972. Part 3, Chapter I of: *Panorama do Poder Maritimo Brasileiro*; Caminha, João Carlos Gonçalves (Vice-Admiral). "Mahan: sua época e suas idéias". *Revista Marítima Brasileira*, July–August–September 1986, pp. 15–70.
[23] Langlois, *op. cit.*; Diaz Buzeta, Santiago (Captain, Navy). *Estrategia Naval*. Imprenta de la Armada, Valparaiso, 1956.
[24] Buse de la Guerra, Hermann. "Influencia del Poder Marítimo en América". Instituto de Estudios Histórico-Maritimos, Lima, 1980. Part II of *Simposium sobre El uso del Mar y Su Influencia en el Desarrollo Nacional*.
[25] Marini, José F. (Colonel). *El Conocimiento Geopolítico*. Circulo Militar, Buenos Aires, 1985; Fraga, Jorge A. (Rear-admiral). *Ensayos de Geopolítica*. Instituto de Publicaciones Havales, Buenos Aires, 1985.
[26] Castro, Terezinha de. "Retrato do Brasil". *Atlas - Texto de Geopolítica*, Biblioteca do Exército, Rio de Janeiro, circa 1986; Flores, Mario César (Captain, Navy). "Poder Maritimo-Conceito e situacao Brasileira". Biblioteca do Exercito-Servico de Documentaçao Geral da Marinha, Rio de Janeiro, 1972. Part 2, Chapter 1 of: *Panorama do Poder Marítimo Brasileiro*; Oliveira Mafra, Roberto Machado de (Lt. Colonel) & Lima Abreu, Carlos Athayades de (Lt. Colonel). "Introducao a Geopolitica". *A Defesa Nacional*, October–November–December 1977.
[27] Pinochet Ugarte, Augusto (General). *Geopolítica de Chile*. El cid, México, 1978 (First published in 1968); Buzeta, Oscar (vice-Admiral). *Chile Geopolítico: Presente y Futuro*. Centro de Estudios de Investigaciones Socio-Económicas de la Compañiía de Jesús en Chile, Santiago, 1978.
[28] Buse de la Guerra. *op. cit.*; Ramirez Canaval, Hugo (Peruvian Rear-Admiral). "Introducción a la Geopolítica". *Revista "Geopolítica* Nr. 19, September 1980, Buenos Aires. Pages 12-31.
[29] See for example, Livezey, William E. *Mahan on Sea Power*. University of Oklahoma Press, Norman, 1947, Chapter XIV, and, Gray, Colin S. *The Geopolitics of the Nuclear Era*. National Strategy Information Center, New York, 1977.

It is worthwhile taking into consideration that, besides the aforementioned literature, Latin American intellectuals in the fields of strategy and geopolitics were also familiar with a number of other classical works such as those by Darrieus,[30] Daveluy,[31] Corbett,[32] and Wegener[33] as well as with the historical works derived from the major wars of the century, particularly, the Russo-Japanese War and World Wars I and II. Many of these books were translated and locally edited. Moreover, Latin American authors produced their own interpretations of these wars.

U.S. Naval Missions.

The U.S. naval missions and advisory groups, as well as the attendance at U.S. naval courses by Latin American naval officers exerted an intellectual influence. In addition, the creation of Naval War Colleges provided another channel of influence in most of the Latin American navies during the century.

The first U.S. naval missions in Latin America were those established in Brazil and Peru, during the closing days of World War I. Over the years, they have provided a continuous flow of American ideas, doctrines, procedures, technology, professional literature, etc., not only in these two countries, but to the whole range of countries which, during the century, had a U.S. naval mission.[34]

By the mid-nineteen thirties, Argentina, in spite of not having a naval mission, requested a U.S. "group of naval advisors" to assist in the establishment and development of its Naval War College. It was no coincidence that, among the first books published by the newly created War College in 1935 were the Spanish translations of Mahan's The Influence of Sea Power upon History and Naval Strategy.[35]

As a first conclusion, it may be stated that Mahan's naval thought was known and accepted among Latin American navies, and his geo-political ideas were and are still influential among other branches of the military and even civilian circles.

The Form of Latin American Navies.

One can see Mahan's influence in the type of navies that have been developed by the Latin American countries since the beginning of the century.

Brazil, Chile and Argentina were, perhaps, the most "battle fleet minded" of the Latin American countries during the first half of the century. Given the prevailing naval theories among the Great Powers, their rivalries and their

[30] Darrieus, Gabriel. La Guerre sur Mer. Agustin Challamel, Paris, 1907.
[31] Daveluy, René. Etude sur la Stratégie Navale. Berger - Levrault & cie, Paris, 1905.
  Daveluy, René. L'Esprit de la Guerre Navale, 3 vols. Berger - Levrault & Cie, Paris-Nancy, 1909-16.
[32] Corbett, Julian S. Some Principles of Maritime Strategy. Longmans, Green & Co, London, 1911.
[33] Wegener, Wolfgang. Seestrategie des Weltkrieges. E.S. Mittler & Sohn, Berlin, 1929.
[34] Scheina. op. cit. Chapter 9.
[35] See notes 12 & 13.

financial position, reasonably better than the rest of Latin America, led to great efforts to create and keep a significant naval power in each one of the three countries.

Brazil. Brazil led the way with its 1904 program calling for two battleships (the first Latin American *Dreadnoughts*), two cruisers and ten destroyers. A third battleship, *Rio de Janeiro*, was later sold to Turkey because of financial problems which also led to the cancellation of its proposed replacement, to be named *Riachuelo*. In addition, three submarines joined the Brazilian Navy by 1914.

Brazilian battleships were later modernized during the 1920's. One of them, *Minas Gerais* was again extensively modified in the 1930's.[36]

There were no significant additions to the surface navy until the late 1930's, at which point Brazil ordered six H-class destroyers from Great Britain. They were never delivered because of the outbreak of World War II.

Prior to this, the Brazilian Navy had tried to purchase or lease some U.S. vessels. Unsuccessful, in part because of Argentinean diplomatic opposition, Brazil started a national shipbuilding program which led to the construction of nine destroyers which were commissioned between the mid 1940's and early 1950's.[37] During the fifties, other important additions to the Brazilian Fleet were two U.S. cruisers of the *Brooklyn*-class and an aircraft carrier (ex-HMS *Vengeance*).

Besides the surface fleet, the Submarine Force, one of the first in South America, was reinforced between the late twenties and thirties, by four Italian built submarines.

The 1960's and the early 1970's gave way to a period in which most Latin American navies were shaped by the transfer of a large number of former U.S. Navy ships, mainly destroyers and submarines.

By the mid-seventies the Brazilian Navy sought an expansion outside the U.S. transfer system. Six frigates of British design (*Niteroi*-class) and three British built *Oberon* class submarines became the core of this program.

The latest additions to the Brazilian Navy are four *Inhahuma*-class frigates and four "209"-class submarines all of which were built in local shipyards.

Argentina. The Brazilian 1904 program generated a swift Argentine answer: two battleships and twelve destroyers were ordered from foreign shipyards. (In fact, because of the outbreak of World War I, only four

[36] Scheina. *op. cit.* Chapter 5; Scheina, Robert L. "Lateinamerikanische Dreadnoughts". *Marine Rundschau*, Nr. 9, 1979, pp. 571-580; Breyer, Siegfried. *Schlachtschiffe und Schlachtkreuzer 1905-1970.* J.F. Lehmanns Verlag, Munich, 1970; Breyer, Siegfried. *Grosskampfschiffe 1905-1970*, Band 3. Bernard & Graefe Verlag, Munchen, 1979; *Conway's all the World Fighting Ships, 1906-1921*. Conway Maritime Press, London, 1985. Pp. 403-407.
[37] Scheina, 1987, *op. cit.* Chapter 9; *Conway's all the World Fighting Ships, 1922-1946*. Conway Maritime Press, London, 1980, pp. 416-418; Almeida Guillobel, Renato de (Captain, Navy). "A Marinha do Brasil na Guerra 1942-1945" (Lecture delivered in 1945), *Subsidios para a Historia Maritima do Brasil*, Volume XXIII - Serviço de Documentação Geral da Marinha, Rio de Janeiro, 1967, pp. 149-150; Vidigal, Armando Amorim Ferreira (Vice-Admiral). "A Evolução do Pensamento Estrategico Naval Brasileiro", *Revista Maritima Brasileira*, August-September-October 1983, p. 37.

destroyers actually joined the Argentine Fleet). The purchase of a third *Dreadnought* was contemplated, as a way to counterbalance the third Brazilian battleship, but, after the latter's cancellation, the Argentine project was discontinued.[38]

The Argentine naval programs of the 1920's and 1930's are, perhaps, the most significant. Argentine battleships were extensively refitted in 1924-1925, where they received most of the improvements derived from the "lessons" of World War I. These improvements included, oil fired boilers, geared turbines and new fire control systems. Additionally three cruisers, twelve destroyers, and three submarines joined the Navy between 1927 and 1939.[39]

In the early fifties, the Argentine Navy received, as did Brazil and Chile, two U. S. built cruisers of the *Brooklyn*-class. These transfers marked the end of Argentine naval dominance in the Southern cone. In fact Argentina had achieved, by the late thirties, a "two power standard", in excess of the "one power standard" prescribed by Storni, one of the Argentine Mahan-inspired naval writers, whose work was previously mentioned.[40]

By the late fifties, the Argentine Navy received its first carrier (ex-HMS *Warrior*), which became the first operational aircraft carrier in South America.

As previously stated in reference to the Brazilian Navy, the sixties and the early seventies were highlighted by the transfers of a large number of former U. S. vessels. However, even in the late 1960's the Argentine Navy turned to Europe, seeking new warships. Two British type 42 DDG's and two German-built "209"-class submarines were ordered. These units were commissioned in the Argentine Navy between the mid-seventies and early eighties.[41]

Moreover, in 1969 the Argentine Navy took advantage of the opportunity of purchasing the Dutch aircraft carrier *Karel Doorman* (ex-HMS *Venerable*), providing the Fleet with the capability of operating jet attack aircraft. Also, three French-built A-69-type corvettes were commissioned between the late seventies and early eighties. The next large procurement effort led the Argentine Navy to add four *Meko*-360-class destroyers, two TR 1700 submarines and three *Meko*-140-class corvettes to its inventory, as well as a squadron of anti-ship missile armed Super Etendard attack aircraft. In spite of serious delays caused by the difficult economic situation in Argentina, four TR 1700 submarines and three MEKO-140 corvettes are still pending completion, as part of this program.[42]

---

[38] *Conway's all the World Fighting Ships, 1947-1982*, part II. Conway Maritime Press, London, 1983, pp. 401-405; Scheina, 1979; *Conway's . . . 1906-1921*, pp. 400-402; Breyer, 1970; Breyer, 1979.

[39] Montenegro, Guillermo J. (Commander). "Die Argentinische Marine seit 1945." *Marine Rundschau*, Nr. 6, 1978, pp. 375-397; *Conway's . . . 1922-1946*, pp. 419-421.

[40] Scheina, 1987, p. 173; *Conway's . . . 1947-1982*, pp. 393 and 401.

[41] Montenegro, 1978; *Conway's . . . 1947-1982*, pp. 393-400.

[42] *Ibid.*

Chile. The Chilean reaction to Brazilian and Argentine shipbuilding programs during the beginning of the century indicated every intention of keeping the pace with its two neighbors. Chile ordered two battleships to be built in Britain, derived from the *Iron Duke*-class but armed with 14" guns. These were taken over by the Royal Navy at the outbreak of World War I. One of them, originally named *Almirante Latorre* served in the Grand Fleet as HMS *Canada*, fought with the British battle line at Jutland and finally was delivered to Chile at the end of the war, reverting to her original name and becoming the only "super-*Dreadnought*" in South America. The second ship, whose intended name was *Almirante Cochrane*, was converted during construction into an aircraft carrier and became HMS *Eagle*.[43] In compensation, the Chilean Navy got six British-built submarines giving birth to the third South American submarine force. In the late twenties, the Chilean Navy improved its capabilities with the modernization of the *Latorre*, and the purchase of six destroyers and three submarines from Britain.[44] Chile also intended to obtain U.S. built cruisers, destroyers and submarines for the Chilean Navy by 1940, but these projects never materialized.[45]

Like Brazil and Argentina, Chile also received two U.S.-built cruisers of the *Brooklyn*-class by the early fifties. In addition to some U.S. transfers in the sixties and the seventies, Chile purchased two brand-new British-built destroyers by the early sixties (one of the few additions of new foreign built vessels to Latin America in the first decades after World War II). Further increases to the Chilean Navy were the ex-Swedish cruiser Göta Lejon in the early seventies, two *Leander*-class frigates and two *Oberon*-class submarines in the mid and late seventies, plus two German-built "209"-class submarines and four ex-British *County*-class destroyers in the eighties.[46]

Peru. The Peruvian Navy, which is now one of the major Latin American naval powers, started this century in a very poor condition. Devastated by the lost war of the Pacific against Chile, Peru was in an extremely difficult economic situation. After World War I, the only significant additions to her navy were four U.S. built "R"-class submarines, which joined the Peruvian Navy in the late twenties. Some authors have argued that Peru attempted to counter Chile's superior surface fleet by creating a significant submarine force following Brazil's example. Brazil had done this to counter the perceived threat from Argentina during the twenties and the thirties, trying to balance with submarines her opponent's superiority in surface forces.[47] In Peru, border disputes with Ecuador caused a difficult relationship between the two countries and actually led to war by the early forties. This was another

[43] Scheina, 1979; Breyer, 1970; Breyer, 1979; *Conway's . . . 1906-1921*, pp. 407-409.
[44] *Conway's . . . 1922-1946*, pp. 422-423.
[45] Scheina, 1987, pp. 85, 163.
[46] *Conway's . . . 1947-1982*, pp. 407-411.
[47] *Conway's . . . 1922-1946*, pp. 416, 423.

impetus to keep a strong Peruvian Navy. Peru obtained a second important enforcement for its submarine force in the fifties, when four brand new U.S.-built submarines of the *Abtao*-class were commissioned. These boats were similar to the U.S. hunter-killer boats of that day. Through the mid-seventies, these Peruvian submarines constituted the most modern units of its kind in South America, as well as being another of the few additions of foreign built "new" vessels to Latin American navies between the end of World War II and the early seventies.[48] On the other hand, the Peruvian surface forces received no significant improvements until the late fifties, when two British-built cruisers of the *Colony*-class were purchased. This led to a sustained expansion from the sixties up to the early eighties, which included two ex-British *Daring*-class destroyers, seven ex-Dutch *Holland/Friesland*-class destroyers, two ex-Dutch cruisers, three *Lupo*-class Italian-built frigates and six French-built PR 72 P-type missile corvettes.[49] The submarine force was also updated, by the purchase of six German-built "209"-class boats.[50]

Venezuela. Venezuela's Navy was a minor force during the first half of the century.[51] In the late forties and early fifties, improved political and economic conditions led to naval expansion. The first important additions were three new construction British-built destroyers, roughly equivalent to the *Battle* and *Daring*-classes, which joined the Venezuelan Navy by the mid-fifties. (These destroyers were another of the few additions of foreign, newly built vessels to South American navies between 1945 and the early 1970's). Further increases in fleet strength, in addition to U.S. transfers, were six Italian-built frigates commissioned in the mid fifties, six Italian *Lupo*-class frigates in the early 1980's and four German 209-type submarines between the late seventies and the early eighties. These additions made Venezuela a significant naval power in the Caribbean region.[52]

Colombia. Colombia's Navy was almost non-existent by the time tensions with Peru arose in the mid-nineteen thirties over boundary disputes. This necessitated a significant effort in order to build up a navy almost from scratch.[53] Two destroyers were purchased from Portugal.[54] Subsequent additions to the Colombian Navy, as far as new ships is concerned, have been relatively minor, *i.e.*: two Swedish-built destroyers in the late fifties and four FS-1500 HDW-built frigates and two "209"-type submarines in the early eighties.[55]

---

[48] *Conway's . . . 1947-1982*, pp. 421-425.
[49] *Ibid.*
[50] *Ibid.*
[51] *Conway's . . . 1922-1946*, p. 415.
[52] *Conway's . . . 1947-1982*, pp. 427-430.
[53] Reyes Canal, Julio C. (Captain, Navy). *Contra viento y marea - Cuaderno Bitácora de la Fundación de una Armada*. Bogotá, 1985.
[54] *Conway's . . . 1922-1946*, p. 415.
[55] *Conway's . . . 1947-1982*, pp. 411-413.

Ecuador. Maintaining that its border dispute with Peru (from the Ecuadorain perception), has not been fully solved, Ecuador has sought to upgrade its navy since the early 1950's and has made significant progress, which has culminated in the commissioning of six Italian-built missile armed corvettes, three missile fast attack craft and two German "209"-type submarines between the late seventies and early eighties.[56]

The remaining Latin American countries kept relatively small naval forces during almost the entire century. In most cases this was due to lack of resources, and, in some others, because of the non-existence of regional tensions, as in the case of Mexico.[57]

Paraguay. Paraguay was a special case. In spite of having no sea coast, the existence of navigable rivers along its borders and across its territory, coupled with a growing tension with Bolivia in the late twenties, which eventually caused a war in 1932-1935, led to the acquisition of two excellent river gunboats, which joined the Paraguayan Navy in 1931.

Mahanian Navies. It should be emphasized that the acquisition and maintenance of the naval forces mentioned in the previous paragraphs represented and still constitute a substantial effort for all the Latin American countries involved. Latin American countries have had first hand experience regarding "having or not having" the adequate amount of sea power to face a crisis or a war situation. These fleets came to life because of tensions and dangers perceived as real, as well as a means to gain diplomatic leverage, whenever necessary.[58]

Moreover, it should be said that several of the aforementioned Latin American naval writers, as well as some others, were advocates of a big navy or showed a distinct concern for a naval balance in the face of prospective rivals.[59]

Therefore, one may conclude that, when tensions were present and resources available, the Latin American Navies favored, and still favor, the Mahanian concept of a strong navy.

Navies and Sea Power. There is another area in which Mahanian inspiration proved significant. This was the continued concern of Latin American Navies in the maritime affairs of their respective countries, giving impulse to their shipyards and fishing industries, their maritime legislation,

---

[56] *Ibid*, pp. 415–416.

[57] *Conway's . . . 1922-1946*, p. 414; *Conway's . . . 1947-1982*, pp. 419–420.

[58] Scheina, 1979.

[59] Dias, Arthur. *O Problema Naval*. Oficina da Estatistica, Rio de Janeiro, 1899; Storni, *op. cit.*; Lagos, M.J. (Rear-Admiral). *El Poder Naval*, Buenos Aires, 1921; Burlamaqui, Armando (Captain, Navy). *A situação Naval Sul Americana em 1921*. Imprensa Naval, Rio de Janeiro, 1921; Burlamaqui, Armando (Captain, Navy). *Esboço da Política Naval Brasileira*, Imprensa Nacional, Rio de Janeiro, 1923; Flores, Mario César (Captain, Navy). *A Marinha de Guerra no Brasil Actual*, Biblioteca de Exercito, Serviço de Documentação Geral da Marinha, Rio de Janeiro, 1972. Part 3. Chapter 2 of: *Panorama do Poder Marítimo Brasileiro*; Ghisolfo Araya, Francisco. "Situación Estratégica Naval". *Revista de Marina*, Valparaiso, 1985, pp. 401–474, 605–644 of: *El Poder Naval Chileno*, vol. II.

etc., trying to put into practice the dictum: "Naval strategy has indeed for its end to establish, support and increase, as well in peace as in war, the sea power of a country".[60]

It should be remembered that, in the beginning of this century, Latin American merchant navies were very small or nonexistent, the indigenous capabilities for ship repairs were minimal, and those for shipbuilding were nil. Therefore, the upgrading of national maritime assets was a colossal task to face.

Latin American Navies have dedicated strong efforts to educate their populations about the advantages of sea power and its meaning. In some cases these policies led to the creation of Navy Leagues, which play an important role in teaching and informing the public about sea power. Naval officers have played a key role in this. In most Latin American countries, important positions concerning the merchant marine, the shipbuilding industry, harbor administration, maritime police, piloting, have usually been held by either serving or retired naval officers.

Another maritime-related field of interest was, and is, the Antarctica. Chile and Argentina were the pioneers, and for many years, they were the only Latin American countries there. However, in the last few decades, a large number of regional countries have encouraged expeditions and/or settled permanent scientific bases there. In all cases, navies have had the most prominent share in each country's efforts to build and maintain a presence in Antartica.

This actual involvement ln the maritime affairs of each country has gone hand to hand with a parallel intellectual effort to influence and to inform the maritime-related community and the general public. Latin American literature about the "Maritime Interests" of each country is really massive.[61]

[60] Mahan, Alfred T. *The Influence of Sea Power upon History-1660-1783*. Little, Brown & Co, Boston, 1940, p. 23.
[61] Some relevant examples are: Flores, Mario Cesar (Captain, Navy). *Panorama do Poder Marítimo Brasileiro*. Biblioteca do Exercito, Serviço de Documentação Geral da Marinha, Rio de Janeiro, 1972. Especially Part 4 - "Marinha Mercante"; Part 5 - "Construção e Reparos Navais"; Part 6 - "Portos"; Part 9 - "O Homen e O Mar"; Storni, *op. cit.*; Fraga, Jorge A. (Rear-Admiral). *La Argentina y el Atlántico Sur*. Instituto de Publicaciones Navales, Buenos Aires, 1983; Casellas, Alberto O. (Captain, Navy). *La Alternativa Oceánica*. Instituto de Publicaciones Navales, Buenos Aires, 1987; Parra Maza, Raul (Captain, Navy). "La Política Marítima Peruana con Proyección al Siglo XXI". *Revista de Marina*, Lima, November-December 1980, pp. 192-206; Indacoechea Queirolo, Alberto (Vice-Admiral). "Los Intereses Marítimos y su Relacion con la Marina de Guerra del Peru hasta 1979", *Revista de Marina*, Lima, November-December 1980, pages 207-212; Carcelen Basurto, Jose (Rear-Admiral). "Los Intereses Marítimos y su Relacion con la Marina de Guerra del Peru en la Decada del '80". *Revista de Marina*, Lima, November-December 1980, pp. 213-222; Leon y Leon, Adolfo. "Situación, posibilidades y metas de la Marina Mercante Nacional". Instituto de Estudios Histórico-Marítimos, Lima, 1980. Part IV of: *Simposium sobre el uso del mar y su influencia en el desarrollo nacional*; Villagran Tapia, Cesar (Captain, Navy). "La Construcción Naval en el Peru". Instituto de Estudios Histórico-Marítimos, Lima, 1980. Part VI of: *Simposium sobre el uso del mar y su influencia en el desarrollo nacional*; Castañon Pasquel, Emilio. "Reseña Histórica de la Pesca e Industrias Conexas - Proyecciones". Instituto de Estudios Histórico-Marítimos, Lima, 1980. Part VIII of: *Simposium sobre el uso del mar y su influencia en el desarrollo nacional*; Scheihing Navarro, Ruben. "Proyeccion Maritima Nacional. Revista de Marina, Valparaiso, 1985, pp. 537-555 of *El Poder Naval Chileno* vol. II; Angulo Budge, Eduardo. "Intereses Maritimos". Revista de Marina, Valparaiso, 1985, pp. 557-603 of *El Poder Naval Chileno* vol. II.

Throughout this century, the majority of the Latin American naval writers have tried hard to influence conditions in the light of these factors that Mahan identified, such as National Character and Character of the Government,[62] which affect the sea power of a country.

Conclusion. Mahan's influence in Latin America was not exclusive, being shared with – and in some cases reinforced by some of the "Outstanding Naval Strategic Writers of the Century".[63] Moreover, his influence had a varying impact upon each individual country, and, was expressed through varying paths. Despite this, Mahan's influence in the region was and remains a real one. For most Latin American navies, he is a *major* prophet, if not the only prophet.

[62] Mahan, A.T., *op. cit.*, pp. 50, 58.
[63] Hunt, Barry D. "The Outstanding Naval Strategic Writers of the Century". *Naval War College Review* September-October 1984, pp. 86-107.

Chapter 9

Low Intensity Conflict in Latin America: Does Mahan have a Place

Robert L. Scheina

Above all else, Alfred Thayer Mahan was *the* Thalassocratic determinist of the United States. For Mahan, national greatness, and even survival, depended upon sea power.

One does not have to be a student of Mahan in order to practice his teachings.[1] Examples exist within Latin America, as elsewhere, of leaders who have employed the theories of noted strategists without having been exposed to their writings.[2]

For three decades Fidel Castro has been employing elements of sea power as defined by Mahan to further Cuba's foreign policy throughout Latin America. On the surface it might seem ridiculous to argue that a country ranked somewhere among the "un-rank" of world naval powers, could seriously challenge the nation possessing the world's most powerful fleet, the United States Navy. This would be ridiculous if sea power were based solely upon navies. However, as Mahan noted, sea power is more than navies for it "includes not only the military strength afloat . . . but also the peaceful

---

[1] And conversely, studying Mahan does not necessarily mean that one has learned from his writings.

[2] The greatness of many noted military teachers lies in the fact that they articulated the obvious before it was espoused by others. This does not necessarily mean that others can not practice the art first or practice it ignorant of the writings of anointed teacher. Since few analysts look to Latin America for military lessons, many of these have gone unnoticed. For example, between 1817 and 1824 General José de San Martín used sea power to carry the war of Independence from Argentina to the center of Spanish power in South America, Peru, with the strategy of liberating Chile first and then transporting his army over the sea to Peru. He came to this strategic concept after witnessing the defeat of three Argentine expeditions led by his predecessors. These had failed to reach Peru by way of the Bolivian highlands. This projection of sea power ashore long preceded the writings of Mahan. A century later during the Chaco War, Marshal José Estigarribia successfully employed a strategy based on mobility against his opponent, General Hans Kundt, who was married to the old doctrine of holding territory. This took place before Estigarribia could have had access to Charles de Gaulle's *Vers l'Armée de Metier*, published in 1934, and Erwin Rommel's *Infanterie greift an*, published in 1937.

commerce and shipping. . . ."[3] As we shall see, merchant ships can haul more than commerce and fishing craft can catch more than fish.

Two factors allow the commercial aspects of sea power to play a major role in modern Latin American history. First, since World War II, "low intensity conflicts" have been the dominant form of warfare throughout the region. Covert action can play a critical role in such fighting. During such warfare, fishing fleets and merchant marines have more opportunities to support national objectives than do navies. Merchant ships and fishing craft may be sent almost anywhere at almost anytime without undue notice. A warship by its nature attracts attention at all times, thus limiting its usefulness for covert operations.

Second, Latin American nations are heavily dependent upon the sea for commerce. More than 90 percent of all international commerce carried among Latin American nations moves by water. No Latin American nation has developed a merchant marine capable of meeting domestic needs. This lack of merchant marines provides others, including Cuba, the opportunity to use their fleets for political objectives within the region.

Most Latin American nations claim exclusive economic zones or territorial waters extending out to 200 miles in order to control the sea's rich bounty. Cuba is the only Latin American nation which has developed a fishing fleet large and sophisticated enough to roam the world's oceans thousands of miles from home. Today, fishing is the third most important industry in Cuba.[4] In about 1980 Cuba even converted a fishing vessel, the *Isla de la Juventud*, into an intelligence gathering ship.[5] Among the remaining Latin American nations, fishing fleets are not even large enough to exploit the harvest within their own territorial waters.

In order to earn much needed hard currency, most Latin American nations find it financially necessary to license foreign fleets to fish in their waters. Cuba and other communist bloc nations are always competitive bidders for these fishing rights. In some cases, such as the current agreement between Peru and the Soviet Union, the foreign fishing fleet has routine access to the ports of the licensing nation.[6]

Ironically, in spite of th fact that Cuba is an island, sea power did not play a major role in bringing Fidel Castro to power. True, Castro and his band of 82 did arrive by boat in 1956 and they did receive significant financial help from sympathizers in the United States. However, during the fighting which

---

[3]Alfred Thayer Mahan, *The Influence of Sea Power upon History, 1660-1783* (Boston: Little, Brown & Co., 1935), p. 28.

[4]The two more significant industries are sugar and the re-export of oil. Dominguez and Hernandez, *U.S.-Cuban Relations in the 1990s* (Boulder: Westview Press, 1989), p. 238.

[5]Baker, *Combat Fleets of the World 1990-91* (Annapolis: U.S. Naval Institute Press, 1990), p. 103.

[6]During the 1970s Peru signed a fishing agreement with Cuba which permitted twelve Cuban fishing vessels to operate in Peruvian waters. Within a few years the agreement was shifted to the Soviet Union because of the significantly greater capacity of its fishing fleets. *Los Convenios Pesqueros entre El Peru y La Union Sovietica en Debate* (Lima: CEPEI, 1989), p. 21.

followed, less than 15 per cent of Castro's logistical support came from outside Cuba.[7] The 1959 Cuban Revolution was an air and ground war.

During his early years in power, Castro undoubtedly learned to appreciate the use of naval power. In June 1959 some two hundred guerrillas sailed from Cuba in two vessels apparently under the escort of three Cuban frigates, holdovers from Batistas Navy. Their objective was the overthrow of Dominican strongman Rafael Trujillo. Although successfully landed, this effort to spread revolution failed.[8] On 17 April 1961 Castro successfully defeated the Bay of Pigs invasion; he, more than anyone, must have understood that this American failure was not caused by lack of adequate naval strength. During this same time Castro openly threatened to support an invasion of Panama by revolutionaries. U.S. naval forces, patrolling the Caribbean coast of northern Panama between 24 April and 4 May, prevented the threat from being carried out.[9] And in October 1962 Castro again witnessed the use of U.S. naval power during the Cuban Missile Crisis. Castro must have appreciated that he could not openly challenge the United States Navy.

Following the Cuban Revolution, Fidel Castro became the champion of Marxists seeking to bring about change through violence. Mario Llerena, a liberal intellectual who had supported Castro during the Revolution, wrote:

> "Revolution, then, came to be Castro's supreme vocation. Castro sees revolution not as a last resort but as a channel for self-expression—an escape valve for his accumulated resentments and hates. He actually needs revolution as the addict needs drugs.[10]

During the three decades following the Cuban Revolution, Fidel Castro supported guerrilla warfare as he searched for a winning strategy. The decade of the 1960s was dedicated to the foco strategy as articulated by Che Guevara. This was followed by years of support for urban guerrilla warfare. And today, we might call the current era the strategy of the united front. Successes have been few; nonetheless, Castro does not seem to have lost his revolutionary enthusiasm.

One constant throughout these three decades has been Castro's use of Cuba's merchant and fishing fleets to support the struggle against non-Marxists governments. For obvious reasons, Castro has attempted to keep secret their operations in support of political objects. However, thirty years of activity can not be made totally invisible.

---

[7]Chapelle, "How Castro Won," 334-35; *Time* (14 July 1958), 29.

[8]Fermoselle, *The Evolution of the Cuban Military: 1492-1986* (Miami: Ediciones Universal, 1987), p. 348-49. During this period other guerrilla groups sailed for Panama, Nicaragua and Haiti. However, no direct Cuban maritime support has been proven.

[9]Robert Scheina, "The Cuban Navy," in *The Soviet and Other Communist Navies: The View from the mid-1980s* ed. by James L. George (Annapolis: U.S. Naval Institute Press, 1986), pp. 324-25.

[10]Mario Llerena, *Unsuspected Revolution* (Ithaca: Cornell University Press, 1978), p. 203. Today, many scholars convincingly argue that Fidel Castro has always been the most generous supporter for revolutionary warfare, at times even contrary to the wishes of the Soviet Union.

During the early 1960s, Castro focused much of his revolutionary activity against the fledgling democratic government of Venezuela. In July 1964 the Venezuelan armed forces discovered three tons of munitions which had been brought by sea from Cuba.[11] In July 1966 and again in May 1967 Castro openly reinforced the Venezuelan Communist Douglas Bravo with arms and fresh guerrillas trained in Cuba. On 18 May 1967 several Cubans were captured landing on the Venezuelan coast. *Granma*, the official Cuban newspaper, responded to Venezuelan charges that Cuba was aiding Communist guerrillas not with denials but admission:

> "We are accused of helping the revolutionary movement, and we, quite so, are giving and will continue to give help to all revolutionary movements that struggle against imperialism in any part of the world, whenever they request it."[12]

By the mid 1960s, Cuba had significantly expanded its fishing fleet, thanks to the help of the Soviet Union, to permit fishing outside the Caribbean. In 1966 two Cuban stern freezer trawlers operated with the Communist-bloc fleet off Argentine's Patagonia coast. The following year, an armada of Communist-bloc fishing vessels appeared off the east coast of South America. Some newspaper reports claimed that there were as many as two hundred fishing vessels. In response, the Argentine government extended its fishing zone out to 200 miles. The Communist-bloc fishing fleet delayed in leaving Argentine waters. As a result, the Argentine Navy used force to seize two large processing ships and a number of catch boats. In early 1971 Brazil also extended its territorial waters to 200 miles, thus making short-lived Cuban fishing in those waters.[13] This also prevented their participation in covert operations in support of urban guerrillas, a serious Brazilian concern at that time. In spite of these setbacks the Communist-bloc fishing vessels, including those of Cuba, continued to operate off the East Coast of South America, outside the 200 mile exclusion zones.

Salvador Allende's election as President of Chile in November 1970 opened new opportunities for Cuba's fishing industry. In February 1971 the newly established Chilean Ministry of Fisheries signed a fisheries technical assistance agreement with Cuba. Under this agreement, Cuban ships were permitted to fish inside Chilean waters if licensed; the possibility of a Chilean marine fisheries school with Cuban instructors was to be studied; and Cuba promised to assist in determining the fisheries stock within Chilean waters. In fact, Cuba proved to be technically incapable of delivering on these promises;

[11]Carbonell, *And the Russians Stayed* (New York: William Morrow and Co., 1989), p. 369.
[12]*Granma Weekly Review* (Havana) 21 May 1967.
[13]In 1972 the Exclusive Economic Zone (EEZ) established by the United Nation's Conference on the Law of the Sea (UNCLOS) had not yet been put forward. The only practical way to guarantee fishing rights was to extend the territorial waters unilaterally. After 1982 Brazil adopted a 12 mile territorial sea with a 200 mile EEZ. Thebberge, *Soviet Seapower in the Caribbean* (New York: Praeger Publishers, 1972), p. 156-57.

however, the necessary know-how was to be provided by the Soviet Union.[14] Soon three Cuban boats were operating in territorial waters off central Chile and six Soviet vessels to the north. According to the Chilean Navy, the first priority of these fishing boats was oceanographic and military intelligence.[15]

On 12 September 1973 an incident occurred which fueled speculation that Cuban maritime activity within Chilean waters was more than commercial. The Cuban merchant ship *Calle Larga* fled Valparaio following the overthrow of the Salvador Allende government. She was overtaken by Chilean destroyer *Blanco Encalada* but permitted to proceed. It is speculated that she had carried arms to the Chilean Communist. Since proof was not immediately at hand, the ship had to be permitted to proceed.[16]

The Communist-bloc fishing fleet did not return to the waters off Chile until 1982. Between 1982 and 1986 the Communist-bloc fishing fleet operated off Chile between 230 and 300 miles out. The Chilean Navy estimated that the fishing catch by the Communist fleet grew from 576,000 tons in 1982 to 1,700,000 tons in 1986.

Cuban maritime assets were important in the arming of Grenada following the rise of the pro-Communist government of Maurice Bishop in March 1979. Grenada contracted with the Soviet Union and East Bloc nations for large quantities of arms. The agreement called for the weapons to be shipped to Cuba and from there they were trans-shipped apparently by Cuban maritime assets to Grenada.[17]

The extent of Cuba's maritime support given to the Sandinistas appears to be modest. Prior to the overthrow of Somoza, apparently Cuban aid was primarily delivered by aircraft. Considering the arms could be flown openly into Costa Rica's San Jose airport and then trucked into Nicaragua, maritime routes offered no advantage. This does not seemed to have changed following the Sandinista seizure of power. During the first three months of 1984 the Contras attacked shipping in Nicaragua's west coast ports. Of the approximately 20 merchant ships damaged by gunfire and mines it appears that only one flew the Cuban flag.[18] Considering that Cuba and Nicaragua had excellent air service and that Nicaragua's principal ports are on the Pacific, the absence of the Cuban merchant marine should come as no surprise. However, sea as well as land and air routes were used to introduce weapons

---

[14]In addition, the agreement did help break down the attempt to isolate Cuba by the Organization of American States. Thebberge, *Soviet Seapower in the Caribbean*, 160-62.

[15]Chilean Navy produced video tape entitled "Soviet Fishing Boat operations in Proximity of Chilean Coastal Waters," no date.

[16]*El Mercurio* (Valparaiso), 13 Septiembre 1973, p. 1.

[17]Agreement between the Government of Grenada and the Government of the Union of Soviet Socialist Republics dated 27 July 1982 published in Uri Ra'anan, *et. al.*, *Hydra of Carnage* (Lexington: Lexington Books, 1986), pp. 364, 379-81.

[18]*Wall Street Journal* (6 March 1985), 20:1.

into El Salvador from Nicaragua. Arms were shipped across the Gulf of Fonseca in small craft.[19]

Probably Cuba's most daring affront to U.S. naval power began in 1982. In that year a department was created within the Interior Ministry the task of which was to smuggle scarce materials from the United States to Cuba. According to radio Havana, which publicly exposed this operation in 1989, "Not a few necessities were resolved this way."[20] A large number of Cuban intelligence agents had been introduced into the United States during the Mariel Boatlift in 1982. These agents routinely crossed between Cuba and Florida in speed boats known as cigarette boats. One of these agents, Mario Estavez Gonzales, described to various committees of the U.S. Congress how it was easy to travel by high speed craft between the two countries. Senator Paula Hawkins asked Estavez, "How many times had you gone back and forth?" The answer, "I would go every month, two or three times." Senator Hawkins continued, "And when you would come back to the United States, did anybody check any of your documents or ask for your identification?" Estevez responded, "This is a very free country. They don't ask for anything here."[21]

According to Eden Pastora Gomez, at the time a member of the Sandinista National Directorate, Fidel Castro decided to enter the narcotics business in 1982 with the objective of introducing drugs into the United States in order to undermine the social fabric.[22] In contradiction, Radio Havana claimed that General Arnaldo Ochoa was fully responsible for Cuba's participating in the drug trafficking.[23] Regardless of which is correct, Cuba tried to coerce drug dealers into using their craft to carry arms to leftist guerrillas in Colombia. Officials in Cuba had agreed to allow their territorial waters to serve as a trans-shipment site for these traffickers in exchange for a share of the profits. The smugglers, Johnny Crump and David Lorenzo Perez, had been unable to pay Cuban officials because one of their boats had to dump its cargo overboard after being detected by the U. S. Coast Guard.[24]

During the 1980s, Cuba continued to transport weapons to guerrillas via water routes. The Colombian Army captured a guerrilla, who a few months earlier had been granted asylum in Cuba. He testified that he had flown from Cuba to Panama and along with other guerrillas and arms had been landed

[19]Testimony of Eden Pastora Gomez, quoted in Uri Ra'anan, et. al., Hydra of Carnage, 329; U.S. Department of State, Special Report 80, 23 February 1981, "Communist Interference in El Salvador," 7.
[20]Granma Editorial on Ochoa-La Guardia Case, 22 June 1989, published in Federal Broadcast and Information Service, LAT-89-120, 4.
[21]Ra'anan, et. al., Hydra of Carnage, 440, see also 437-38, 448-49.
[22]Eden Pastora Gomez states that Castro said during the 1982 meeting, "we are going to make the people up there (the United States) white, white with cocaine." Uri Ra'anan, et. al., Hydra of Carnage, 330.
[23]Granma Editorial on Ochoa-La Guardia Case, 22 June 1989, published in Federal Broadcast and Information Service, LAT-89-120, 1-8.
[24]Ra'anan, et.al., Hydra of Carnage, 459, 462.

from a boat named the Freddie on the coast of Colombia.[25] As a result of this and other Cuban activity, the Colombian government suspended diplomatic relations with Cuba 23 March 1981. On 14 November of the same year the Colombian Navy intercepted and sank the boat *El Karnia* attempting to land guerrillas and weapons on that nation's Pacific Coast.[26]

Cuba's attempt to promote revolution during the 1980s was not limited to the Caribbean. In August 1986 the Chilean government discovered a large cache of arms at four isolated locations along the northern cost of Chile. In mid June the Chilean coastal fishing boat *Chompalhue* had picked up weapons from a Communist-bloc fishing fleet operating outside the Chilean 200 mile fishing zone. The weapons were landed using inflatable boats. The procedure was repeated by the Chilean coastal fishing boat *Astrid Sue* on 6 August. The weapons included more than 3,000 U.S. made M-16 assault rifles, 114 Soviet-made rocket launchers, almost two million rounds of ammunitions, and large quantities of C4 and TNT explosives. One of the three guerrillas captured at that time had been trained in Cuba.[27]

It would be ridiculous to argue that Fidel Castro is a Thalassocratic determinist in the tradition of Alfred Thayer Mahan. Above all else, Castro is a pragmatic revolutionary not wed to any military strategy. However, it would be accurate to say that Castro appreciates that the commercial aspects of sea power, the merchant marine and fishing fleets, are important tools for spreading revolution. For Mahan, merchant marines and fishing fleets are economic resources. Castro has broadened their use to include political and military tasks during times of "Low Intensity Conflict."

Does Mahan have a place in low intensity conflict? Fidel Castro would seem to think so.

[25]Ra'anan, *et. al.*, *Hydra of Carnage*, 452. Among the captured guerrillas were members of the 19 April Movement (M-19) who had seized a group of diplomats at the Dominican Embassy in Bogota. As part of a negotiated settlement, the guerrillas had been flown to asylum in Havana where they received additional training in guerrilla warfare. Robert S. Leiken, *Soviet Strategy in Latin America*, 89-91.

[26]Germán Castro Caicedo, *El Karina* (Bogotá: Plaza & Janes Editores, 1987).

[27]Chilean Navy produced video tape entitled "Infiltration of Arms," no date. The M-16s had been sent to South Vietnam by the United States between 1967 and 1969. These fell into the hands of the Hanoi government after the fall of Saigon in 1975. "Chile Intercepts Soviet Arms Aimed for Rebels," *The Mexican City News* (12 August 1986), 8.

PART III:
THE MAN AND HISTORIAN

Alfred Thayer Mahan was the son of Dennis Hart Mahan, Dean of the Faculty and Professor of Civil and Military Engineering at West Point. He was born September 27, 1840 and probably in this house on the grounds of the U.S. Military Academy. The house, which was also home to Mahan's five brothers and sisters, no longer exists.

Copy of photograph in the U.S. Military Academy Archives.

"Marshmere," the Mahan family summer residence in Quogue, Long Island built in 1909. During the four months of winter, the Mahans' generally rented in New York City or toured abroad. Mahan's private study in "Marshmere" was soundproof, since he demanded absolute silence when engaged in writing.

Courtesy of the Quogue Historical Society and Mr. & Mrs. Shuttleworth.

Chapter 10

My Parents,
Rear Admiral and
Mrs. Alfred Thayer Mahan

Lyle Evans Mahan
(Edited and Annotated by John B. Hattendorf)

To his contemporaries as well as to later students of his writings, the personality of Alfred Mahan has been remote and difficult to understand. Held in awe by some and ridiculed by others, there has been no consensus. In these previously unpublished recollections, Mahan's youngest child and only son sketches his view of his parents. Despite some minor inaccuracies, these impressions provide useful insights into Admiral Mahan's character and personality.

Lyle Mahan went on to a successful legal and financial career in New York after having graduated from Groton School and Columbia University in 1902. He wrote the recollections of his father in 1935, more than 20 years after his father's death. Then in his mid 50s, he may well have been responding to a request from Captain W.D. Puleston, who was then writing a biography of Mahan. Lyle wrote the reminiscences of his mother in 1936, nine years after her death, apparently in response to a separate request from an unidentified source.

These reminiscences are reprinted by permission of the Special Collections Department, U.S. Military Academy Library. The original typescripts are dated as follows: 11 July 1935 for the recollections of Admiral Mahan, and 30 January 1936 for the recollections of Mrs. Mahan. These documents complement the "Recollections of Ellen Kuhn Mahan," Lyle's sister, which are printed in Robert Seager II and Doris D. Maguire, Letters and Papers of Alfred Thayer Mahan (Annapolis: Naval Institute Press, 1975), vol. 3, pp. 719-730.

My Father

At the time of my birth in 1881, my father was over forty years of age. While I was still a baby, he went to sea on the *Wachusett*, which, as I recall, was on duty in the Atlantic and for a time was stationed at the port of one of the Central American Republics in which there was a revolution. He did not return from this cruise until I was about four years old, so that my first recollections of him are at about that date.[1]

I remember standing in considerable awe of him, and, as a matter of fact, the same frame of mind continued until I was almost grown up, because, while never unkind, he always insisted on strict and implicit obedience. He was, however, always absolutely just. I never was on the terms of intimacy with him that I could have wished. There was a certain reserve in his character that seemed to prevent this, and the unfortunate situation may have been accentuated by the fact that he was in his later middle age before I knew him at all.

At the time my father returned from the cruise on the *Wachusett*, my mother and sisters and I were living with my mother's mother, Mrs. Manlius G. Evans, at the Hotel Hanover, 2 East 15th Street, New York City. Shortly after that time, my father was appointed to the Naval War College at Coasters Harbor Island, Newport, R.I. In *From Sail to Steam* my father gives an account of his experiences at that time in opening the sessions of the War College and getting the necessary furnishings, etc.[2]

The building, as he said, was formerly an alms house. It was an unpretentious structure and was divided into two separate portions. The westerly one, looking towards Narragansett Bay, was assigned to my father and his family. The easterly portion was occupied by Commander Duncan Kennedy and his wife and son. Just what his duties were, I do not know.[3]

The lower floor of my father's house, if it may be so called, were the living quarters. Of the upper floor, I only remember one room which was a large room with three exposures in which the lectures were given and in which my father worked. It also crosses my mind that one or two card parties were held there.

My principal memory of my father at this period is seeing him make the maps or plans of the various battles which he discussed in the lecture room. He had large pieces of red and green paper or very thin cardboard which he cut out roughly himself in the shape of ships and pasted on to large sheets

[1] Lyle Evans Mahan was born on 12 February 1881 in a house which the Mahans had rented on 11th Street, just off of Fifth Avenue, in New York City. At that time, the forty-year old Commander Mahan was serving as navigation officer at the Brooklyn Navy Yard. In August 1883, when Lyle was two years old, Mahan left New York to take command of USS *Wachusett*, based at Callao, Peru. When Mahan arrived on the South Pacific station, it was the fifth and final year of the War of the Pacific. In March 1885 Mahan and *Wachusett* were at Panama City when the Panamanians revolted against Colombia. The following month he cruised off El Salvador at the time when Guatemala was attempting to annex Nicaragua, Costa Rica and El Salvador. He rejoined his family in September 1885 enroute to assignment at the Naval War College.

[2] A.T. Mahan, *From Sail to Steam: Recollections of Naval Life* (New York: Harper Brothers, 1907), see pages 239-300.

[3] Built in 1820 by the city of Newport as an alms house, it is now Founder's Hall at the Naval War College. Today it houses the Naval War College Museum. Kennedy, then a lieutenant, was on the administrative staff at the Naval War College in 1887.

of heavy paper to show the positions of the ships in the battles. This was something I had to imitate so I always wanted to cut out ships and paste them on paper too, which is undoubtedly why I recall this so well.

When my father was in deep thought, he would pace up and down the room with his head sunk forward a little bit and generally with his hands clasped behind him. He was slightly over six feet in height and very spare. His weight, I think, averaged between 150 and 160 pounds. His carriage was erect except that his head was apt to be bent slightly forward. On the whole, his carriage was graceful and easy.

I have heard it said, and I believe it is true, that my father was a strict disciplinarian on ship, although entirely just there as at home. My son,[4] who was nine years old when my father died and who could take more childish liberties with him than I ever dared to, and in that way probably knew him better, and who was also very observant, said that there were two people in the world whom he knew who he thought were actuated only by what they believed to be right in their every action. One being his grandfather, and the other the Rector, meaning Reverend Endicott Peabody, Headmaster of the school which both my son and I attended.[5]

I recollect two incidents with regard to my father's disciplinary measures on shipboard which I heard in my childhood and which might have been told to me by him or by my mother who heard them from him. In one instance, there was a sailor who was always late in coming on deck. My father asked him what the trouble was and he said that he did not have time to get dressed. When my father told him that he would be called a half hour before the rest of the watch, the trouble did not recur.

In the other instance, there was a sailor who habitually failed to keep his feet clean. After several warnings, my father had one or two of the other sailors wash them with a broom, which cured this particular failing.

I believe that my father naturally had a violent temper but he had worked hard all his life to get it under control. I can only recollect two incidents of what I should call loss of temper on his part, both occurring when I was a well-grown boy or young man. In the first case, the incident was connected with a stage driver. In Quogue [Long Island], where the family has spent the summers ever since 1893, the station was a mile or so from the village, and anybody who wanted to go to New York before the days of the automobile, went to the station by stage. Each house in the village was supplied with a red flag which was hung up when the stage was wanted. My father wanted to go to the station one day and hung up the flag, but the stage driver did not see it. My father accordingly had to go to the station on his bicycle on a very hot day, and seeing the stage driver when he got about

---

[4] Alfred Thayer Mahan, II (1905-1989).
[5] Groton School.

fifty yards from the station, began to berate him in no uncertain language, although not in the least profane. I know that he was very sorry for it afterwards and I believe apologized.

The other incident is connected with myself. We had a new waitress who had done something that startled my mother, I have forgotten just what it was, and my mother started to scold her, which I thought unfair and at which I remonstrated. My father told me to stop talking, which I refused to do, and he raised his voice very markedly to make me stop. These were the only two incidents which I remember of his having lost his temper even momentarily.

I never remember my father using any profane language beyond perhaps a very mild "darn." One of my cousins who recently died, told me that my father had used such language on occasions and intimated that it might have been usual with him on shipboard. He said that once when his own father or uncle, I forget which, was walking along the waterfront with him, a boat was upset and a man fell into the water, and my father jumped into a boat in which there were some oarsmen, and in order to get them to hurry, swore at them roundly. This is a second- or third-hand account of what happened and I cannot vouch for its truth. I am merely trying to put down everything that may show any sidelight on my father's character.

About 1889[6] we moved to New York City taking an apartment at 75 East 54th Street, which was the northwest corner of 54th Street and Park Avenue. We were on the top floor, the 5th, and there was no elevator. In those days, Park Avenue was very different from what it is now; the railroad tracks not being covered over so that every train that passed was very audible and sometimes in the early morning an engine would stop under our window and let off steam. I was sent to school in 42nd Street opposite what is now the site of the Public Library, which was then occupied by the old reservoir. It was very customary for my father to walk down with me at least as far as 42nd Street. I do not know for what purpose except that it was probably to exercise our dog, who was very much a part of the family. We had owned his mother and could not think of the family apart from the dog. He was a bull terrier, quite a bit larger than the average, and not of the present Boston type, but with a pointed nose. His name was Jomini, after the French General, author of *The Art of War* which exercised a very profound influence on my father's writings. My father either was very fond of walking or thought that he ought to take exercise. At any rate, he took the dog out every morning and afternoon, as far as I remember, and it seems to me in these walks he was more relaxed than at most other times. I remember that there was a small boy, I should say about six years old, who caused him a great deal of

---

[6] Mahan and his family moved to this address on 1 October 1890, after having spent July through September at Hall Cottage, Merton Road, Newport, RI.

amusement. He wore a derby hat and we passed him frequently on the way down. My father also got a great deal of amusement because when Jomini first went out in the morning, he would make a dead-set at the birds in the street, and there were always quite a few of them. Once, to his great surprise, he caught one and immediately let it go. My father always urged him on his usually abortive charges.

My father took great pains with our religious training. He was a very devout Episcopalian himself, not one of the lip-service kind, but one who read the Bible and studied it very, very carefully. This is shown by his book *The Harvest Within*[7] which has been praised by a great many churchmen. We were all taught to catechism, and each Sunday, one year, I had to learn by heart the collect for that day. One day I remember saying that I could not learn the collect and was told that that was all right, but that I would not go out to play until I did. I soon mastered it.

Not content with the catechism, my father himself got up what might be called a supplementary catechism explaining various things and the meanings of certain words used frequently in the church service, but which would be entirely unfamiliar to children. This I was also required to learn by heart.

When my father again resumed work at the Naval War College, a new building had been built, as narrated by him in *From Sail to Steam*.[8] It was a very nice stone building, as I remember it, very close to Narragansett Bay, that is, on the west side of the island. His quarters again overlooked the Bay.

I cannot remember the exact time that we were in this place, but it was there, I believe, that my father was first urged to publish his lectures in book form. I think it must have been about 1890 and 1891. Of course, I was too young to know much about what was going on, but I afterwards learned that my father sent *The Influence of Sea Power Upon History* to several publishers, I believe about eight or ten, and that it was consistently turned down.[9]

It would be impossible to write anything about my father's life without saying a great deal about my mother.[10] To my mind, they constituted a perfect team. I can never remember a cross word being spoken on either side. The few occasions on which my father ever expressed any annoyance was when he thought that my mother was doing too much work and tiring herself unnecessarily. She was a woman of very strong character and absolutely indomitable determination. She was also a wonderful manager. The problem of bringing up and educating properly three children on a captain's shore pay

[7] *The Harvest Within: Thoughts on the Life of a Christian* (Boston: Little, Brown and Co., 1909).
[8] The new building, now named Luce Hall, is mentioned only in passing in *From Sail to Steam*, p. 313. Mahan took charge of the new building on 22 July 1892. The College re-opened for classes on 6 September of that year, having been closed since 1889.
[9] Mahan began to look for a publisher in September 1888, offering it first to Charles Scribner's Sons, who had published his first book, *The Gulf and Inland Waters* (1883). Finally, in October 1889, through James R. Soley, Little Brown and Co. agreed to publish it. The finished book appeared in the first week of May 1890.
[10] Ellen Lyle Evans Mahan (1851-1927).

of $3,500 a year was quite a serious one even in those days. During the early part of her married life, my mother kept a strict account of literally every penny that was spent. My father always turned his entire pay over to her each month and she gave back to him whatever he needed. This was because of no insistence on her part, but because he preferred to have it that way. He knew that she had excellent business sense and was very careful, and the care of money was something that he was glad to be relieved of. I don't think he even had a bank account until the latter part of his life. I remember my mother telling me once that she had never spent more in a month than my father's pay for that month, that is, up to the time that their income was increased from his writings and other sources, but that in one month she spent only seven cents less than the amount of his pay.

In addition to taking care of the house and the children, she was only too glad to turn her hand to anything that would help my father. When he started to write his lectures, it soon was evident that they would have to be typewritten. Without ever having had any experience, my mother bought a typewriter and learned to operate the machine by herself, and I believe that she personally transcribed every word written by my father that he published, certainly by far the greater part of it. This, I am very certain, was her own suggestion. She could deny herself any luxury or even necessity if the occasion demanded, but she would do anything for her husband and children.

I do not believe that my father's books would ever have been published if it had not been for my mother's determination that they should. He was easily discouraged and had a very humble opinion of himself and his own abilities. She was, as I have said, indomitable and had supreme confidence in him. She was absolutely determined that what he wrote should be published and kept at him to make sure that he left no stone unturned.

Mr. James Russell Soley was Assistant Secretary of the Navy at about this time or shortly before. He was a successful New York lawyer and had published a book which I read with avidity when young called *The Boys of 1812*. It was a history of the naval war of 1812 between this country and Great Britain. My father came to know Mr. Soley when the question of the continuance of the War College was discussed, or he may have known him before, I am not quite sure.[11] At any rate, he happened to tell Mr. Soley of his difficulties in having the books published, and Mr. Soley, who believed in the value of his works, said, "Take them to my publisher, Little, Brown and Company of Boston, and I am sure that they will publish them." My father told me that Little, Brown and Company said that if Mr. Soley said

---

[11] Soley, onetime Naval Academy instructor and international lawyer, became Librarian of the Navy Department Library in 1882. In 1885 he became the first civilian instructor at the Naval War College, lecturing on international law through 1889. In July 1890 he became Assistant Secretary of the Navy, becoming the foremost spokesman in Washington for the work of the War College.

the book was valuable, they would publish it without reading the manuscript. In this way the *Influence of Sea Power* was brought out, and my father always insisted on giving Little, Brown and Company the right to publish any of his books if they wanted to. The sale of books in England was taken care of by Messrs. Sampson, Low, Marston and Company, and Mr. R.B. Marston of that firm in London became a warm friend of my father's.

When my father was ordered to the *Chicago*, we moved permanently to New York. About 1891 or 1892, my father and mother bought a house, 160 West 86th Street, where the family lived until about 1905 or 1906.[12] Both my father and mother had a horror of owing any money except current bills which were always paid promptly on the first of the month. They carried this feeling to the extent of insisting upon paying for the house entirely in cash. The idea of owing money, even when it was secured by a mortgage, was thoroughly distasteful to both of them. The first summer that my father was away, we went to Quogue, Long Island, for the first time. This, I think, was in 1893, and we had a small and by no means water-proof house in what is known as Quogue, which is separated from Quogue proper by a small body of water known as Quantuck Bay. My oldest sister[13] had several friends living there and my mother liked the place so much that she decided to build a house there, even in my father's absence. This shows very clearly the thorough understanding between them, that she should undertake something of this kind without consulting him except by letter. Of course, he approved of everything that she did. I say that the bringing up of the children and all matters relating to the household were always left to my mother without question. My father considered that his job was to see that everybody did as my mother wanted them to do, although he would never hesitate to make a decision in an important matter where one had to be made, but on the whole, my mother was the manager, my father, the president, and felt that his main duty was to say "yes."

I remember the first summer the house at Quogue was built,[14] my mother's brother came down to stay with her and he used to recall with glee the conversation he had with her at that time. He said, "Ellie, Alfred will hate this place," to which she replied, "Well, then we'll move away." He said, "What will you do with the house?" She answered, "Sell it." My uncle always said, "By jove, she would and would make a profit on it too." He was a successful business man himself, but this showed his confidence in my mother's business judgment. His own opinion as to my father hating Quogue was

---

[12] The family remained in the rented apartment on East 54th Street from 1890 until June 1895. They moved into the newly purchased house at 160 West 86th Street in February 1896. They lived there during the winters until September 1905.

[13] Helen Evans Mahan (1873-1963).

[14] "Slumberside," the house at Quogue, was completed in the late spring of 1894.

entirely wrong. He loved the place from the moment he saw it and as the years rolled by, the family steadily spent more time there.

During the years of my father's absence on the *Chicago*, we were naturally very much interested in his letters. Of course, as I remember, he told us about dining with the Queen of England and the Emperor of Germany, and also of some of the other honors which were conferred on him, but I fear that he did not do the various occasions justice. He was by nature an extremely modest man. It was very difficult even for his family to get him to talk about himself or what he had done. I knew, for instance, that he had been in the engagement at Port Royal during the Civil War, but I never could get him to tell me anything about it, nor did he say much of his other experiences. This accounts for the fact that I am able to tell so little about his earlier life.

He was modest too in other ways; for instance, at Quogue the men's bathhouse quarters and the women's were entirely separate and were so built that it was impossible to see into either of them from outside. Most of the men took advantage of this after bathing to take what we always call a sun bath, each man lying in the sun for periods varying from five minutes to an hour, in a state of nature or at the most with only the protection of a small bath towel. I know that my father thought this disgusting, to use his own words, although I am sure that very few men will agree with him. When I was approaching adolescence, he attempted one day to tell me something about the nature of the sexes, but it embarrassed him so that I hardly got any idea at all of what he was driving at and my knowledge had to be obtained from outside. Fortunately, it came in a way that was not at all injurious.

To return to the trip on the *Chicago*, I cannot remember anything of my father's letters distinctly, except that I do recall that he told, either in a letter or personally, after he came home, that one of the undergraduates at Oxford called down from the gallery, where they sat during the conferring of the degrees, "Look at the red man from the West." This was supposed to be very appropriate, since the persons upon whom the degrees are conferred wear red gowns. If I remember right, my father was the first American who was honored with the degree of D.C.L. by Oxford.

My father had always seemed to me lacking in affection, but I believe that this was due to an inability on his part to show affection or it may have been some idea that demonstrations of affection were not the proper thing. He returned in March or April, 1895. I was just recovering from a very severe illness of which I almost died. My mother had not let him know that I was ill because she was afraid that it would worry him too much on his return voyage, but I remember that when he did return, one evening while I was lying in bed in a room adjoining the living room, that my mother told him about my illness. He certainly was terribly shocked and asked over and over again if she was sure that I was all right now. It was the first inkling I had of the feeling which lay beneath the surface.

The house on 86th Street was bought shortly after this and from that time until my marriage in 1904, our winters were spent there and our summers in Quogue in the house which my mother built during my father's absence. This is not the house in which my sisters live now,[15] which was built in 1908 or 1909, but a smaller one on what is known as Quaquanantuck Lane. The only break in this routine was in 1898 when we took a trip abroad. My father had planned this trip for a long time, having retired from the Navy in 1897, I think it was, after completing forty years of service. War with Spain was in the air, but my father made particular inquiries of the Navy Department as to whether it was proper for him to go under the circumstances and was assured that it was. He had planned this trip with the utmost care. We were to be gone for six months, returning in the latter part of September from Southampton. I believe that all the tickets both ways had been bought before we left, and the itinerary mapped out exactly with each place that we were to stay and the dates set down.

We went by the South Atlantic to Naples arriving there early in April and making a short trip through southern Italy. We returned to Naples after about ten days or two weeks, and either there or at our next stop which was Rome, a cablegram came to my father calling him back to serve on the Board of Naval Strategy. Of course, he left us immediately, travelling through England and from there under an assumed name, taking a liner to the United States, but at his express wishes, the rest of the family finished out the trip as originally planned with very slight variations.[16]

A day or two after my father left, a cablegram came from William Randolph Hearst offering him a dollar a word to write as much as he cared to about the war. My mother immediately cabled back, "No," knowing that my father would not write for Hearst under any circumstances, and I may say that he entirely approved what she did. He was convinced that Hearst was an undesirable citizen and would not, under any circumstances, accept his money or write for his papers, and would never allow a copy of any of Hearst's papers to be brought into the house. Sometimes he seemed almost fanatical upon certain subjects of this kind, but his feelings were always based on what he believed to be his duty, and he felt that to aid in any way the circulation of papers which he believed were doing harm was a sin on his part, even if it were to spend a cent, the price of the paper in those days, for a copy of one of the papers or even to seem to give them his approval by allowing a copy in the house.

I remember another circumstance which is not particularly appropriate at this spot, but which just came to my mind, this was during Wilson's

---

[15] "Marshmere," built in 1909.

[16] Mahan and his family left New York on a six month's leave of absence on 26 March 1898. He received the order to return to Washington at Rome on 25 April, departing Rome on 27 April and arriving in Washington on 9 May, for duty on the Naval War Board.

administration when Daniels forbade the use of grog in the Navy. My father
was highly incensed at this. He was not a drinking man, although he
occasionally enjoyed a glass of wine, but to deprive a sailor of his grog was
to him unthinkable. In fact, I believe that he strongly disapproved of any
legislation designed to control people's private lives beyond preventing them
from committing crimes.

The doings of the Naval Strategy Board[17] are a matter of history so that
all that I need to remark on is the heat which my father displayed at home
with regard to the so-called Sampson-Schley controversy. As I remember it,
without referring to any documents, not only did the question arise of whether
Sampson or Schley should be given credit for the victory over Cervera's fleet,
but whether either or both of them should be made vice admirals. My father,
of course, was absolutely convinced that the credit belonged to Sampson as
Commander-in-Chief, even though he was not with the fleet at the time that
the Spanish ships came out of port. He said that all arrangements for possible
contingencies had been made by Sampson before he left on a short trip for
a conference, and that his orders were strictly carried out by everybody,
except possibly Schley. He had never had any confidence in Schley, who was
almost a contemporary of his, and said that he had caused the Strategy Board
two days of intense anxiety because of disobedience of orders prior to the
time of the battle. He felt that no credit was due to Schley any more than
any of the captains in the fleet, possibly even less, although Schley was in
temporary command. I remember at the time that he told us that at the Naval
Academy in referring to Schley they used to say "Schley by name and 'sly'
by nature."

The anxieties of the Strategy Board were not alleviated by the fact that
they had an intensely hot summer in Washington that year.

In 1899, my father was appointed as the Naval Delegate of the United States
at the Peace Conference at The Hague. With regard to this, the only
noteworthy feature that comes particularly to my mind is his account of what
happened when the final draft of the document prepared for the signatures
of all the powers was submitted to the American Delegation.

That Delegation had agreed, from my father's insistence, that a reservation
should be made that the United States would not submit to arbitration any
matter arising under the Monroe Doctrine. When the final draft came in,
this had been omitted, and the document had almost received the approval
of the American Delegation without noticing the omission, which was
apparently due to an error of Holls,[18] the Secretary of the Delegation. My
father, however, noticed that it was omitted and in considerable excitement

---

[17] Mahan's "The Work of the Naval War Board of 1898: A Report to the General Board October 29,
1906," is printed in Seager and Maguire, *Letters and Papers*, vol. 3, pp. 627-643.
[18] George Frederick William Holls, New York lawyer, non-voting secretary and legal counsel.

brought it to the attention of Mr. White,[19] the Chairman of the American Delegation, so that the omission was corrected in time.[20]

From that time on, our lives were comparatively uneventful. My father, having retired from the service, was not called to any active duty and spent his entire time at home, either in New York or at Quogue. He had very few amusements. He liked to take exercise, but only in the form of walking in the winter and either walking or bicycling in the summer. He also went in bathing, with considerable regularity, in the summer and thoroughly enjoyed it. Most of the time in the water he spent floating, and particularly enjoyed floating with his head towards the sea and letting the waves break over him. He always wore a jersey cap with a cork sewed on it so that he would be able to retrieve it if it was washed off, which was frequently the case.

He was extremely regular in his habits. Breakfast was supposed to be at 8:00 o'clock in the morning, and all of the family was expected to assemble for family prayers at that time, promptly, after which we had breakfast. Promptness was also the rule for all meals.

One of his regular duties, as he considered it, was exercising the dogs in winter. In summer, of course, they exercised themselves. Having them with him and seeing them play gave additional pleasure to his walks, which were generally along Central Park. He was certainly a home-loving man in every sense of the word, hating to be separated from his family and enjoying trips only if they were along, but if they were with him, he thoroughly enjoyed them.

I was married in 1904 and after this, unfortunately, saw very little of my father. The house in 86th Street was rented shortly after that time, and from then on most of the year was spent in Quogue and the family only came to New York for three or four months in the winter. Owing to the friction that unfortunately existed between my wife and my parents, I did not see nearly as much of them as I should have, for which, of course, I was largely to blame.

I think this concludes about all of my recollections. My father died on December 1, 1914, while in Washington. His death was unexpected and I was not informed of the seriousness of his condition in time to see him before he died. I do not think, however, that even the doctors expected the end to come as suddenly as it did. My father had not been in the best of health for several years, but when I last saw him, in the August before he died, there was nothing to indicate that he might not live for several years longer.

---

[19] Andrew D. White, historian, diplomat and former president of Cornell University.
[20] This incident involved Article 27, which as originally written would have required *all* nations to become involved in the disputes of any two nations. While others in the American delegation approved the wording, Mahan alone saw that it was a violation of the intent of the Monroe Doctrine, and quickly persuaded his colleagues to introduce a clause exempting the United States and the Monroe Doctrine.

At this particular time, the World War had just broken out, and he was, of course, intensely interested and had written two or three articles for newspapers and magazines. It is well known that within a few weeks of the outbreak of the War,[21] orders were issued that no Naval officer, either on the active or retired list, should write any article commenting on the War. This was to uphold Wilson's policy of neutrality in word and deed. My father was the only officer, so far as I know, who had written anything up to the time of the promulgation of this order, and he considered it a direct slap at him, especially as the order came to him not through the usual channels by way of the Brooklyn Navy Yard, but direct from Washington.

It also was widely known that he disapproved of the Administration's policies with regard to the Navy. He was a very nervous and sensitive man and this direct slap, as he considered it, preyed on his mind, and was, I am certain, the cause of his early death.

While he had been ill, he was quite hardy, and I am sure that he would have overcome his ailments and lived for a long time in the natural course of events. A manuscript which he had started for a new article remained unfinished. He obeyed the order so far that he would not even set pen to paper to write, even though he would not have thought of publishing what he had written.

My father was half Irish, as I believe that both of my Grandfather Mahan's parents were fullblooded Irish people. On his mother's side, however, there is a mixture of blood—English, French and Dutch. With the exception of his mother's father, who was English by birth, the rest of his ancestors had been in this country for many generations . . .[22]

. . . he was related to the Van Countlandts and Jays in New York, but the relationship is not very generally known due to the fact that his great grandfather, James Jay, was never legally married to his great grandmother. James Jay lived in what is now Tenafly, New Jersey, and, as I am informed, took to live with him the daughter of some prosperous farmers in New Jersey. Neither he nor she believed in marriage, although at one time, at the solicitation of John Jay, the first Chief Justice of the United States, acting for himself and other members of the family, James did offer to marry his consort. She refused, saying that she had agreed to live with him as the lady of his household as long as they both wanted to continue the relationship, and that she would abide by that agreement, but that if he insisted upon a marriage, she would leave him immediately. Whether or not one agrees with her ideas, one must admire her courage, and the relationship was certainly far more moral than that of 75% of modern marriages.

---

[21] On 6 August 1914.
[22] Omitted here is a reference to an attached genealogical chart.

James Jay and his consort lived together in love and harmony until her death, but because of the lack of a ceremonial marriage, as I understand, the relationship with the other members of the Jay family was never recognized.

My Mother

My mother's maiden name was Ellen Lyle Evans. She was the daughter of Manlius G. Evans and his wife, who was formerly Ellen Kuhn. She was born on November 27, 1851. She always had a very strong character and will and was positive in everything that she did. She was also, in her younger days, very alert mentally and physically. She was quite tall, about five feet nine inches, and also broad and heavy-set. I know very little about her earlier life except some fragments which she told me and which emphasized what I learned myself in later life. She was extremely punctual and very quick in everything that she did. In her earlier years, certainly she did not have the vice of procrastination to any degree.

Her family used to go to Sharon Springs, New York, in the summer, and I believe that it was there that my father and mother first met. My father, of course, was extremely religious, and he was drawn to my mother not only for her personal attractions, but because he could see the same trait in her. I believe that my mother was quite an attractive woman when she was young and was very popular among the young men at Sharon Springs.

My father was eleven years older than she was. The match, I know, was very distasteful to my grandfather.[23] I believe this was because he did not feel that a naval officer would make a good husband both for financial reasons and also because he would be away from home so much. In any event, my mother has told me that he would not have that damned naval officer around his house. However, when my mother made up her mind to do anything, she generally went through with it and she had made up her mind that she was going to marry my father. I believe that she was not yet twenty when they met. The probabilities are that this was in the summer of 1871 or possibly 1870,[24] although I believe it is the later date. When my grandfather saw that her mind was made up, he finally said that he would consent to the marriage if they would agree not to see each other for a year so that my mother could be sure that she knew her mind. This was agreed to and my grandfather, when he saw that my mother had definitely made up her mind, ended the probation period after six months. They were married on June 11, 1872.

Shortly after the marriage, my father went to South America and took my mother with him. Captain Puleston[25] stated that he was attached to the

---

[23] Manlius Glendower Evans, a Philadelphia businessman.

[24] They met in July 1870. Mahan proposed to her 14 August 1871.

[25] This may refer to a draft chapter of Captain William D. Puleston, *Mahan: The Life and Work of Captain Alfred Thayer Mahan, USN* (New Haven: Yale University Press, 1939).

U.S.S. *Wasp* with headquarters, I believe, at Montevideo.[26] They were there until after the birth of my oldest sister, Helen Evans Mahan, who was born at Montevideo on August 6, 1873.

My mother was, among other things, a very excellent household economist. They were determined that they would not accept any help from her family who, at that time, were in a position to give it if they had wanted to, which they probably would not have done, and always lived on less than my father's pay, keeping account of every cent that she spent. She told me once that the nearest she ever came to living beyond her income was one month when she spent seven cents less than the amount of my father's check.

Shortly after my oldest sister's birth, but I do not know exactly when, yellow fever broke out in Montevideo and my father felt that my mother and my sister should leave there. I do not know whether he was relieved from the South Atlantic station[27] or just how it occurred, but they crossed the Atlantic from Rio to Bordeaux to spend some time with my grandfather, grandmother, and aunt, who had then moved to Pau, France.[28] It was there that my younger sister, Ellen Kuhn Mahan, was born on July 10, 1877. Some time later they returned to New York, and I was born in that City on February 12, 1881.

Living on a naval officer's salary with three children, even in those days when money went further than it does now, is no joke, but I never have heard of my mother making any complaint about any hardships that she suffered from lack of money. Although she had been brought up in an environment bordering on luxury, she appeared to demand nothing for herself and when clothes were to be bought, she always considered her children first, not to speak of her husband. My father, I know, was frequently very annoyed because she went around wearing shabby clothes. Indeed the only times in his life that I can ever remember his being annoyed with her was because she was sacrificing herself for the other members of the family.

My father was unquestionably a man of very fine character and a great deal of determination, but he did not begin to have the driving power that my mother did. My earliest clear recollections in life were when my father was stationed at the Naval War College on Coasters Harbor Island, Newport,

---

[26] Mahan took command of *Wasp* on 17 February 1873.

[27] Mahan passed on command of *Wasp* at Montevideo on 2 January 1875.

[28] In order to reduce living costs following his financial losses in the Panic of 1873, Glendower Evans moved his family to Pau, in the department of Basse-Pyrennes in the south of France. Between duty stations, Mahan and his wife took a six-month leave of absence to visit her family there. They returned to the United States in May 1875 and Mahan later took up an assignment at the Boston Navy Yard. In December 1876, following the disputed election of Rutherford B. Hayes, outgoing Secretary of the Navy Robeson punished Mahan for his outspoken views, and forced him into taking a leave of absence. On half-pay, he could only afford to live with his in-laws in France, so he returned to Pau in January 1877 with his wife, then three months' pregnant. They remained there only until September 1877, when the new administration recalled Mahan to be head of the Department of Ordnance and Gunnery at the Naval Academy. He remained there until July 1880, when he received orders to the Brooklyn Navy Yard.

Lyle Evans Mahan, Mahan's only son, was born February 12, 1881, attended Groton School and Columbia College (1902) and went on to a successful law practice in New York City.

R.I. This was when the War College was in the old insane asylum building. I can remember my mother pounding away on the typewriter. This was done at her own suggestion. My father probably chanced to say that he wished he could have his manuscript typewritten and that was enough for her to undertake to do the typing herself, although she had never touched a machine in her life. She bought one I think secondhand and started to work. I doubt if my father ever wrote a word for publication that she did not type. It has always been a source of amusement to me that frequently my father would ask my mother to read his own handwriting, words that he could not make out himself, but she always was able to do it.

When it came time to publish his books, it was my mother's driving power that kept him to it. After one or two publishers had refused them, he began to get discouraged, but I do not think that in those days she knew what the word meant. She had the utmost confidence in my father's ability, and, in addition to that, the assurances of the officers who had listened to his lectures, and she knew that my father had a message for the naval world that ought to be published. My father just did not seem to feel that people in general would be interested in what he wrote, but my mother had a decidedly opposite opinion.

My mother's willingness to do anything to lighten my father's burden is shown by the fact that when he was on the *Wachusett*, the rest of us lived with my Grandmother Evans and my aunt in order to save expense. Later on, when my father had returned, we spent a winter with his mother and sister in Elizabeth, New Jersey. This, I know, was a great trial to my mother although I was only six years old at the time, but I am very sure that she never complained about it.

In January, 1894, when I was at boarding school, my father was abroad in the *Chicago*. I was taken very seriously ill with measles and pneumonia. My mother came up and spent about six weeks at the school, leaving my sisters alone in New York. It was a tremendous ordeal for her as it was a very cold winter and she had to live in a boarding house outside of the school grounds. She came over every day, of course, and spent most of the time with me. I can remember one time when the doctors had small hope of my getting well that she fainted on a couch in the room. I was sufficiently conscious to be worried by it, but did not know just what had happened, and they told me that she had fallen. I was so much worried that the headmaster gave her a room in the school building, but in spite of all the anxiety and strain, she did not let my father know that I was ill as she did not want to worry him. The first he knew of it was when he got back to New York in April.

The family's fortunes were considerably augmented about this time because my Grandmother Mahan[29] died in 1893 leaving my father a small amount of money, and my Grandmother Evans, in 1894, leaving my mother a considerably larger amount. Nevertheless, while we were more comfortable, the strain was not entirely eased, as my education was quite a drain. However, about the time I entered college in 1898, an uncle of my mother's died and left her a very considerable amount of money so that after that there was little financial worry. The first house in Quogue was built with my father's inheritance in 1894, and in 1898 a house was purchased in New York.

I presume it may have been largely a reaction from this strain that affected my mother's health. She had always had a certain amount of rheumatism. She was then over forty-five years old. From that time on, she was constantly going to the doctor and had lost a great deal of her alertness. Her will, however, remained as strong as before, although her body was weakened very considerably. I do not think she ever got over the habits of economy which had taken such a strong hold of her during her early married life, as she always seemed to feel that she was hard up, although there was little ground for that feeling. She never would spend any money on herself and always dressed in the simplest possible clothes. She was extremely warm-blooded and would frequently go out in a skirt and blouse when other women were wearing heavy coats. This is a characteristic which I have inherited from her. In hot weather, she suffered very considerably.

You have asked me to give you a description of my mother. I believe that her eyes were gray and she had fairly regular features with a rather prominent though straight nose. Her hair was quite dark when she was young, although ever since I have any clear recollection it was gray, being white when she died. Her face and forehead were always very wrinkled since I can remember, which seems to be a family characteristic. Her hair was naturally wavy though not curly.

There is no picture of my mother in existence so far as I know. She had an unconquerable aversion to being photographed, an aversion shared by my father although he had to submit to it occasionally; she never did. I cannot remember ever having seen even a snapshot of her.[30] She did have a tintype taken of her when she was a girl, but I do not know even the whereabouts of that.

---

[29] Mary Okill Mahan (1815-1893), widow of Dennis Hart Mahan (1802-1871). There is a brief recollection of her by Lyle Mahan in this same collection, not printed here.
[30] A photograph of her, with her daughter, may be found in Robert Seager II, *Alfred Thayer Mahan: The Man and His Letters* (Annapolis: Naval Institute Press, 1977), p. 313.

Mahan family plot in the Quogue, N.Y. Cemetary.
Courtesy of the Quogue Historical Society and Mr. & Mrs. Shuttleworth.

Chapter 11

Christianity and the Evangelist for Sea Power: The Religion of Alfred Thayer Mahan:

Lieutenant Commander Reo N. Leslie, Jr.
Chaplain Corps, U.S. Navy

Introduction

After serving five years as Secretary of War (1940-1945), Henry L. Stimson reflected upon what he called "the peculiar psychology of the Navy Department" which according to him "frequently seemed to retire from the realm of logic into a dim religious world in which Neptune was God, Mahan his prophet, and the United States Navy the only true Church. The high priests of this Church were a group of men to whom Stimson always referred as 'the Admirals'."[1] Such religious language is indeed fitting for "the prophet" named by Stimson. Alfred Thayer Mahan was a man whose ideas about religion influenced his thought and behavior.

Mahan's Personal Faith

In the Episcopal, Church of the Atonement at Quogue, Long Island, New York, there is a memorial tablet to Rear Admiral Alfred Thayer Mahan (1840-1914). It reads:

Great among the nations as an expounder of sea power. Greater in the Kingdom of God as an example of a Christian man.

From his earliest days at the Naval Academy Mahan showed a "tendency to religious reflection" that was "an inheritance from both sides of his family."[2] While only nineteen, his letters to Samuel A. Ashe reveal Mahan's interest in matters of the spirit. In commenting on a Presbyterian pastor's sermon in the Academy Chapel he said, in a letter dated February 7, 1859:

---

[1] Henry L. Stimson and Mc George Bundy, *On Active Service In Peace and War*, (New York: Harper and Brothers, 1948), p. 506.
[2] W. D. Puleston, *Mahan*, (New Haven: Yale University Press, 1939), p. 23.

He gave a very good sermon, a little too much hell-fire and damnation in it. I can't stand what looks like an effort to bully you into religion. I have never yet heard a minister who preached the Word of God as I should wish to preach it if I were one myself. A man who is religious because he fears to go to hell is as despicable as one who remains irreligious because he fears the world's opinion. My idea of the loveliness of religion is the thought of a being who shows His love less in the physical comforts of life, than in His sympathy for our sufferings, and I believe the great God would rather have us look on Him as a friend than as a benefactor.[3]

A letter written to Ashe a week earlier, February 1, 1859, concludes with a reflection on Holy Scripture:

Do you ever read the Bible? What a beautiful passage this is that I met the other day in a book. "Or ever the silver cord be loosed, or the golden bowel be broken, or the pitcher be broken at the foundation, or the wheel broken at the cistern - then shall the dust return to the earth as it was, and the spirit shall return unto God who gave it." And what more sublime than the fortitude and courage of Job when he had lost all - "Naked came I out of my mother's womb and naked shall I return thither; the Lord gave and the Lord hath taken away; blessed be the name of the Lord." Sam, I am not religious but does it need religion to appreciate the beauty and sublimity of such poetry as that?[4]

On February 20, 1859 this young midshipman who considers himself "not religious" and "irreligious" again comments on the Bible and Biblically - based faith:

I admire the Bible as a book of great beauty, and those passages I cited and others like them, as poetry more sublime than you can find elsewhere, and as portraying a degree of moral heroism and triumph of principle over human weakness that must find sympathy and admiration in every manly heart. Totally irreligious as I acknowledge myself to be and utterly devoid of any intention or wish to be otherwise, yet if I wished a young man to be induced to act from the loftiest motives as a man not as a Christian I would make him read the actions and words of the great men of the Bible.[5]

Despite his self-awareness as one "devoid of any intention to be religious," Alfred Thayer Mahan grew into a man who professed Christ as "the power who works in us to 'sanctification'."[6] No doubt his uncle, the Reverend Milo Mahan, professor of ecclesiastical history at the General Theological Seminary, with whom he had lived for two years in New York City, had influenced him.[7] Until his death in 1870, this Anglo-Catholic minister and church historian served as his nephew's spiritual advisor.[8] One can imagine the theological discussions that took place when Mahan lived with his uncle

---

[3] Robert Seager II and Doris D. Maguire (editors), *Letters and Papers of Alfred Thayer Mahan*, (Annapolis: Naval Institute Press, 1975), vol. 1, p. 57-58.

[4] *Ibid.*, p. 56.

[5] *Ibid.*, p. 61

[6] *Ibid.*, volume 3, p. 336.

[7] Phillip A. Crowl, "Alfred Thayer Mahan: The Naval Historian," Peter Paret, ed., *Makers of Modern Strategy From Machiavelli to the Nuclear Age*, (Princeton: Princeton University Press, 1986), p. 445.

[8] *Ibid.*

while attending Columbia College. An example of such a dialogue is represented in a letter from Milo Mahan to his nephew in 1864:

> Things happen to us constantly, which proves that *God* rules, or else that chance rules. But if I must choose between Chance or God, to solve the mysteries of life, it is certainly reasonable to refer things to God of whom I can form *some* idea, rather than to *Chance* of which I can form no idea whatsoever. God may be mysterious. His ways may be dark and past finding out. But Chance is not mysterious merely it is utterly unintelligible (italics are Rev. Mahan's).[9]

In a letter dated September 20, 1870, written after his uncle's death, Mahan laments to Ashe about the loss of his beloved spiritual guide:

> You do my uncle no more than justice, in your surmises as to the loss he has been to us and to the church. The latter is greater than the former, for during many years we have all been much separated. For myself I am quite at a loss to know to whom to turn for the advice and the information that I used to get in matters of theological, rather than religious, interest -and during my last cruise I had accumulated several points upon which I wished instruction. The loss of course is irreparable, for though I might find equal ability, I cannot have the same familiar freedom of intercourse. It is gratifying to our affection that two memorial windows are now erected to him.[10]

Another family influence on Mahan's spiritual development was certainly his mother, Mary Helena Okill Mahan. In raising her son, she planted seeds which sprouted in the fertile soil of his intellectual and spiritual struggles. In a letter to Ashe dated October 30, 1858 Mahan states:

> I should not be surprised if I fetched up in the ministry one of these days, for Mother often told me before I entered the service, that, from the time I was born she had dedicated me to God's service, and that it had been the prayer of her life since. "The prayer of a righteous man," the Bible says, "availeth much," but I hope that in this I may be allowed by Providence to suit myself, for a greater horror of anything I could not have than I have of that same profession.[11]

Although the ordained ministry was not in the plans of Providence for Alfred Thayer Mahan, he still would have his "pulpit" to preach the Gospel. In 1909 he published a real labor of love. With numerous articles and books to his credit on sea power, history and international politics, Mahan also authored a work on Christianity entitled *The Harvest Within: Thoughts on the Life of the Christian*. The book reveals the decades of study in Holy Scripture and systematic theology Mahan had engaged in. *The Harvest Within* includes abundant use of Bible verses, spiritual counsel and inspirational illustrations. In the preface Mahan discusses his motivation for writing this work making him an evangelist for Christianity as well as an evangelist for sea power:

> One clear duty of old age, whether as regards personal character or unfulfilled purposes, is to gather up fragments that remain; to redeem lost time and lost opportunity; to utilize

---

[9] Quoted in Charles C. Taylor, *The Life of Admiral Mahan*, (New York: George H. Doran Company, 1920), p. 266
[10] Seager and Maguire, *op. cit.*, vol. 1, p. 358.
[11] *Ibid.*, pp. 10-11.

what is left of powers which may have begun to fail, and the remnants of thought or knowledge lying still at loose ends.[12]

Mahan believed that he should share his own spiritual insights gained through an experience through his life with "the riches of Christ." "The riches of Christ are unsearchable," said Mahan, but chief among them is the gift of love for Himself. It is a gift, not an acquisition."[13] Not only did his sense of Christian duty inspire Mahan to write about his faith, but the great theorist of sea power lived out his Christianity in daily life.

Mahan's Involvement in His Church

Mahan was an actively involved layperson of the kind that would please the pastor of any congregation. His Christian witness was manifested in his personal devotional life, church membership and participation in mission efforts of the Protestant Episcopal Church. Mahan's Bible study and theological reflection have already been mentioned. In addition to the question of whether to interpret the Bible literally, he also struggled with how to be a positive spiritual influence in the lives of the men he commanded. Mahan consulted his uncle on both questions and received this answer:

> The best influence in your position, is that of a quiet consistent life accompanied with as much of courtesy, gentility and consideration in dealing with your men as the nature of the Service will allow. . . . Let punishment be administered when really needed; but till the need comes, men should be treated, as if punishment never could be needed. An officer who commends his Christian character by observing this rule will find that a smile, a cheerful word, or occasionally a few words of friendly expostulation will do more in the long run, than any more ambitious or obtrusive efforts. (On the second matter) Find a solution if possible; but if a thoroughly satisfactory solution can not be found, do not accept a half-solution, rather let the matter rest, in short wait till the solution comes of itself.[14]

Mahan continued his struggle with Scripture and discipleship while at sea. When underway at the hour when service was being held at his home church, he would break away when possible from his duties as captain of the ship, and retire to his cabin. There he would have a service of private worship and read the Episcopal Daily Service.[15] Prayer, worship, Bible study and personal reflection were central to Mahan's spiritual life at sea and ashore. In a diary entry dated January 1, 1869 Mahan outlines what he calls his "Rules For My Life":

Rules for My Life:
1) Rule for Drinking.   A glass of sherry before and a pint bottle at dinner.
2) Rule for Prayer.   Reading and prayer at 11:30; 11 on fast day, etc; also short prayers at 9,1,and 3. Each to be accompanied with a distinct recalling to mind God's presence.

[12] Alfred Thayer Mahan, *The Harvest Within*, (Boston: Little, Brown and Company, 1909), p. vi.
[13] *Ibid.*, p. viii.
[14] Puleston, *op. cit.*, p. 37.
[15] Taylor, *op. cit.*, pp. 262-263.

3) Rule for Duty.	Regular inspection at morning quarters and after-with constant carrying of a memorandum book.
4) Almsgiving.	Seventeen dollars per month to be put in, upon my monthly drawing.
5) Fast & Feast Days.	When a Collect or Gospel is appointed, meditation thereupon for half an hour at 3 P.M.

Rules to be deliberately & prayerfully read at my morning devotions; & a prayerful self examination in the evening.

I allow myself as having an unsettled life for sufficient cause to anticipate or postpone a fast or feast day.

Rules not to be added to before Lent.[16]

Not only was Christianity a private matter of devotion for Mahan, but it was a public commitment. He was an active member of the Protestant Episcopal Church in attendance, lay ministry and leadership in mission efforts.

Mahan was a "cheerful giver" in the Biblical sense. As his fourth "Rule For My Life" indicated, while only twenty-eight years old he had already developed the discipline of giving seventeen dollars a month in charity. At the end of the Civil War Mahan made a voluntary offering of all the means at his disposal to help Southern naval officers in financial trouble. Throughout his life he often answered private requests for donations to churches or workers of the Church. One note dated November 2, 1911 gives an example:

Nov. 2, 1911. Sent Mr.—cheque for $100 named January, 1913, for repayment, but said sum would be given or returned to some church work. He was, therefore, to consider himself in debt to the Church, rather than to me, and on that basis to contrive repayment.

In case of my death authorised him to pay the amount to Bishop——for missionary work in diocese.[17]

Mahan's authorship of *The Harvest Within*, called his spiritual autobiography by many, was well received, as were his other writings on religious matters. Responding to an article entitled "Twentieth Century Christianity" which appeared in the April, 1914 issue of *North American Review*, Bishop Gailor of Tennessee wrote: "I thank God for a layman who can state the faith as you have declared it."[18]

After reading to the same article, Secretary of the Navy Josephus Daniels wrote to Mahan:

"It is most helpful to the younger men to read your clear call to hold fast to the ancient landmarks our fathers set."[19]

Mahan was a frequent speaker on spiritual matters at professional organizations, churches and church-related groups. As his mother envisioned, he was at home in a pulpit. In an address delivered at Holy Trinity Episcopal

---

[16] Seager and Maguire, *op. cit.*, vol. 1, p. 256.
[17] Taylor, *op. cit.*, quoted on p. 261.
[18] *Ibid.*, p. 263.
[19] *Ibid.*

Church in Brooklyn in March, 1899, Mahan stated the value of Christianity in his life:

> Here let me briefly say-to define my position at once clearly-that my experience of life is that of one who has based his practice upon a full intellectual acceptance of the Christian Faith, as explicitly set forth in the historic Creeds-the Apostles' and the Nicene Creeds. In those, and in the Word of God, I have found, and find, not merely comfort and strength but intense intellectual satisfaction.[20]

At the conclusion of this same address, Mahan included in his remarks the importance of his lay ministry as a Christian public speaker:

> I thank you greatly for listening to me, and your Rector for asking me to speak. I value beyond words the opportunity, once in my life, before God's people, to avow my faith, that to me He is, and has been, - not in my imperfect service, but in His own perfect faithfulness,-Alpha and Omega, the Beginning and the End, the First and the Last. I rejoice that once at least I am able publicly to lay at His feet in words-however poor my deeds-the confession that all that I have, all that I am, all that I have accomplished, has been of Him and through Him, and that, as the end draws near, there abides, what only my own demerit can forfeit, the Hope, which experience of His faithfulness renews day by day.[21]

In recognition of his support of Foreign Missions, Mahan was elected to the Board of Missions in 1900.[22] He served in this capacity until 1910. Mahan was an active member of the Board of Managers of the Seaman's Church Institute of New York from 1867 until his death in 1914.[23] After his death, the Board called him "a man of God of superior intellect, and with profound religious convictions; a great Churchman and ardent patriot."[24] A resolution adopted on December 3, 1914 by the Trustees of a home mission effort speaks of Mahan's activities in other areas of ministry:

> RESOLVED, that the Board of Trustees of the American Church Institute for Negroes desire to express their sense of the very great loss which they have sustained in the death of Rear-Admiral Mahan. He was always most deeply interested in the work of the Institute, and was one of the most regular attendants at its meetings. His counsel and advice were always greatly prized, and it will be difficult if not impossible to find anyone to fill his place.

> DAVID H. GREER,
> President
> American Church Institute for Negroes.[25]

---

[20] Seager and Maguire, *op. cit.*, vol. 3, p. 599.
[21] *Ibid.*, p. 602
[22] *Ibid.*, vol. 3, p. 657.
[23] Taylor, *op. cit.*, p. 265
[24] *Ibid.*
[25] *Ibid.*, pp. 265-266.

In another area of religious work Mahan was consulted about the Episcopal Prayer Book. He wrote several articles on the subject in the religious journal *The Churchman*.[26]

Mahan acted out his religious beliefs, as well as holding them in a personal faith. His understanding of Christianity also influenced the military philosophy, view of politics and approach to geopolitical thinking that the evangelist of sea power developed.

The Morality of the Use of Force in International Relations

In a letter to Silas McBee dated November 27, 1898, Mahan asked a question in a postscript: "Do Churchmen, even Bishops and Priests, practically consider the gift of the Holy Ghost, and the powers of the world to come to be potential factors in a nation's politics and welfare?"[27] Whether they did or not, he certainly did.

Mahan's view of the world was rooted in the idea found in Judaism and Christianity that human history was directed by God toward a divinely-ordained fulfillment in the future. In his Presidential address to the American Historical Association on December 26, 1902, he defined history as "the plan of Providence."[28] This concept of history as a divine drama orchestrated by God had an impact on how Mahan looked at war and the use of force in the relations between nations.

Mahan's view of the place of force in global politics was influenced by his religious views. In essays and speeches like "Thoughts on the Righteousness of War" (1913), "War From the Christian Standpoint" (1900) and "The Place of Force in International Relations" (1912), he explained his views on the nature of war in human affairs.

The authority to wage war had been granted to earthly political authority by the God of the Universe. Force, according to Mahan, was a regrettable but necessary instrument in maintaining order, defending national interests, avenging wrongdoing and administering righteous justice. Since humanity was "far removed from human perfection," war was a "necessary evil" in its use as "a remedy for greater evils, especially moral evils."[29] Although he rejected going to war for conquest, dynastic succession and impure motives, Mahan believed that "the obligation to destroy the evil and the evildoer, if need be, still exists" when injury or self-defense requires "the result of war."[30] In "War From the Christian Viewpoint" he stated:

---

[26] *Ibid.*, p. 263.
[27] Seager and Maguire, *op. cit.*, vol. 3, p. 617.
[28] Alfred Thayer Mahan, *Naval Administration and Warfare*, (Boston: Little, Brown and Company, 1918), p. 267.
[29] Alfred Thayer Mahan, *Some Neglected Aspects of War*, (Boston: Little, Brown and Company, 1907), p. 99.
[30] *Ibid.*, p. 100

I affirm that War, under conditions that do and may arise, is righteous; and further, that under such conditions it is distinctly an unrighteous deed to refrain from forcibly redressing evil, when it is in the power of thine hand to do so. I have affirmed that under some conditions it is unrighteous not to use force to that extent of War.[31]

Mahan challenged those who interpreted the Bible and Christian theology to support non-resistance and pacifism to consider other neglected aspects of Scripture, Christ and Christianity. As well as being the "Prince of Peace" (*Isaiah* 9:6), Christ also "in righteousness does judge and make war" in command of "the armies of heaven" with "a sharp sword with which to smite the nations" (*Revelation* 19:11-15). The commandment "Thou shalt not kill" is not for capital crimes or holy wars in the Old Testament. Christ used force himself to expel the immoral money changers from the Temple in Jerusalem (*Matthew* 21:12, *Mark* 11:15, *Luke* 14:45, *John* 2:15). When centurions like Cornelius converted to Christianity (*Acts* 10) they were not required, or even advised, to leave their military profession. Christ counseled the purchase of swords by his disciples (*Luke* 22:36-37) and rebuked Peter only because he used his sword prematurely (*Matthew* 26:52-54, *John* 28:10-11).

Although Mahan understood how Christian conscience could lead one to pacifism, his own belief was quite clear. Christ, since his Kingdom was "not of this world" had assigned the sword to the authority of nations in "the physical coercion of material evil" within the earthly sphere.[32] "Every independent state is a kingdom in this world," he said, "Its subject or citizens, if confronted by the prospect of innocent blood being shed, or of their Ruler being slain (their government destroyed) are justified in resisting by force."[33]

A favorite Biblical passage of Mahan in articulating his view of the morality of using force in international relations was *Romans* 13. Verse 4 was especially useful in his exegesis for it says "for he [the Ruler] does not bear the sword in vain; he is the servant of God to execute his [God's] wrath on the wrongdoer." The sword, Mahan believes, "must defend the right" of nations. The answer is clear, Mahan said, if the question is "should the nation do right (go to war) and suffer or do wrong (appease evil) and be at ease?" After all, he says, "is militarism really more deadening to the spirit than commercialism or than legalism?"[34]

Since the sword of military power was assigned to nations by God, Mahan was suspicious of efforts to restrict or prohibit the use of force in international relations. "Legislative enactment" and the "external compulsion" of arbitration could not replace "the fidelity of Conscience" inherit in the righteous use of war to right wrongs and do justice, for "even the material

[31] *Ibid.*, pp. 100-101.
[32] *Ibid,* p. 112
[33] *Ibid.*, p. 108.
[34] *Ibid.*

evils of war are less than the moral evil of compliance with wrong."[35] Those who place too much faith in international arbitration, Mahan states, fail to recognize "how far force daily enters into the maintenance and execution of law."[36] The danger Mahan sees in "undiscriminating advocacy of arbitration" is that "it may lead men to tamper with equity, to compromise with unrighteousness, soothing their conscience with the belief that war is so entirely wrong that beside it no other tolerated evil is wrong."[37]

In his own spiritual development, Mahan had reconciled his personal faith and his commission as a naval officer believing that Christianity was a religion that reinforced his military profession. Force and faith were not antagonistic, but complimentary:

> Power, force is a faculty of national life; one of the talents committed to nations by God. And this obligation to maintain right, by force if need be, while common to all states, rests peculiarly upon the greater in proportion to their means. So viewed, the ability speedily to put forth the nation's power, is one of the clear duties involved in the Christian word "watchfulness," readiness for the call that may come, whether expectedly or not. Until it is demonstrated that evil no longer exists, or threatens the world, which cannot be obviated without the recourse to force, the obligation to readiness must remain; and where evil is mighty and defiant, the obligation to use force, that is, war arises.[38]

Although Mahan's language may seem bellicose by current religious standards, he was certainly within the mainstream of the popular Christianity of his period. His views are also consistent with the theories of just war formulated in Christian theology by Ambrose, Augustine and Aquinas. This was, after all, a period of American history when President William McKinley stated publicly that his decision to annex the Philippines came to him in a religious experience after seeking counsel from God in prayer.

Geopolitics and "Christian Civilization"

Mahan, in addition to being a devoted Christian, naval strategist, evangelist for sea power, historian and author, was also a great global geopolitical thinker. Before Mackinder presented his ideas of "the Pivot Area," "the Heartland" and the need to prevent a single continental power from gaining control of the Eurasian "world island," Mahan had discussed similar concepts in his book *The Problem of Asia* published in 1900. In his essays Mahan identified Russian expansionism as the greatest threat to the stability of China, global peace and security of the world.[39] Mahan also saw what he called a zone of "the debatable and debated ground" that stretched from Northeast Asia to

---

[35] Alfred Thayer Mahan, *Lessons of the War With Spain and Other Articles*, (Boston: Little, Brown, and Company, 1918), p. 215.
[36] *Ibid.*, p. 222.
[37] *Ibid.*, pp. 236–237.
[38] *Ibid.*, pp. 232–233.
[39] Robert Seager II, *Alfred Thayer Mahan: The Man and His Letters*, (Annapolis: Naval Institute Press, 1977), p. 463.

the Balkans.[40] He predicted that the sea powers Japan, Germany, the United States and the United Kingdom would unite in alliance to contest the Russians in the zone of "debatable and debated ground," contain Russian imperialist expansion and control China.[41] Thus, at the turn of the century, Mahan predicted the policy of "containment" and global alliances like the U.S. - Japan Security Treaty and Nato that would become the cornerstones of American national strategy half a century later.

However, Mahan's interest in the Pacific Rim and East Asia was more than political alone. Mahan's great interest in Christian missionary efforts saw in American acquisition of the Philippines in the Spanish - American War of 1898 and Western trade with China, Korea and Japan an opportunity to spread Christianity among Asian peoples. As already mentioned, Mahan served ten years on the Board of Missions of the Episcopal Church. The Church recognized his labor by naming the Mahan School in Yangchow, China, as a memorial to him.[42]

Mahan was concerned that either the Russians, Chinese or both would one day rise to challenge the West. He called "the stirring of the East" and its "entrance into the field of Western interests" a "vital" and "significant" event.[43] He thought that although the potential conflict might be inevitable, it was avoidable if Eastern nations were brought into the "Christian civilization" of the West:

> We stand at the opening of a period when the question is to be settled decisively, though the issue may be long delayed, whether Eastern or Western civilization is to dominate throughout the earth and to control its future. The great task now before the world of civilized Christianity, its great mission, which it must fulfill or perish, is to receive into its own bosom and raise to its own ideals those ancient and different civilizations by which it is surrounded and outnumbered, the civilizations at the head of which stand China, India, and Japan.[44]

Mahan expected Western political, religious and material civilization to lift up the "ancient nations" of the East which were "deficient" in intellectual, social and political organization.[45] In order to be successful in this spiritual offensive-defensive strategy, the Western nations must return more to their own Christian values and ideals to facilitate their growth in other lands:

> If our own civilization is becoming material only, a thing limited in hope and love to this world, I know not what we have to offer to save ourselves or others; but in either event, whether to go down finally under a flood of outside invasion, or whether to

---

[40] Alfred Thayer Mahan, *The Problem of Asia*, (Boston: Little, Brown and Company, 1900), p. 22.

[41] Seager, *op. cit.*, p. 463.

[42] *Ibid.*, p. 577.

[43] Alfred Thayer Mahan, *The Interest of America in Sea Power*, (Boston: Little, Brown, and Company, 1906), p. 235.

[44] *Ibid.*, p. 243.

[45] *Ibid.*, p. 252.

succeed, by our own living faith, in converting to our ideal civilization those who shall thus press upon us, - in either event we need time, and time can be gained only by organized material force. Nor is this view advanced in any spirit of unfriendliness to the other ancient civilizations, whose genius admittedly has been and is foreign to our own.[46]

Mahan believed the Philippines would provide not only a geo-strategic base for pursuit of U.S. interests in Asia, but also serve a similar purpose in spreading Christianity to the Asian mainland. The acquisition of the Philippines by the U.S. was guided by "the hand of Providence" in the view of Mahan and many others.[47]

The religion of Islam did not fare any better than the religions of the East in the eyes of Mahan. Although, in a July 30, 1867, letter to his father Mahan lauded the temperance of the Muslim inhabitants of the Comoro Islands,[48] he considered nations under "Mahometan government" to be politically and culturally backward.[49] Mahan saw the liberation of the Balkan states from "Turkish misrule" as the start of the decline of Islam as "a political power" and "a religious power."[50] He attributed Turkish political despotism not to their ethnicity, but to their religion, saying "Turkish misrule is not because they are Turks, but because Mahomet has blinded their eyes to the Person of Christ, and to the Cross which showed His courage and fidelity."[51]

In addition to supporting the spread of Christianity and Western culture in Asia through public advocacy and institutional church work, Mahan made a significant personal effort also. In response to a request by Lieutenant Commander K. Asami, a Christian in the Imperial Japanese Navy, Mahan wrote an introduction to Asami's biography of Japanese Vice Admiral Tasuka Serata. Admiral Serata, also a Christian, graduated from the U.S. Naval Academy in Annapolis. In the introduction, Mahan not only praises Serata and his Christian faith, but presents Christianity to the Japanese people. Mahan also compliments the Japanese for progress and entices them with the "universal" nature of Christian civilization:

Japan has recognized the progress of Christendom, has adopted its fruits, and since so doing has herself contributed to the development much which the European world fully and explicitly admits.

It is the glory of that faith which Admiral Serata professed, in which he lived, and in which he died, that it impresses upon the group of nations in which it is held a solidarity, a unity, which survives and transcends all differences between them. It has the quality of immortality, of universality, and of unity of character, which is to be found in no other feature of their various national lives.[52]

---

[46] Ibid., p. 246.
[47] Mahan, The Problem of Asia, p. 175.
[48] Seager and Maguire, op. cit., vol. 1, p. 108.
[49] Ibid., vol. 3, p. 511.
[50] Ibid., p. 683.
[51] Ibid., p. 690.
[52] Ibid., p. 690-691.

Mahan thought of geopolitics not only in terms of national, economic, commercial and military strategy, but also spiritual strategy. The Open Door to China was considered one for evangelization as well as trade. The sea powers (United States, Britain, Germany and Japan) must insure, Mahan told Theodore Rossevelt in a March 12, 1901 letter, that China provides "simple, but entire, liberty of entrance for European thought, as well as European commerce" in order for China to "be saved."[53] It is indeed fascinating to see, particularly in our contemporary *milieu* where religion plays such a significant role in international politics, the religious element of Mahan's geo-political thinking. He felt Christianity could unite the East and the West in both political and spiritual kinship.

National interests of the West are served, Mahan said, by bringing "Asian peoples within the compass of the family of Christian states; not by fetters and bands imposed from
without, but by regeneration promoted from within."[54]

Conclusion

Alfred Thayer Mahan was a man who possessed a dynamic faith. Spiritual reflection, involvement in national and international mission efforts, historical analysis, personal values, lay ministry, geo-strategic thinking and political advocacy all grew from the fertile soil of his Christian beliefs. As Charles Carlisle Taylor says in his biography of Mahan:

> No portrait of Alfred Thayer Mahan which failed to emphasize his deeply religious nature would faithfully reflect his true personality. It would be difficult to exaggerate the intensity of his convictions or his lifelong devotion to things spiritual.[55]

The evangelist of sea power was a complex man with many interests and views. The Christian faith he professed and practiced provided an underpinning for his outlook and vision and is evident in books published and letters written.

From his time at the Naval Academy he consistently pondered on what it meant to live a Biblically-based faith in a modern environment. The questions raised in his letters show, despite his chosen military profession, Mahan had a spiritual sensitivity that informed his decision making process.

His sense of God behind history convinced him that his native land had a role of greatness to play on the stage of time. His advocacy of America's interest in sea power and international conditions was motivated by this belief. Mahan's understanding of the just war tradition in Christianity led him to the conviction that there were no Biblical or religious constraints on the use of force in international relations. On the contrary, his reading of the Holy

[53] *Ibid.*, p. 708.
[54] Mahan, *The Problem of Asia*, p. 154.
[55] Taylor, *op. cit.*, p. 266.

Scriptures made him certain that the proper moral course mandated the resistance of evil by force if necessary, rather than acquiescence to wrong motivated by a misguided ethic.

Mahan's sense of missionary Christianity was at the root of his geo-political analysis of "the problem of Asia." He desired the Open Door Policy for China more for the conversion of the Chinese people than the commercial interests of the West. Mahan envisioned an apocalyptic war between the East and the West if China, India and Japan were not brought into Christendom. There was no separation between religion and politics in the strategic thought of Alfred Thayer Mahan. Religion and strategy were interwoven in his views on Christian civilization.

In his political, spiritual, military and intellectual life Mahan sought to reflect his beliefs for Christ. He was an evangelist of his faith as well as an evangelist for sea power. A look at his life indeed reveals the truth of the memorial plaque in his honor at the Church of the Atonement in Long Island. With religion growing as a factor in international relations perhaps the union between spiritual affairs and national security affairs evident in Mahan's thinking can help broaden our understanding of how global issues are viewed.

After his return from the South Pacific Station in the fall of 1885, Mahan took up residence with his family in New York City and continued his research in the Astor Library for his Naval War College lectures on naval history and tactics. He continued his work until August 1886, technically under Rear Admiral Stephen B. Luce's order, but enjoying what in effect was a leave of absence from the Navy. Most of his lectures for the 1886 College course were completed during this period.

Copy of *Harper's Weekly* illustration courtesy of the Redwood Llibrary.

Chapter 12

Alfred Thayer Mahan on the War of 1812

William S. Dudley

More than 175 years after the War of 1812, James Fenimore Cooper, Theodore Roosevelt and Alfred Thayer Mahan, all nineteenth century authors, are still considered the pre-eminent naval historians of that event. Cooper was a contemporary and near participant in the events of those days, but Roosevelt and Mahan lived in the declining years of the age of sail and viewed the successive phases of its decline, as steam technology, more powerful guns, and armor plate influenced warship design. In the quarter century between 1882 and 1905, Roosevelt and Mahan made lasting contributions to the field of 1812 studies in different ways. I propose to compare the treatments by Roosevelt and Cooper to that by Mahan in order to highlight the distinctive approaches of each historian, to make some more extensive remarks on Mahan's method and biases, and to give some impression of the way Mahan's version of the war has influenced later authors.

Naval wars in the days of sail involved a theory and practice of ship construction, rigging and sail technology, the science of maneuvering, and a maritime dialect that was difficult for landsmen to understand. Then, a greater proportion of Americans lived near the sea and depended on it for their livelihood. These skills are now irretrievably lost to all but a handful of our population. Many history professors would be hard put to explain the necessity of "seeking the weather gauge" before closing with the enemy. Perhaps we have come to a time when the war cannot be taught because we have lost the means of communicating how it was fought. It will be a real challenge to bridge this gap. When historians undertake this task, time and again they must have recourse to Cooper, Roosevelt and Mahan.

James Fenimore Cooper was the first and in some ways the best of the 19th-century historians of the U.S. Navy. Before him came some men who scribbled, cut, and pasted, but none before him had created a comprehensive and coherent portrait of the American navies from 1775 to 1815.[1] When Cooper published his *History of the Navy of the United States*, in 1839, he was already an established writer who took pains with his craft. As one of the first men of American letters, he had over a period of twenty years published a critically-acclaimed variety of fiction and essays. He consciously included the American national experience in his works. High-spirited as a youth, he entered Yale at an early age, but was expelled after using gun powder to blow the lock off a dormitory door. His father, Judge William Cooper, consented to his signing as an ordinary seaman on board the merchant ship *Sterling* for a year of preparation (1806-1807) before joining the Navy. He served for three years (1808-1811) as a midshipman. While under the orders of Lieutenant Melancthon Woolsey on Lake Ontario, Cooper helped to supervise the building of the brig *Ontario*. This task completed, the Navy Department sent Cooper to Lieutenant James Lawrence's *Wasp* in New York harbor. Lawrence assigned Cooper the frustrating task of recruiting seamen in New York City. During this time, Cooper came to know other officers, such as William Branford Shubrick, a lifelong naval friend. Cooper resigned his commission in 1811 to administer his deceased father's estate and to marry Susan DeLancey who made it known she did not want an absentee husband.

Cooper had inherited his father's vast estates in central New York and for a while tried farm management, but soon he turned his hand to novels to supplement his income. As the years passed, he kept his eyes toward the sea, and created America's first sea fiction.[2] He kept in touch with his naval friends,

---

[1] Cooper's predecessors include Thomas Clark, who compiled a mixture of narrative, excerpted documents, laws and statistics. In *Naval History of the United States*, Clark took advantage of the naval enthusiasm of 1812 to glue together this pastiche of the first few months of the war and boldly predicted a second volume which was incompletely published in early 1814. There were no further volumes. Clark went on to publish a series of Latin textbooks more suited to his talents.

Some excellent naval writing appeared in the *Analectic Magazine*, edited by Washington Irving, who was personally acquainted with a number of naval officers. It is thought Cooper was among the contributors of these unsigned pieces. The years following the war saw the appearance of numerous edited collections of military and naval documents, such as Abel Bowen, *The Naval Temple. Containing a complete history of the battles fought by the navy of the United States from 1794-1816* (Boston, 1816); Horace Kimball, *Naval Battles: being the complete history of the battles fought by the United states from 1794* (Boston, 1816); and John Brannan, *Official Letters of the Military and Naval Officers of the United States during the War with Great Britain in the Years 1812, 13, 14, & 15* (Washington, 1823). Many of these titles boasted completeness and status as histories. To a great extent, the narratives contained hyperbole and the texts were haphazardly edited.

Another account that preceded Cooper's is Charles Washington Goldsborough's *United States Naval Chronicle* (1824). It is not a history but is rather what the title indicates, a ponderous chronology, running from 1775 to 1801, and unfortunately, there he stopped. He was very knowledgeable about the management of the Navy Department, and he knew many of the leading officers, having served as chief clerk of the department under Robert Smith (1802-1809) and Paul Hamilton (1809-1812). When William Jones assumed the post of Secretary of the Navy in January, 1813, he brought in his own appointee, Benjamin Homans, as chief clerk. Goldsborough was brought back as chief clerk by Secretary Benjamin Crowninshield in 1815. Goldsborough also served as secretary to the Board of Navy Commissioners.

[2] *The Pilot* (1824), *The Red Rover* (1827), and *The Water Witch* (1830) are commonly called "nautical romances;" his later nautical novels, such as *The Wing and Wing* (1842), *Two Admirals* (1842) and *Afloat and Ashore* (1844) were written in a more realistic vein. For a thorough discussion of these novels, see Thomas Philbrick, *James Fenimore Cooper and the Development of American Sea Fiction* (Cambridge, Mass.: Harvard University Press, 1961).

was moved to write a critical essay on the *Somers* mutiny, and finally set himself the task of researching and writing the history of the U.S. Navy, not just since 1798, but the whole story since 1775. The result was very different from what one might expect from the story-teller of the "Leatherstocking Tales."

For a man lacking historical training, Cooper had an advanced idea of the historian's role. In research, he used primary sources and oral history whenever possible. He sent questionnaires to naval officers he could not interview so as to reflect differing viewpoints. He was widely read in the secondary sources as well. He judiciously compared published sources with eyewitness accounts and arrived at his own judgement of events by careful reasoning and analysis of these sources. In writing history, Cooper shunned the popular tendency to place naval heroes on a pedestal. Memorable phrases supposedly uttered by naval leaders rarely find their way into Cooper's narrative. On the other hand, he was a man of his age, and would have approved of Thomas Carlyle's emphasis on biography and the role of the individual in history. His theme, when it emerges, is the high character of the American naval officer. Those he admired were to serve as models for emulation. Still, he attempted to keep above the fray. In writing about the Battle of Lake Erie, he chose not to take up cudgels against Master Commandant Jesse D. Elliot, the commanding officer of the brig *Niagara*, whom many officers had criticized for failing to support Commodore Perry's brig *Lawrence* at a critical time. Rather, Cooper based his description on Perry's earliest reports which praised Elliot rather than those he wrote later which condemned him. Perry's shipmates pilloried Cooper in the press and he replied. He later blamed the slow sales of his *Naval History* on the festering of the Perry-Elliot feud.[3]

The works of Cooper, as both novelist and historian, have been undergoing reappraisal for the past thirty-five years. He had been neglected, since the late nineteenth century, as a relic of the romantic era. The historian Walter Muir Whitehill, writing in 1954, was of the opinion that "there can be no question about the importance of Cooper's place as a naval historian. He was, after all, the first to make any systematic attempt to cover the whole field from the earliest colonial sea fights onward." He praised Cooper's "detached

---

[3] Captain Daniel Dobbins, an old Lake Erie hand who served under Perry gave Cooper his due, however, when on May 11, 1843, he wrote: "Having read your Naval History, as also the Biography of Como Perry by Capt. A.S. MacKenzie, the biography of Capt. Jesse D. Elliot by a Citizen of N. York, and the commencement of your life of Perry in the May number of Graham's Magazine, I would beg leave to say that none of them are entirely free of errours; but I must say, you treated matters and things with much the most candour . . . ." Cooper replied on May 20, "I never flattered myself with having written a history without errors; such a phenomenon, the world never yet saw. Still, I believe myself to be nearer to the truth than any other writer on the subject of the Battle of Lake Erie . . . ." James Franklin Beard, *The Letters and Journals of James Fenimore Cooper*, 4 vols. (Cambridge, Mass.: Harvard University Press, 1960), vol. 4, pp. 383-384.

and abstract impartiality" and his "dignified disregard of that which attracted popular attention."[4]

This is an impressive statement when one realizes Cooper's own capacity for invective and his willingness to attack opponents in pamphlets and in the law courts. For example, in addition to his balanced view of Elliot in the Perry-Elliot feud, he defended Commodore Chauncey's failure to cooperate with the army in 1814 on Lake Ontario. He is but mildly critical of Rear Admiral Cockburn's behavior in the Chesapeake Bay campaigns of 1813-1814 and is also even-handed in his treatment of Captain James Hillyar's attack on Captain David Porter's frigate ESSEX in Chile's territorial waters. In accounts by other American authors of the day, these matters were treated with bias and indignation.

Cooper's approach to naval history was, first of all, episodic and narrative. He dwelled on sea actions, related the role of principal officers, explained the methods of rating ships, and appraised the balance of the forces engaged in battle. With his own naval background and in consulting his human sources, Cooper arrived at penetrating evaluations of decisions and tactics. Of the three historians under consideration, he paid the most attention to the human factor, including biographical detail, to enlighten the reader. Good examples are his annotation portraits of Captain James Lawrence of the frigate *Chesapeake* and Captain Johnston Blakeley of the *Wasp* who was lost at sea after a very successful cruise in 1814.[5]

Theodore Roosevelt's *The Naval War of 1812*, published in 1882, was a product of an energetic personality and a brilliant, eccentric mind.[6] His study of the War of 1812 had nothing to do with his academic work at Harvard, except it was there that he first read British historian William James's account of the war.[7] Roosevelt's book was not, as some have thought, an expansion of his senior thesis. Roosevelt's interest, as an undergraduate, lay in the Natural Sciences. He was, however, a voluminous reader in every area and enjoyed rowing and sailing in small boats on Long Island Sound. Perhaps this is where he found his maritime inspiration. Somehow, Roosevelt managed to squeeze his research into a life teeming with social engagements, 25-mile hikes, his first marriage, a European honeymoon, involvement in Republican Party politics, and his first year at Columbia Law School.

The writing was not easy, for like Cooper, Roosevelt was untrained as an historian, and unlike Cooper, he was not a literary man, used to organizing

---

[4] Walter Muir Whitehill, "Cooper as a Naval Historian," in Mary E. Cunningham, ed. *James Fenimore Cooper: A Reappraisal* (Cooperstown, N.Y., 1954), pp. 105. Among many other works, Whitehill wrote a biography of Admiral Ernest J. King and was Chairman of the Secretary of the Navy's Advisory Committee on Naval History for many years.

[5] Cooper, *History of the Navy*, pp.181-182, 212-213.

[6] Theodore Roosevelt, *The Naval War of 1812* (New York: G.P. Putnam's Sons, 1882).

[7] William James, *An Inquiry into the Merits of the Principal Naval Actions between Great Britain and the United States* (London, 1816) and *Naval History of Great Britain from the Declaration of War by France to the Accession of George IV*, 6 vols., (London, 1822-24).

and editing vast amounts of written material. Still, he developed a method to go with his obsession. According to David McCullough, he "forced himself to master every nuance and technical term of seamanship . . . he plowed through everything in print on his subject, tracked down original documents, amassed volumes of statistics on fighting ships, armaments and crews. He had started out knowing no more on his subject than anyone else and with no experience or training in historical research." Then, too, there were the natural interruptions of family life. He was hard at work one afternoon, in the library of the Roosevelt family's New York townhouse, his wife Alice burst in on his study and cried out to her sister-in-law, "we're dining out in twenty minutes and Teddy's drawing little ships."[8]

There came a time in 1881, when Roosevelt felt overwhelmed by his subject, perhaps because of the vast amount of research he had done. He and Alice were in Europe on their honeymoon, residing in The Hague when his worries emerged. "I have plenty of information but I can't get it into words; I wonder if I won't find everything in life too big for my abilities. Well, time will tell."[9] But help was near at hand in the person of Teddy's uncle, a former U.S. Navy and Confederate States Navy officer, James D. Bulloch.[10] During the war, he had successfully arranged for the purchase and outfitting in Liverpool of several ships that became Confederate high seas cruisers, including *Florida*, *Alabama*, and *Shenandoah*. This renowned figure suffered notoriety after the war because of the *Alabama* claims arbitration, during which the United States successfully obtained a judgement against Great Britain for the part she had played in aiding the Southern cause. Roosevelt spent several weeks receiving advice and sympathy in Bulloch's company. Much encouraged, Roosevelt soon completed his work and arranged for its publication through the firm of Col. George H. Putnam, a family friend. Coincidentally, Roosevelt "invested" $10,000 in Putnam's firm as a "silent partner" in 1883. Whether this was a shrewd move to assist publication of his book or simply a means of creating income is unknown.[11]

Roosevelt's approach to the War of 1812 is combative in instinct. From the earliest pages, he makes it clear that he is out to square accounts with Englishman author William James, whose history of the war he holds in contempt for its inaccuracy and pro-British bias. Although Roosevelt's study is not without errors, it is basically reliable. He gives the enemy his due and strives, without entire success, to establish a fair and dispassionate view. We see this in his evaluation of James: "an invaluable work, written with fullness

[8] David McCullough, *Mornings on Horseback* (New York: Simon & Schuster, 1981), pp. 235, 247.
[9] TR to [his sister] Anna Roosevelt, as cited in Pringle, *Theodore Roosevelt: A Biography* (New York: Harcourt, Brace, 1931), p. 47.
[10] James D. Bulloch (1823-1901), a native of Savannah, Georgia, and former U.S. Navy officer who joined the Confederate States Navy and became the Confederacy's agent in England. His exploits are recorded in *The Secret Service of the Confederate States in Europe* (2 vols., 1884).
[11] Henry F. Pringle, *Theodore Roosevelt* (New York: Harcourt, Brace, 1931), p. 64.

and care; on the other hand, it is also a piece of special pleading by a bitter and not over-scrupulous partisan." Unfortunately, Roosevelt found it necessary to lash out at Cooper, in a condemnation that carried through until recent years. He acknowledged his debt to Cooper, backhandedly. James' work, he wrote, can be "partially supplemented by Fenimore Cooper's *Naval History of the United States*. The latter gives the American view of the cruises and battles; but it is much less of an authority than James', both because it is written without regard for exactness and because all the figures for the American side need to be supplied from Lieutenant (now Admiral) George E. [H.] Emmons' statistical History of the United States Navy. . . ."[12]

Roosevelt's study of the war is indispensable for anyone working on the subject, but his opinion of Cooper is both unfair and inaccurate. It is one of the few times when the question of Roosevelt's maturity becomes relevant. It is as though he felt the necessity to denigrate his predecessor in order to promote his own accomplishment. He wrote that "much of the material in the Navy Department has never been touched at all. In short, no full, accurate, and unprejudiced history of the war has ever been written."[13] If he meant that Cooper and others had not used Navy Department dispatches and commanding officers' action reports, he was wrong. Cooper had access to the printed versions in *Niles' Register* and other periodicals and officers' retained copies of letters to the department. He wrote letters to survivors, interviewed them, and his notes on these matters are contained in Yale University's Beinecke Library. Recently, Edward K. Eckert's otherwise informative introduction to a new edition of *The Naval War of 1812* failed to examine Roosevelt's opinion of Cooper and mistakenly calls Cooper's work "pro-American but no more credible [than James']."[14] To draw out the comparison, Roosevelt became so exasperated with James' description of American sailors' "fear" because they used helmets and multi-barreled guns [probably a Chambers gun]. Roosevelt wrote: "such a piece of writing as this is simply evidence of an unsound mind; it is not so much malicious as idiotic . . . any of James' unsupported statements about the Americans . . . are not worth the paper they are written on."[15] Roosevelt had earlier claimed Cooper was less exact and much less an authority than James. Are we now to infer that Cooper's writings were more "unsound, "idiotic," and worthless than James'? Roosevelt's narration and presentation of facts are sound, but in matters of opinion he partially undermines his own history of the war.

---

[12] Roosevelt, *The Naval War of 1812*, p. iv. Emmons' work, is a synthesis of battle results between American public and private warships, dependent on many primary and secondary sources, including Cooper's *History*.
[13] Roosevelt, *Naval War*, p. iv.
[14] Theodore Roosevelt, *The Naval War of 1812*, Intro. & ed. Edward K. Eckert, (Annapolis, Md.: U.S. Naval Institute, Classics of Naval Literature Series, 1987), xi-xxxii, p. xiv.
[15] Roosevelt, *Naval War*, p. 333.

On the other hand, Roosevelt's history is valuable for its attention to minor as well as major naval actions. He based his research on original documents sent from the Navy Department to the Astor Library for his use. Roosevelt proceeds carefully, comparing the American and British versions of each action; he takes issue with his sources on occasion and does not hesitate to express his judgement of officers' actions. He is as critical of Perry for his tactics as of Elliot for his failure to support his commodore. Commodore Sir James Yeo is as culpable as Commodore Chauncey for avoiding a decisive fleet action on Lake Ontario in Roosevelt's view, though Yeo was instructed by Governor General Prevost's orders to fight defensively. Roosevelt spends much time comparing the throw-weights of ships' batteries and numbers of crew at the time of certain battles in order to refute James' arguments. He also deplored the tendency of American historians to avoid censuring Captain James Lawrence for his flawed handling of the *Chesapeake* in her fatal combat with *Shannon*. Where the common view was one of Lawrence's extraordinarily bad luck, Roosevelt wrote that it was simply a matter of Shannon fighting better, regardless of the usual American excuses.[16]

The Naval War of 1812 was generally well-received, and it was soon adopted as a text by the Naval War College. Written at the nadir of post-Civil War American naval power, Roosevelt urged that the moral of the War of 1812 was lack of preparation. Had the nation been adequately prepared, the war might have been forestalled or would have been fought with greater success on land and sea. Roosevelt was acutely conscious of the U.S. Navy's weakness in the early 1880s and this informs his presentation.[17] According to his memoir (1925), Roosevelt wrote *The Naval War of 1812* not just for its own sake but as a means of drawing attention to the need for a stronger navy, so the nation could to play a significant role on the world's stage. In this sense he was a precursor of Mahan, whose own history of the War of 1812 had not been conceived when Roosevelt's appeared.

By the time Mahan commenced work on *Sea Power in its Relations to the War of 1812* in 1902, he had already reached the pinnacle of his career. Alfred Thayer was an 1859 graduate of the Naval Academy, a veteran of the Civil War, and a capable sea officer, but he had early shown a preference for writing on naval history and strategy rather than the usual routine of command at sea. He assisted Rear Admiral Stephen B. Luce in establishing the Naval War College at Newport and in defending it against its naval and congressional critics.

He began to mature as a writer in the late 1870s. His first work, *The Gulf and Inland Waters*, the last of Scribner's histories of the navy in the Civil War, was published in 1883. In this book, Mahan showed his abilities as a self-taught,

[16] Roosevelt, *Naval War of 1812*, pp. 189–190.
[17] Theodore Roosevelt, *An Autobiography* (New York, 1925), p. 205.

practicing historian, by using original documentation and writing to survivors, much as Cooper did, in order to reconcile conflicting accounts. His book was commended by others, brought him favorable attention, and began his remarkable career as a man of naval letters.[18] After publishing this work, Mahan's strategic concept of sea power, for which he is so well-known, developed rapidly. In preparing lectures for the Naval War College, Mahan absorbed the great military writings of earlier ages, especially those of Jomini and applied what he learned to the study of naval history in an original way.

In the early 1890s, he wrote his most famous books, *The Influence of Sea Power upon History, 1660-1783* and *The Influence of Sea Power upon the French Revolution and Empire.* Mahan had intended at that time to publish a work on the War of 1812 as the third in his sea power series. For various reasons, he put off the task for almost ten years. He was called to sea duty, against his will, by the Bureau of Navigation and put in command of the cruiser *Chicago.* Now famous, he was in constant demand as a columnist and speaker on international and naval affairs. His friendship with Theodore Roosevelt blossomed in the mutual admiration of one navalist for another. The Spanish-American War and its aftermath made many demands on his time and abilities, as American sea power moved from theory to practice.

Underlying all these imperatives was Mahan's curious reluctance to confront the War of 1812. The comment in his memoir *From Sail to Steam* was apt: "I had foreseen that the War of 1812, as a whole, must be flat in interest as well as laborious in execution; and upon the provocation of other duty, I readily turned from it in distaste."[19] When he did get started, it took three years to obtain the result, and he was diffident about the effort even then, as he wrote to his old friend Samuel Ashe: "I am at present at work on the War of 1812. It is a very old story, often told, and not a brilliant episode, nor one of which as a whole the United States can be very proud. It remains to be seen whether I can give any such novelty of presentation as to justify another telling."[20] With this attitude, one is surprised he finished the work. Yet he kept at it, and when the book (2 volumes) appeared, some readers were critical. Theodore Roosevelt, whose own work preceded Mahan's by 33 years, wrote: "I was as disappointed as you with Mahan's *War of 1812.* He is a curious fellow, for he cannot write in effective shape of the navy or of the fighting of his own country."[21]

---

[18] Captain W. D. Puleston, USN, *Mahan: The Life and Work of Captain Alfred Thayer Mahan, USN* (New Haven: Yale University Press, 1939), pp. 56-65.

[19] Alfred Thayer Mahan, *From Sail to Steam: Recollections of Naval Life* (New York: Da Capo Press, 1968; reprint of Harper & Bros. edition of 1907), p. 313.

[20] Mahan to Samuel A. Ashe, 12 April 1903, as printed in Robert Seager and Doris D. Maguire, eds. *Letters and Papers of Alfred Thayer Mahan,* vol. 3, (Annapolis, Md.: U.S. Naval Institute Press), III, p. 58.

[21] Roosevelt to James Roche, 7 March 1906, as printed in Elting E. Morrison and John Blum, eds. *The Letters of Theodore Roosevelt,* 8 vols., (Cambridge, Mass., 1951-54), vol. 5, p. 173.

At the outset, in reading Mahan's 1812 study, one realizes that he is not only re-writing the history of the war but also searching for justifications of his theories of sea power. Hindsight plays a major role in this method. He opens his study with a ponderous discussion of the legal precedents for impressment of seamen and the economic necessity of Britain's interruption of the American neutral trade to Napoleonic Europe. Viewed from this distance, it appears that Mahan, in writing this study, was considering the possibility that Britain could soon be at war with Germany.[22] The United States might again play the neutral role, an event which he, as an anglophile, hoped to discourage.

The causes of the War of 1812, for Mahan, were entirely maritime, and he justified the declaration of war against Britain considering the humiliations borne by the United States. His criticism is most harshly aimed at Presidents Jefferson and Madison for their ineptness in handling the diplomatic aspects of the Chesapeake-Leopard affair of 1807, their failure to prepare for war, and their policies of commercial retaliation. Mahan's descriptions of the frigate engagements are brief, in contrast to his treatment of the diplomatic entanglements before the war. One gains a much better appreciation of ship-maneuvering and the balance of the opposing forces from Roosevelt and Cooper. Mahan admired Commodore John Rodgers's cruising strategy which forced the British to concentrate their own relatively weak forces during the first months of the war. Yet he is puzzled that Rodgers's combined squadron was relatively unsuccessful in capturing enemy prizes, as compared with the single cruising frigates *Constitution* and *Essex*.[23] Mahan's correspondence with Admiral Luce shows that Mahan despised what he considered the "useless" spilling of blood in the high seas frigate engagements because there was no positive strategic result for the United States.[24]

Mahan is at his best in demonstrating the strategic inter-relationship of land and sea operations on Lakes Ontario, Erie, and Champlain.[25] Had the planned combined military and naval operations been skillfully and consistently carried out, American objectives might have been attained. Mahan is least effective in his account of the British 1813 and 1814 campaigns in the Chesapeake and seems to have been diverted from his analysis by the American propensity to trade with the enemy. He also suggests, without explanation, that the campaign of Admiral Warren and Rear Admiral

---

[22] William E. Livezey, *Mahan on Seapower* (Norman, Oklahoma: University of Oklahoma Press, 1947), pp. 224-225.

[23] Mahan to Luce, 12 May 1903, as printed in Seager and Maguire, *Letters and Papers*, vol. 3, pp. 61-62.

[24] Mahan to Luce, 13 January 1903, as printed in Seager and Maguire, *Letters and Papers*, vol. 3, p. 52 and 52n. Mahan replied to Luce's letter of 31 December 1902 which began with the sentence "It is my hope that in your next book you will dispose of the popular delusion that "we whipped England" in the War of 1812. See Albert Gleaves, *Life and Letters of Rear Admiral Stephen B. Luce, U.S. Navy* (New York: G.P. Putnam's Sons, 1925), pp. 289-290.

[25] Mahan, *Sea Power, in its Relations to the War of 1812*, vol. 2, pp. 101, 125, 299-309, 370-382.

Cockburn in the Chesapeake "cannot be regarded as successful."[26] Although this view could be contested by inhabitants from tidewater Maryland and Virginia, Mahan may have been suggesting that the British should have brought larger land forces to cut communications between Baltimore and Philadelphia and hence New York, perhaps even repeating the invasion and occupation of Philadelphia as in 1777.

Admiring British naval flexibility, Mahan emphasized the virtues of preparation, the disproportionate effect a few American ships-of-the-line might have had on British policy makers and the effectiveness of the British blockade in 1813-14 in undermining the American economy.

In appraising the value of Mahan's predecessors, one is bound to acknowledge the worth of all three to a comprehensive view of the naval war. Cooper's account thrives on action, is rich in biographical detail and strives for fairness to both sides at a time when objectivity was the exception rather than the rule in histories of the second Anglo-American war. He, like Roosevelt and Mahan, recognized the weakness of the American position before the war but blamed Congress as much as presidents for that situation. Roosevelt, using Cooper and James as foils, concentrated all his efforts on the war, wasted little time on its antecedents (spending only half a paragraph on *Chesapeake-Leopard*), and provided as much detail as possible in recounting the ship-to-ship combats. These attributes make his work, perhaps more than Cooper's, an essential reference for those working deeper in the subject. If Roosevelt's study is flawed by his aggravation with William James' history, Cooper is a good antidote in his dispassionate use of sources. He, too, was familiar with James' inaccuracies but chose to answer them, vigorously, in a separate piece.[27] Roosevelt's work has enduring value for the student of the War of 1812, and it probably also had a lasting influence on the United States Navy in that it permanently focused Roosevelt's attention on the issue of preparedness.[28] This preoccupation resurfaced during his terms as Civil Service Commissioner, as Assistant Secretary of the Navy and as President of the United States.[29]

Without question, the utility of Mahan's War of 1812 study is intrinsic to his view of the conflict's larger issues and its strategic aspects, absent from Cooper's book, though present in some degree in Roosevelt's. Strangely, Mahan never publicly acknowledged Roosevelt's contribution as an inspiration for his own approach to the War of 1812, although he certainly knew the work and Roosevelt's strong views on the subject. Luce had invited

---

[26] *Ibid.*, pp. 171-177.

[27] James Fenimore Cooper, Review of William James's *Naval History of Great Britain* in *United States Magazine and Democratic Review*, Vol. 10, New Series, (1842), pp. 411-435 and 515-541.

[28] Roosevelt, *Naval War*, ed. E.K. Eckert, xxxi-xxxii.

[29] See Richard Turk's valuable discussion of Roosevelt and Mahan and their views on the War of 1812 in *The Ambiguous Relationship: Theodore Roosevelt and Alfred Thayer Mahan* (Westport, Connecticut: Greenwood Press, 1987), pp. 57-70, 104-105.

Roosevelt to lecture at the Naval War College, which he did in August 1888.[30] Although Mahan mentions *The Naval War of 1812* in a letter to Luce, it is by way of explaining that he "purposely refrained from studying his [Roosevelt's] reasons till I shall have my independent conclusions."[31] This is a curious admission, possibly reflecting Mahan's desire to distance himself from Roosevelt's interpretation of events.

Mahan's bias, a predilection for the British use of sea power to defend her island kingdom and empire, has both its strengths and weaknesses in an analysis of the American way of naval war. Mahan is applying a seventeenth-century paradigm of fleet warfare between well-developed national polities to a nineteenth-century naval contest between mother country and former colony, an infant republic, researched and written under the baleful influence of early twentieth-century empire building. The hundred years naval war between Britain and France (1715-1815) was in its final stages when the War of 1812 issued forth, brought into existence by James Madison and his Congress as the ultimate of desperate moves to satisfy national honor. The American Revolution had not yet completed its work; it was as if Americans felt that, ready or not, they could hold Canada hostage with Britain preoccupied in staging the collapse of her continental rival.

The war-making demons created by the administrations of Jefferson and Madison worked in no logical strategic manner. It is the naivete of these gentlemen and their cohorts that has so troubled most naval historians of the United States. If a nation depends on commerce for its national income and commences war without a considerable naval force against a kingdom possessing the world's largest navy, she will surely suffer the closing of her ports and the disastrous decline of national finance. Mahan's dismay at having to write the story of these events was produced by a psychological predicament. As a patriotic American naval officer, he disliked writing of national events conducted in a foolhardy manner against a worthy foe the descendants of whom he greatly admired. In 1896, when the Venezuelan crisis posed the possibility of another Anglo-American War, he wrote "My own belief has long since passed . . . from faith in and ambition for my country alone, to the same thing for the Anglo-Saxon race."[32] This sentiment was uttered nine years before the publication of his War of 1812 "Sea Power" study. The variance of his approach from Roosevelt's is seen in Mahan's silent dependence on William James' version of naval engagements because of his painstaking accuracy.[33] Although Roosevelt had invested considerable time

---

[30] Turk, *Ambiguous Relationship*, p. 15. Turk adds that although the two men met on that occasion, "what either man thought of the other on the basis of this initial contact remains a mystery to this day."
[31] Mahan to Luce, 17 June 1903, as printed in Seager and Maguire, *Letters and Papers*, III, pp. 64-65.
[32] Robert Seager, *Alfred Thayer Mahan: The Man and His Letters* (Annapolis, Md.: Naval Institute Press, 1977), p. 334.
[33] Turk, *Ambiguous Relationship*, p. 105.

in contradicting James' prejudiced versions of events, Mahan proceeded as if Roosevelt had never written *The Naval War of 1812*.[34]

While historians often revisit the multiple causes of the War of 1812, it is still acknowledged that one of the most important of these was the ideological one of national honor, and immediately following this, the American belief in the phrases "free trade" and "freedom of the seas," inherited from the British. In the seagoing America of those days, these issues were tantamount to a maritime declaration of independence. The officers and men of the frigate *Chesapeake* were not the only ones who believed in the motto on Lawrence's battle flag "Free Trade and Sailors' Rights," protesting the seizure of American merchant vessels and seamen by British men of war.

When Mahan arrived at the point of discussing the virtues of this position, he could not, because he was morally incapable of asserting the argument. So convinced is he by the international politics of the late 1890s that Britain's trade will suffer in a future Anglo-German war while Germany would benefit from an internationally-condoned neutral trade, that he publicly and privately advocated that the rights of neutral trading nations should not be recognized in the Hague Conferences of 1899 and 1908.[35] During the interim period, Mahan researched, wrote, and published his *Sea Power in its Relations to the War of 1812*. Its most labored part is the 280-page introductory chapter discussion of the legal justifications for Britain's non-recognition of neutral American trading rights during the Napoleonic Wars.[36]

As difficult as it was for Mahan to face the realities of the War of 1812, he grudgingly acknowledged that it made some sense for the United States to encourage privateering and to use her navy in commerce raiding. He noted the success of privateers in annoying the enemy, especially during the waning months of the war when our larger naval vessels were blockaded in port. He acknowledged that Secretary Jones was more impressed with the faster, more maneuverable design of the Baltimore clippers than by heavy frigates and ships of the line that were so slow to build and difficult to man. In 1814, Jones recommended to Congress that this be the next basic naval ship design so that squadrons of several could operate under men such as Porter and Perry. Had the war continued, the navy might have taken this shape in 1815.

---

[34] There is little doubt that Mahan used both James and Roosevelt, as can be seen from internal references in Mahan's correspondence with Rear Admiral Luce but he makes no overt citations to either historian. Some of Mahan's other printed sources are listed in an enclosure of a letter to Charles W. Stewart, Chief Clerk of the Library and Naval War Records, Navy Department, Washington, D.C. See Seager and Maguire, *Letters and Papers of Alfred Thayer Mahan*, vol. 3, 1902-1914, pp. 65-66.

[35] Turk, *Ambiguous Relationship*, 71-74. In letters to Theodore Roosevelt (Dec. 27, 1904) and Elihu Root (Apr. 20, 1906) Mahan encloses excerpts from his "forthcoming War of 1812" containing his historical arguments against the exemption of private property from capture at sea. Mahan here displays the tendency to manipulate history for reasons of state policy in order to derail the proposed American position at the approaching Second Hague Conference. See Seager and Maguire, *Letters and Papers*, vol. 3, pp. 112-113 and 157-158.

[36] Seager, *Mahan: The Man and His Letters*, p. 569, believes this is one of the "freshest and most useful sections of the book."

In considering the U.S. Navy's cruising strategy, Mahan rightly perceived that more naval frigate commanders should have tried their luck in English seas, as did Captain William Henry Allen in the brig *Argus*.[37] Not enough American commanders took so bold an approach to warfare. Witness Captain John Smith wasting his time and his ship in months of fruitless cruising off the Guianas in 1812-1813. Mahan spares Commodore John Rodgers whose squadron failed to capture any significant prizes because the squadron's mere existence had a strategic effect. In 1812, while the Rodgers' and Decatur's combined squadrons unsuccessfully chased the frigate *Belvidera*, Captains Porter and Hull captured, burned or sent in almost two dozen prizes while cruising independently. On the other hand, when on a later cruise, Rodgers had an ideal opportunity to raid in the chops of the channel or the Irish Sea, he chose to avoid those busy seaways and to cruise off northern Norway to the North Cape taking but a few desultory prizes. But, in Mahan's eyes, despite Rodgers' "bad luck," the commodore made the right strategic move early in the war by concentrating his ships. This forced Commodore Broke to keep his small squadron intact in pursuit and allowed free play for a number of American privateers and independent frigates early in the war.[38]

Mahan the historian did do research in original documents, but he also made ample use of the friendly assistance of other specialists in constructing his version of events. He consulted John Bassett Moore regarding the legalistic argumentation on maritime rights. Rear Admiral Luce helped him with the frigate combat actions and criticized sections of a draft dealing with these engagements. He frequently called on John Franklin Jameson and Andrew McLaughlin for advice in writing the work. But "at no time in spite of all the assistance he received did Mahan succeed in effectively suspending his anglophilic tendencies."[39]

The influence of Mahan's *Sea Power in its Relations to the War of 1812* was not as great as his earlier works on European sea power. There was and is little international interest in the American "War of 1812" even though his book appeared on the eve of the centennial of the conflict. On the other hand, Mahan's work has been influential among many generations of American historians of the war, for most of them are not maritime historians. They have depended on Mahan heavily for his interpretation of events at sea while they spent their efforts explaining and reinterpreting the Madison administration's 'policies, military operations on land, and the political and economic impact of the war. For some examples, a recent major work on the War of 1812 is J.C.A. Stagg's *Mr. Madison's War: Politics, Warfare and Diplomacy in the Early Republic, 1783-1830* (1983), based heavily on correspondence of political and military figures. But Stagg virtually ignores

---

[37] Mahan, *Sea Power*, vol. 2, pp. 217-220.
[38] *Ibid.*, vol. 1, pp. 324-327.
[39] Seager, *Mahan*, p. 567.

naval documentation. When he needs a citation, he leans on Mahan, and the papers of Secretary William Jones, Albert Gallatin, and James Madison and Edward Eckert's slim monograph on Jones, *The Navy Department in the War of 1812.*⁴⁰ He never offers a qualitative comment on Mahan's approach or method and does not cite Theodore Roosevelt's *The War of 1812.* An older but still better work than Stagg's for its balance between military and naval coverage is Reginald Horsman's *The War of 1812.*⁴¹ In his "bibliographical note," Horsman describes Mahan's work as "essential reading for an understanding of this period," but also adds that Theodore Roosevelt's *Naval War of 1812* is particularly useful for its analysis of comparative strengths in the various naval engagements of the war.⁴² The newest research on the war will be found in Donald R. Hickey, *The War of 1812: A Forgotten Conflict* (1989). Hickey prefers Roosevelt as "the best account of the war at sea" and a "judicious work" which is a good antidote to the ill-tempered standard British account" by William James. Hickey considers Mahan's a valuable work "though Mahan had a tendency to rework quotations from his source material so they read better."⁴³

In summary, Alfred Thayer Mahan's *Sea Power in Its Relations to the War of 1812* is alive and well in academe, despite any shortcomings it may have in terms of bias and "present-mindedness." Those who use it should also consult Roosevelt for his appreciation of tactical detail and better balance between American and English source materials. Cooper, too, should be kept in mind for his lively appreciation and apt expression of American naval efforts. None of these authors provides much insight into the institutional, administrative, logistical, or social history of the U.S. Navy of the early republic, but this is a contemporary concern of our own time and was not of great interest to earlier naval historians. This is the arena in which future "Mahans" will have to make their mark.

---

⁴⁰ For example, see Stagg, p. 325, n.74, referrence to *Sea Power*, vol. 2, 63–69; Stagg, p. 341, n. 135 reference to *Sea Power*, vol. 2, 51–56; Stagg, p. 391, n. 12 reference to *Sea Power*, vol. 2, 324–328.
⁴¹ Reginald Horsman, *The War of 1812* (New York: Alfred A. Knopf, 1969).
⁴² See Horsman, *The War of 1812*, pp. 273.
⁴³ Donald R. Hickey, *The War of 1812: A Forgotten Conflict* (Urbana & Chicago: Illinois University Press, 1989), p. 321.

PART IV: ON REFLECTION

THE

INTEREST OF AMERICA IN INTERNATIONAL CONDITIONS

BY

A. T. MAHAN, D.C.L., LL.D.

CAPTAIN, UNITED STATES NAVY

Author of " The Influence of Sea Power upon History," " The Interest of America in Sea Power," etc.

BOSTON
LITTLE, BROWN, AND COMPANY
1910

Title page of the first edition in the Collections of the Eccles Library, Naval War College.

Chapter 13

Mahan on World Politics and Strategy: The Approach of the First World War, 1904-1914

John H. Mauer

Introduction

Alfred Thayer Mahan's reputation as a strategic thinker rests primarily on his famous books on *The Influence of Sea Power*. Scholars examining Mahan's writings tend to concentrate on these histories about naval operations during the great wars between the end of the seventeenth and the beginning of the nineteenth centuries. As a consequence, Mahan is now best remembered as a naval historian and a theorist of naval operations.[1]

But this perspective on Mahan is too narrow. In addition to his contribution to understanding naval history and operations, Mahan was a political scientist and policy analyst. This facet of Mahan's thought can especially be seen in his writings from the period 1900-1914, which are often only glanced at for surveys of his writings. It is perhaps not surprising that this is the case, since Mahan's writings are difficult to study. He was a celebrated and prolific writer for almost a quarter of a century, and during that time he changed his views on a number of important issues. Moreover, he failed to provide his readers with a systematic treatment of his own views on politics and strategy. As a consequence, his more famous early historical writings that highlight naval operations are emphasized in examinations of his thoughts, while his theories about international politics are relatively neglected. This is unfortunate, because some of Mahan's most seminal thoughts were expressed in his later writings about international politics and strategy.

To use the language of modern-day international relations theory, Mahan's thought belongs within the realist tradition for the study of relations between states. This tradition traces its lineage back to Thucydides, and includes such prominent modern thinkers as Hans Morgenthau and Henry Kissinger. Indeed,

---

[1] Philip Crowl's article in the new *Makers of Modern Strategy* in an example of this way of surveying Mahan's writings. Philip A. Crowl, "Alfred Thayer Mahan: The Naval Historian," in *Makers of Modern Strategy from Machiavelli to the Nuclear Age*, edited by Peter Paret (Princeton: Princeton University Press, 1986), pp. 444–477.

many of Mahan's tenets about world politics and strategy are mainstays of contemporary international relations theory, and it is useful to identify at the outset some of the most important of these tenets.

First, Mahan saw anarchy as a distinctive attribute of world politics. Since no supranational organization existed that could control the international system, individual states needed to provide for their own security in a Darwinian struggle for survival. Because states struggled to find security, Mahan was dubious of the ability of states to promote cooperation between themselves by peaceful means. Arbitration agreements between states and the establishment of norms for conduct in the international arena were likely to work only so long as the issues at stake were limited. Once a state saw that its important interests were threatened, however, international agreements to promote cooperation could not take the place of armed force in providing for its security. To use Kenneth Waltz's apt phrase: "Self-help is necessarily the principle of action in an anarchic order."[2] Nor did Mahan think that the international system was likely to change in the near future. His scathing comments on Norman Angell's *The Great Illusion* show how far Mahan was from the view that great power rivalries were atavistic and suicidal and that they stood in the way of greater international cooperation and material progress. Mahan argued that the "entire conception of the work is itself an illusion based on a profound misreading of human action."[3] So long as human nature remained unchanged, Mahan thought that the threat of war could never be banished from international relations. In Mahan's view, the best way to prevent war was to be so well-armed that potential adversaries would be deterred from risking a conflict.[4]

Second, hierarchy was in Mahan's view a distinguishing feature of world politics, and the international system was directed by the decisions of the great powers. Mahan contended that the great commercial states in particular would play a leading role in world politics because of the wealth they generated from international trade. To Mahan, Britain's leadership of the international political system during the nineteenth century rested in large part on its position as the world's leading trading state and naval power.

Third, Mahan theorized from his study of history that the cause of war and change in world politics was rooted in underlying shifts in the power relationships between states.[5] Thus, the international system's leading states

---

[2] Kenneth N. Waltz, *Theory of International Politics* (Reading, Massachusetts: Addison-Wesley Publishing Company, 1979), p. 111.

[3] See Robert Seager II, *Alfred Thayer Mahan: The Man and His Letters* (Annapolis: Naval Institute Press, 1977), pp. 586-591. Hereafter cited as Seager, *Mahan*.

[4] See Mahan's short article "Why Not Disarm?" in Robert Seager II and Doris D. Maguire, *Letters and Papers of Alfred Thayer Mahan* (Annapolis: Naval Institute Press, 1975), volume 3, pp. 685-687. Hereafter cited as Seager and Maguire, *Mahan Papers*.

[5] On this theme in world politics, see the two thought-provoking studies: Robert Gilpin, *War and Change in World Politics* (Cambridge: Cambridge University Press, 1981); and Paul Kennedy, *The Rise and Fall of the Great Powers* (New York: Random House, 1987).

had in the past been challenged by more rapidly growing powers, and these challenges carried with them the potential for war. During the period examined by Mahan in his histories of sea power, Spain, the Netherlands, England, and France had struggled with one another for leadership of the international system. In the decade before the First World War, Mahan saw the rise of Germany as the major challenger to Britain's leading position in world politics. Indeed, Mahan considered the decline of British power in the face of challenges from other great powers as the cardinal feature of the international system in the early twentieth century.

Fourth, Mahan was concerned with the balance of power. It was an important tenet of his views on world politics that the great powers needed to prevent any one of their number from achieving hegemony within the international system. Mahan was concerned not only with the European balance of power but with the global equilibrium. The imperial rivalries between great powers in Asia and Latin America were linked with the European balance in a global system. In his assessment of power balances between states, Mahan gave prominence to five indicators: territory, population, armed forces, commerce, and the ability of governments to develop and carry out long-range planning and to mobilize their country's resources.

A fifth factor that was prominent in Mahan's thoughts about world politics and strategy is that competing states adopt similar strategic doctrines and force structures. In the early twentieth century, this principle was nicely illustrated by the general competition between the great powers in the building of battleships and their adoption of the strategic doctrine of battle-fleet concentration. Mahan attached a great deal of importance to the relationship between a country's foreign policy and its naval power. A great power eager to pursue an expansionist foreign policy—or a country trying to contain the expansion of rivals—required naval power. Thus, Mahan gave particular attention to the great-power battleship building rivalries and the strategic doctrines guiding the deployment of their navies in his analyses of developments in world politics.

In this essay, I will examine Mahan's views on world politics during the ten-year period before the outbreak of the First World War. My purpose is to show the relationship between Mahan's theoretical understanding of world politics and his policy prescriptions. In particular, three policy issues are examined in this essay: Mahan's assessment of Britain's declining position in the international system, the importance of shifts in the global balance of power for the United States, and the naval competition between the great powers and the associated strategic doctrine of battle-fleet concentration.

Mahan on the Rise and Fall of Great Powers

Like many statesmen and political commentators of his era, Mahan thought that world politics in the twentieth century would be characterized by a global rivalry between the great powers for commercial and naval supremacy. These struggles for empire, world power, and naval mastery were viewed by Mahan and others as a twentieth-century replay of the wars that he had described in his volumes on *The Influence of Sea Power*. During the course of these struggles, dramatic shifts were likely to take place in the power balances between the great powers.

In particular, Mahan was concerned with Britain's ability to hold its position in world affairs against rising great-power challengers. It was an axiom of world politics at the turn of the century that the imperial rivalry between Britain and Russia throughout Asia and the Middle East—the so-called "Great Game"—must sooner or later result in a diplomatic showdown and perhaps war. A corollary to this axiom held that Britain would not be able to contain Russia's expansion in Asia without the support of major allies. In the United States, such prominent national leaders and commentators on world affairs as Theodore Roosevelt, Henry Cabot Lodge, Brooks Adams, as well as Mahan subscribed to this axiom and its corollary. This group wanted the United States to take a more active role in world politics in support of Britain's position. Thus, Brooks Adams, in his book *America's Economic Supremacy* published in 1900, advocated that "America must more or less completely assume the place once held by England, for the United States could hardly contemplate with equanimity the successful organization of a hostile industrial system on the shore of the Pacific, based on Chinese labor."[6] Mahan agreed with this assessment, arguing that the United States should align itself with Germany and Japan to assist Britain in containing Russia. This bloc of "Sea Powers" should seek to prevent Russia from gaining "preponderant political control" of China.[7] But this historical precursor to what after 1945 would be called a strategy of containment failed to come about. The Russo-Japanese War of 1904–5 revealed that Russia's power had been overestimated.

Russia's defeat, however, did not mean that Britain's position was secure from challengers. In place of Russia, Germany's rise as a great naval power and Japan's success over Russia heightened Mahan's concern about the balance of power in Europe and Asia. Thus, far from being united in purpose, the coalition of Britain, Germany, Japan, and the United States, which Mahan had proposed in *The Problem of Asia*, was actually made up of rival great powers. In particular, Germany had emerged by 1908 in Mahan's eyes as the most serious challenger to Britain's position in world politics. "The rivalry between Germany and Great Britain today," Mahan told his readers, "is the danger point, not only of European politics, but of world politics as

---

[6] Quoted in Howard K. Beale, *Theodore Roosevelt and the Rise of America to World Power* (New York: Collier Books, 1962 edition), pp. 226–227. On Roosevelt's views that the United States might be drawn into a war with Russia, see *ibid.*, pp. 263–4, and Seward W. Livermore, "The American Navy as a Factor in World Politics, 1903–1913," *The American Historical Review*, volume 63 (July 1958), p. 877.

[7] See A.T. Mahan, *The Problem of Asia and Its Effect upon International Policies* (Port Washington, New York: Kennikat, 1970 edition), passim. Mahan's book *Problem of Asia* first appeared in 1900.

well. . . . No such emphasized industrial and maritime competition between two communities has arisen since the time of Cromwell and the later Stewart kings, when England wrested from Holland her long possessed commercial supremacy, supported by a navy until then unconquered."[8]

What political and strategic indicators led Mahan to this assessment? One factor was Germany's rapidly rising population and industrial production. To Mahan, Germany's dramatic demographic and industrial growth meant that it would demand overseas territories as an outlet for its growing population and as markets for its products. But perhaps the single most important indicator that triggered Mahan's alarm about Germany was that country's naval challenge to Britain. Germany's stated program of naval construction and its decision to follow the lead of Britain and the United States in building "all-big-gun" or dreadnought battleships showed the seriousness of the German challenge. Mahan pointed out: "The huge development of the German Navy within the past decade, and the assurance that the present rate of expenditure—over 20,000,000 annually—will be maintained for several years to come, is a matter of great international importance."[9] Mahan saw an intimate connection between Germany's industrial growth, rise as a naval power, and drive for imperial expansion. As Mahan put it, there is "an inevitable link in the chain of logical sequence: Industry, markets, control [of overseas territories], navy, bases."[10]

The famous 1909 "naval panic" in Britain, in particular, heightened Mahan's concern about Germany's foreign policy goals. Prompted by the naval panic in Britain, Mahan tried to alert his American readers to the political significance of the growing German battle fleet in an article for *Collier's Weekly*, entitled: "Germany's Naval Ambition: Some Reasons Why the United States Should Wake Up to the Facts About the Kaiser's Battleship-Building Program—Great Britain's Danger Exaggerated, But Not Her Fright." He reminded his readers of the German involvement in Venezuela in 1902—"a condition almost sure to arise" again—and warned that Germany would "have the whip hand" in a future crisis if it possessed "a decisively superior navy." Mahan asked whether the Monroe Doctrine should be "dependent upon the uncertain indulgence of a foreign state, which is notoriously thirsting for colonization in the supposed interest of racial development?" Only by building "a navy adequate to prevent such humiliation" could the United States be prepared for the crisis to come. According to Robert Seager, in the years between 1909, when he sounded the tocsin in "Germany's Naval Ambitions" for *Collier's Weekly*, and his death

---

[8] A.T. Mahan, *The Interest of America in International Conditions* (Boston: Little, Brown, and Company, 1918 edition), pp. 163-164. This book first appeared in 1910.

[9] Admiral A.T. Mahan, "Britain and the German Navy," *The Daily Mail*, July 4, 1910.

[10] Mahan, *Interest of America in International Conditions*, p. 87.

on 1 December 1914, Mahan acted as "a journalistic Paul Revere" alerting his English-speaking audience "to the fact that the Germans were coming."[11]

Germany's naval and colonial ambitions led Mahan to advocate that the United States support Britain in defeating this challenge. Why did Mahan champion this course for U.S. foreign policy? Mahan might have recommended, for example, that the United States attempt to play Britain and Germany off against each other. This is what Germany's foreign policy attempted to do at the turn of the century when Britain and Russia were rivals in Asia. By attempting to hold the balance of power between London and Saint Petersburg, Prince Bernhard von Bülow, Germany's foreign secretary and later chancellor, wanted to increase German prestige and influence in world politics.[12] But instead of suggesting that the United States do likewise and seek to exploit the growing Anglo-German antagonism, Mahan advocated that it help Britain contain German expansion. Why did Mahan, whose writings reveal such a pronounced Darwinian character, not call for the United States to take advantage of Britain's embarrassment and help partition the British empire, thereby establishing the United States as the leading world power? Answering these questions helps shed some light on Mahan's theories about world politics.

First, Mahan believed that cultural and ideological affinities promoted cooperation between Britain and the United States. Britain's heritage was part of America's history. One consequence of these common traditions was that the governments in both countries were committed to promoting "the liberty of the individual."[13] This acted to dampen their rivalry.

Second, Mahan did not see where Britain represented a threat to the United States. To Mahan, Britain was a satiated power, which was not likely to challenge the United States in the Western Hemisphere. Britain's actions in acquiescing in the control of the Panama Canal by the United States demonstrated this proposition.[14] Moreover, Canada was "open to land attack,"

---

[11] Captain A.T. Mahan, "Germany's Naval Ambitions: Some Reasons Why the United States Should Wake Up to the Facts About the Kaiser's Battleship-Building Program—Great Britain's Danger Exaggerated, But Not Her Fright," *Collier's Weekly*, volume 43 (April 24, 1909), pp. 12-13; Seager, *Mahan*, p. 468. On the Venezuelan Crisis of 1902-3 between the United States and Germany, see Beale, *Theodore Roosevelt and the Rise to World Power*, pp. 357-358; and Seward W. Livermore, "Theodore Roosevelt, the American Navy, and the Venezuelan Crisis of 1902-1903," *The American Historical Review*, volume 51 (April 1946), pp. 452-471.

[12] On Bülow's foreign policy, see Peter Winzen, *Bülows Weltmachtkonzept: Untersuchungen zur Frühphase seiner Aussenpolitik, 1897-1901* (Boppard am Rhein: Harald Boldt, 1977), passim; and Klaus Wormer, *Russland and Deutschland: Studien zur Britischen Weltreichpolitik am Vorabend des Ersten Weltkriegs* (Munich: Wilhelm Fink, 1980), pp. 64-140.

[13] Mahan, *Interest of America in International Conditions*, pp. 93-101.

[14] On Anglo-American relations in this period, see Bradford Perkins, *2The Great Rapprochement: England and the United States, 1895-1914* (New York: Atheneum, 1968); Kenneth Bourne, *Britain and the Balance of Power in North America, 1815-1908* (Berkeley: University of California Press, 1967); Samuel F. Wells, Jr., "British Strategic Withdrawal from the Western Hemisphere, 1904-1906," *Canadian Historical Review*, volume 49 (December 1968), pp. 335-356; and Stephen R. Rock, *Why Peace Breaks Out: Great Power Rapprochement in Historical Perspective* (Chapel Hill: The University of North Carolina Press, 1989), pp. 24-63.

and thus Britain possessed a vulnerability that the United States could exploit to check British ambitions.[15] Britain, then, had already conceded hegemony to the United States in the Western Hemisphere and was playing the main role in upholding the balance of power throughout Europe and Asia.

Third, in Mahan's opinion, the rapid collapse of British power would result in the strengthening of Germany's position. Unlike Britain, Germany was in Mahan's opinion aggressive, expansionist, and seeking new colonies. The growth of German power might result in a challenge the United States' position in the Western Hemisphere.

Given these considerations, Mahan argued that the United States was better off strengthening Britain's position than in undermining it. Indeed, if the United States aligned itself with Britain, it would be in a better position to contain German expansion. Faced by this alignment, Germany might even be deterred from seizing colonies in the Western Hemisphere, so long as the United States developed a powerful fleet.

Mahan's sympathies for Britain were not uncommon for naval officers of this era. The General Board of the Navy, for instance, suggested a naval alliance with Great Britain directed against Germany. In a letter to Secretary of the Navy Charles Bonaparte, dated September 28, 1906, the General Board warned that Germany would strike to seize colonies in the Western Hemisphere as soon as her fleet was ready. Since British leaders were also alarmed by German naval and colonial expansion, the General Board advised the Roosevelt administration to consider an understanding with Britain along the lines of the Anglo-Japanese Alliance of 1902: if the United States faced only Germany, Britain would remain benevolently neutral; but if Germany attacked with the aid of an ally, Britain would enter the war on the side of the United States. The General Board believed such an agreement would deter Germany from attacking across the Atlantic because their own home coasts would then be denuded of battleships and open to British attack. In the General Board's opinion: "The two English speaking nations seem detained to exert a great influence on the further progress of the world, and the conduct of war."[16]

But a formal alliance was outside the bounds of practical politics within the United States, and Mahan urged instead a foreign policy of tacit cooperation with Britain. This alignment entailed that the United States build a powerful navy, while at the same time eschewing any policy of provoking a naval competition with Britain. It is important to note that Mahan did not urge that the United States acquire a battle fleet as large as that maintained by Britain. What Mahan wanted was for the United States to direct its energies to keeping abreast of Germany in modern battleships. Given

---

[15] Mahan, *Interest of America in International Conditions*, p 162.
[16] Admiral George Dewey to Bonaparte, September 28, 1906, General Board Letterpress, General Board Papers.

Germany's naval ambitions, the cost of achieving even this goal was going to be substantial. Mahan also advocated that the United States mass its force of battleships on the east coast, where it could be more readily assembled to defeat a German move to seize territory in the Western Hemisphere.

Mahan sought to impress upon American readers the threat posed by the German battle fleet for the security of the United States. He warned, again and again, that the growth of the German battle fleet was rapidly overturning Britain's naval supremacy. In 1910, in *The Interest of America in International Conditions*, Mahan told his fellow countrymen that they could not remain unconcerned to this German challenge to Britain because it might prove successful. Americans must ask themselves "whether they can afford, to exchange the naval supremacy of Great Britain for that of Germany; for this alternative may arise." Once the European balance was overturned, "a German navy, supreme by the fall of Great Britain, with a supreme German army able to spare readily a large expeditionary force for over-sea operations, is one of the possibilities of the future."[17]

In *Naval Strategy*, published in 1911, Mahan drew attention to the importance of the decline of British power for the United States. "The power to control Germany does not exist in Europe," he wrote, "except in the British Navy; and if social and political conditions in Great Britain develop as they now promise, the British Navy will probably decline in relative strength, so that it will not venture to withstand the German on any broad lines of policy, but only in the narrowest sense of immediate British interests . . . for it seems as if the national life of Great Britain were waning at the same time that of Germany is waxing." Mahan argued that "it is this line of reasoning which shows the power of the German Navy to be a matter of prime importance to the United States." Germany might be able to use its fleet as a political lever to keep Britain and the United States from acting in concert with each other to maintain the existing balance of power. By separating Britain from the United States, Germany might seize an opportunity to acquire territory in the Western Hemisphere.[18]

For Mahan, then, it was essential that Britain and the United States attempt to defeat Germany's naval challenge. But Mahan was not sanguine that either Britain or the United States—despite his estimation that they possessed superior economic resources— would be able to keep ahead of Germany in this naval rivalry. Mahan was concerned that governments representative of the people might not be able to pursue a viable long-term strategy. Despite their superior resources, Britain and the United States appeared incapable of harnessing them. Germany's government, on the other hand, seemed to Mahan to be better able to mobilize the resources of the country to support

[17] Mahan, *Interest of America in International Conditions*, pp. 161-162.
[18] Captain A.T. Mahan, *Naval Strategy Compared and Contrasted With the Principles and Practice of Military Operations on Land* (Boston: Little, Brown, and Company, 1911), p. 110.

its foreign policy aims. "The two English-speaking countries," Mahan wrote, "have wealth vastly superior, each separately, to that of Germany; much more if acting together. But in neither is the efficiency of the Government for handling the resources comparable to that of Germany." Mahan argued that "the habits of individual liberty in England or America [do not] accept, unless under duress, the heavy yoke of organization, of regulation of individual action, which constitutes the power of Germany among modern states."[19] Mahan, then, questioned whether democratic governments would be able to make and carry out a long-term strategic plan.[20]

It was Mahan's fear that the United States would not build a sufficient number of modern battleships to match the German program. Mahan lamented in 1909:

> The German Navy will in 1912—in three years—have a stronger battle fleet in A[ll]-B[ig]-G[un] ships than we. What then shall we say, upon what shall we rely, if she, on occasion arising, defy us in the Monroe Doctrine? How do we propose to keep that national idol on its feet without a superior navy?[21]

Mahan's anxiety that Germany was rapidly outstripping the United States in naval strength was shared by the U.S. Navy's General Board. The General Board argued that the United States needed to maintain a condition of at least rough parity with Germany's battle fleet. But this standard of naval strength was unlikely to be obtained in a future clash, so long as the United States did not keep pace with Germany in the building of capital ships.

The result of losing the naval arms race with Germany might be German colonial gains in the Western Hemisphere. For the readers of *The New York Times* on 2 April 1912, Mahan even devised peace terms that Germany would impose on the United States at the conclusion of some future war:

> What terms? Well, to name three principal, omitting others: the surrender of the Panama Canal, the admission of Asiatic labor immigration, and the abandonment of the Monroe Doctrine. These may be stated as (1) the surrender of a vital link in our coastwise communications, the principal end for which the Canal was undertaken; (2) the constitution of a population predominately Asiatic on the Pacific slope west of the Rocky Mountains—a new race problem; and (3) the suppression of a national policy, the salutary aim of which has been to exclude foreign wars from propagation to the American Hemisphere.[22]

When war engulfed Europe in the summer of 1914, Mahan worried that this prediction might soon come about if Germany defeated her enemies. He told interviewers from *The New York Evening Post*:

---

[19] Mahan, *Naval Strategy*, p. 109; and Mahan, *Interest of America in International Conditions*, p. 163. Given Germany's chaotic decision making structure in this period, Mahan's view that Germany possessed these attributes of governmental efficiency is dubious.
[20] On this theme, see Mahan's hard-hitting piece "Britain and the German Navy," in *The Daily Mail*.
[21] Mahan to Charles W. Stewart, March 19, 1909, Seager and Maguire, *Mahan Papers*, volume 3. pp. 290-2.
[22] Seager and Maguire, *Mahan Papers*, volume 3, p. 453.

> If Germany succeeds in downing both France and Russia, she gains a respite by land, which may enable her to build up her sea power equal, or superior to that of Great Britain. In that case the world will be confronted by the naval power of a state, not, like Great Britain, sated with territory, but one eager and ambitious for expansion, eager also for influence. This consideration may well affect American sympathies.

To one of his English correspondents, Mahan expressed the fear "that if Germany wins by a big margin she is likely to be nasty to us [in the United States]."[23] Thus, Mahan's sympathies for Britain in the World War were clear at the time of his death. Moreover, he deeply resented the Wilson administration's gag order, which prevented him from arguing the case for containing German power.[24]

Battleship Building and Naval Concentration

The concentration of naval forces into powerful battle fleets was a distinguishing feature of early twentieth century strategic theory and war planning. In Germany, for example, a critical component of Tirpitz's strategy was the concentration of Germany's battleship in home waters. By concentrating Germany's most powerful warships, Tirpitz aimed at increasing their operational readiness and magnifying their political impact.[25] The United States and Britain followed and also took steps to concentrate their battleships.[26]

In the United States, the Naval War College played a critical role in promoting the strategy of naval concentration. A study prepared by naval officers attending the summer conference of the Naval War College in 1903 recommended that the United States concentrate all its battleships in naval bases and ports on the east coast. The study made clear that the strategic rationale for this concentration was the need to match Germany's battle fleet. Since all of Germany's battleships were massed in the North Sea, while the United States had three of its battleships in the Pacific, an American battle fleet in the Caribbean would amount to only 70 percent of the German strength in battleships at the outbreak of hostilities. This disparity in numbers meant that the German battle fleet would probably win the critical initial engagements in any future war. To restore the naval balance, the War College study recommended:

---

[23] Seager and Maguire, *Mahan Papers*, volume 3, pp. 551-669.

[24] Seager, *Mahan*, p. 689, note 31.

[25] On Tirpitz's strategy, see Paul Kennedy, "Strategic Aspects of the Anglo-German Naval Race," in *Strategy and Diplomacy, 1870-1945; Eight Studies* (London: George Allen and Unwin, 1983), pp. 127-160.

[26] For the debate in the United States about naval concentration, see John H. Maurer, "American Naval Concentration and the German Battle Fleet, 1900-1918," *The Journal of Strategic Studies*, volume 6, number 2 (June 1983), pp. 147-181. Britain's naval concentration is analyzed in R.F. Mackay, "The Admiralty, the German Navy, and the Redistribution of the British Fleet, 1904-1905," *Mariner's Mirror*, volume 56 (1970), pp. 341-346; Paul M. Kennedy, *The Rise and Fall of British Naval Mastery* (Atlantic Highlands, New Jersey: The Ashfield Press, 1983 edition), pp. 205-237.

The battle fleet should at all times be concentrated in the Atlantic. . . . Habitual concentration is Blues's [that is, the United States] only safeguard unless the battle fleet is at least one and one-half times the strength of Black's [Germany]. It is particularly noticeable that such concentration is the policy of Black and of all other great powers except Great Britain, which maintains a small battleship squadron in the East.

The War College made this recommendation even though the entire Pacific would be without a single American battleship.[27]

The War College recommendation calling for the withdrawal of all American battleships from the Pacific ran into strong opposition from some members of the General Board of the U.S. Navy. To resolve this dispute over the distribution of the Navy's battleships, the Board debated the proposals of the War College study between 20 November and 4 December 1903. Captain Charles S. Sperry, President of the Naval War College, argued that the concentration in the Atlantic should take place. Rear Admiral Henry Taylor presented the opposing view that the current battleship deployment in the Pacific had to be maintained. Great-power rivalry throughout the Far East—especially the acute tension then existing between Russia and Japan—Taylor argued, made it unwise for the United States at that moment to move its battleships out of the region. This clash between strategic dogma and foreign policy considerations could not be resolved, and instead the debate ended in a compromise. While the General Board recognized that "the proper military policy, taken as a general principle . . . is the concentration of all battleships in the Atlantic," it advised that "under present conditions, *vis.*, the imminence of war between Russia and Japan, the presence of a battle squadron in the East is necessary; and so long as the very unsettled condition shall continue in the East, the detail of not less than three battleships in the Pacific is advisable." On 5 December 1903, Secretary of the Navy William H. Moody accepted the Board's recommendation on the deployment of battleships.[28]

As part of this debate, Admiral Taylor asked Mahan to give his opinion of the Naval War College's proposed shift of all United States' battleships to the Atlantic. Although it arrived too late to be used in the General Board's debate on deployment, Mahan agreed with Secretary Moody's decision to retain a squadron of battleships in the Pacific, even though this ran counter to the strategic principle of naval concentration. Mahan argued that international political conditions required that the United States retain a strong squadron in the Pacific. At the end of 1903, Mahan did not consider Germany to represent much of a threat to the Western Hemisphere. But Russia's actions in the Far East seemed to portend a war in the Pacific. Mahan argued that the United States must be ready to protect its interests if war

---

[27] "Solution, Problem of 1903," pp. 34, 35, 65, Record Group 12, Naval War College Archives.

[28] *Proceedings*, November 20-December 4, 1903; Admiral George Dewey to Secretary of the Navy, December 5, 1903, General Board Papers, File 420-1.

occurred, hence the requirement for a squadron in the Pacific.[29] What this episode highlights is that Mahan did not at this time hold the principle of battle-fleet concentration to be a strategic imperative. Instead, international political considerations and not operational doctrines were the driving force behind naval deployments.

The major war in the Far East that Mahan and the General Board foresaw began on February 8, 1904, when Japan attacked without warning the Russia fleet based at Port Arthur. The experience of the Russo-Japanese War highlighted the strategic importance of battle-fleet concentration. At the war's beginning, the battleships of the Russian Navy were distributed between its fleets in the Baltic Sea and Black Sea, as well as in the Far East. By the time the Baltic Fleet of seven battleships had reached the Far East (only to be defeated in the Tsushima Straits), the seven battleships of Russia's Pacific Fleet had already been destroyed in Port Arthur. This had all been accomplished by a Japanese fleet that never numbered more than six battleships. Had it not been for the dispersion of its naval forces, the Russian Navy would have possessed greater than a two-to-one advantage in battleships—a crushing superiority. Russia's error in the initial deployment of its naval forces was taken to heart by naval planners in other countries.[30]

This lesson was not lost on naval planners in the United States. Even before the Russo-Japanese War had ended, the 1905 summer conference at the Naval War College renewed the call to mass all of the battleships possessed by the United States in the Atlantic: "The battle fleet should at all times be concentrated in the North Atlantic. The policy of concentration is paramount. Concentration is the policy of all the great powers." Only with the fleet in the Atlantic would it be possible to defeat an advancing German force "near the edge of the Caribbean before Black has had an opportunity to coal his battleships and tune them up to battle speed after the long passage, and before Black has been able to establish and fortify a temporary shelter for his transports."[31] With Russian naval power effectively destroyed, Secretary Charles J. Bonaparte agreed with the War College that all battleships should be in the Atlantic. In his annual report for 1905, Bonaparte called the dispersion of the Navy's battleships "injurious" to the nation's security. "The business of the fleet is to fight," the report continued, "and anything which interferes with the training for that purpose detracts from the attainment of that object." Without any further debate, Bonaparte ordered the withdrawal of American battleships from the Far East during the summer of 1906.[32]

---

[29] Seager and Maguire, *Mahan Papers*, volume 3, pp. 79-80.
[30] For these naval actions, see Denis Warner and Peggy Warner, *The Tide at Sunrise: A History of the Russo-Japanese War, 1904-1905* (New York: Charterhouse, 1974), passim.
[31] "Solution, Problem of 1905," Part II, pp. 8-9, and Part III, p. 29, Record Group 12, Naval War College Archives.
[32] William R. Braisted, *The United States Navy in the Pacific, 1897-1909* (New York: Greenwood Press, 1969), pp. 188-190.

President Roosevelt fully supported the concentration of the United States battleship strength into a single fleet located in the Atlantic. In a letter to Assistant Secretary of the Navy Truman H. Newberry, Roosevelt argued that if "any one lesson is taught by the Russo-Japanese War, and indeed by naval history generally, it is that in the effort to protect even two important points a division of force may mean the failure to protect either and the final loss of the war." Because the Russians had divided their naval forces before the war, Roosevelt explained, they "were obliged to wait until the Japanese had destroyed their Pacific battle fleet, and then to see them destroy the Atlantic [that is, Baltic] battle fleet when it got out there [to the Far Eastern theater of war]." Roosevelt wanted to make certain that a similar fate did not befall the United States in some future conflict in the Atlantic or the Pacific. He told Newberry: "I do not intend to run the slightest risk of any such disaster. . . . I want our fleet to be a unit."[33]

Mahan also believed that Russia's experience in the war with Japan contained a lesson for the United States. In an article for *National Review* in March 1906, he noted that the number of battleships in the Russian Navy "outweighed decisively" those available to Japan. By foolishly dividing their battleship strength, Russia's leaders had permitted the Japanese victories at sea. Mahan feared that "an irresolute or militarily ignorant Administration" in the United States might repeat the Russian blunder and "divide the battleship force into two divisions, the Atlantic and the Pacific." If a war suddenly occurred, "with the fleet divided between the two oceans, one half may be overmatched and destroyed, as was that of Port Arthur; and the second, on coming, prove unequal to restore the situation, as befell Rozhestvensky." Americans must "understand the simple principle that an efficient military body depends for its effect in war— and in peace—less upon its position than upon its concentrated force." Mahan concluded by clearly expounding the lesson he wanted his readers to learn:

> Concentration protects both coasts. Division exposes both. It is of vital consequence to the nation of the United States that its people contemplating the Russo-Japanese War, substitute therein, in their apprehension, Atlantic for Baltic, and Pacific for Port Arthur. So they will comprehend as well as apprehend.[34]

Thus, by the end of the Russo-Japanese War, Mahan had converted to the international strategic dogma of battle-fleet concentration.

The strategic issue of battleship deployments acquired some urgency in the fall of 1906, when a diplomatic crisis caused by the decision of the San Francisco School Board to segregate Japanese students threatened to erupt into a conflict between the United States and Japan. Since the United States battle fleet was now located in the Atlantic, the Japanese Navy would not

---

[33] Roosevelt to Newberry, quoted in Newberry to Rear Admiral J.P. Merrell, August 8, 1907, General Board Papers, File 420-1.
[34] A.T. Mahan, "Retrospect Upon the War Between Japan and Russia,

face any significant opposition until it could be shifted to the Pacific— an operation that would take at least three months.[35] With the heightened threat of war with Japan, stories began appearing in American newspapers saying that the Roosevelt administration intended to divide the battle fleet and send a squadron of battleships back into the Pacific. One article, reporting that four battleships would go to the Pacific, prompted Mahan to write a letter to President Roosevelt warning against such a move. "In case of a war with Japan what can four battleships do against their navy? In case of war with a European power, what would not the four battleships add to our fleet here?"[36]

Roosevelt wanted no lesson from Mahan about the principles of naval strategy. The president indignantly replied:

> Don't you know me well enough to believe that I am quite incapable of such an act of utter folly as dividing our fighting fleet? I have no more thought of sending four battleships to the Pacific while there is the least possible friction with Japan than I have of going there in a rowboat myself.[37]

This brief exchange of letters between Mahan and Roosevelt shows how deeply ingrained the dogma of naval concentration had become in the two men.

But not everyone in the United States subscribed to the necessity of strategic concentration. Roosevelt could not simply ignore the call from inhabitants of the west coast and their representatives in Congress, as well as the opinion of respected advisers, such as the influential General Leonard Wood and Army Chief of Staff General J. Franklin Bell, that a force of battleships was essential to protect American territory in the Pacific from a Japanese offensive. Even from within the Navy there appeared some sentiment for moving battleships back to the Pacific. The likelihood of war and the weakness of United States' naval power in the Pacific led the officers attending the summer conference at the Naval War College in 1907, for example, to rank Japan for the first time ahead of Germany on its list of potential enemies. The General Board itself declared that "our interests in the Atlantic and Pacific ocean are each such as to require protection by a battle fleet, and, the distance between these oceans being so great as to preclude the possibility of a single fleet giving adequate protection to both, the military interests of the United States require that we should possess two fleets, one in each ocean." The General Board did not mean this to imply that it was "departing from the principle of fleet concentration," only that

---

[35] On the difficulties of moving the United States' battle fleet to the Pacific, see Michael E. Vlahos, "The Naval War College and the Origins of War Planning Against Japan," *Naval War College Review*, volume 33 (July-August 1980), pp. 23–41.

[36] Letter Mahan to Roosevelt, dated January 10, 1907. Seager and Maguire, *Mahan Papers*, volume 3, p. 202.

[37] Elting E. Morison, editor, *The Letters of Theodore Roosevelt* (Cambridge: Harvard University Press, 1951-1954), volume 5, pp. 550-551. Hereafter cited as Morison, *Roosevelt Letters*.

they wanted to "emphasize the inadequacy of the present fleet to meet the demands upon it, and to indicate the direction towards which our building program should tend." There was little hope, however, that the Congress would appropriate the funds to build the General Board's "two-ocean" navy.[38]

While the battleship concentration would not be disrupted, the danger of war with Japan seemed greater than a German threat in the Atlantic. To put this problem in modern parlance, the Board had to meet commitments in two oceans with a one ocean fleet. To resolve this debate on where to place battleships, a paper compromise was reached in a report issued by the Joint Army and Navy Board on 21 February 1908. Concentration would continue, but the battle fleet would be deployed in the "region where the greatest danger exists." The main task now confronting naval planners was how, before the completion of the Panama Canal, to move the fleet from the Atlantic to the Pacific. Those favoring concentration had to demonstrate that the battle fleet could be moved from one ocean to the other in a reasonably short period of time. Yet it was by no means clear whether this "swing strategy" would work. To Roosevelt, it "became evident . . . from talking with naval authorities, that in event of war they would have a good deal to find out in the way of sending the fleet to the Pacific." Roosevelt's solution was to "send the fleet on what would practically be a practice voyage. . . . I want all failures, blunders, and shortcomings to be made apparent in time of peace and not in time of war." This decision to give the fleet a "practice voyage" to the Pacific was later expanded into the famous cruise of "The Great White Fleet" around the world.[39]

But the calls to disrupt naval concentration did not die down with the movement of the battle fleet to the Pacific. In June 1908, when the fleet was still on the west coast, one member of the General Board, Captain Sydney A. Staunton, prepared a memorandum calling for the deployment of 16 battleships in the Pacific, while keeping only nine older battleships in the Atlantic. Staunton argued that the presence of this force in the Pacific would deter Japan from attacking the United States and its possessions. While no further action was immediately taken on this proposal, in February 1909, less than two weeks before the incoming Taft administration took office, the General Board agreed with Staunton that the defense of United States' territory in the Pacific required a large force of battleships. At a meeting on 20 February 1909, the General Board decided that the United States now possessed enough battleships to form a separate battle fleet for the Pacific.

[38] Braisted, *Navy in the Pacific, 1897-1909*, pp. 199-239; and Rear Admiral John P. Merrell to Acting Secretary of the Navy Truman Newberry, August 2, 1907, and Merrell to Newberry, August 15, 1907, General Board Papers, File 420-1.

[39] General Board memorandum for the guidance of the naval members of the Joint Board, February 18, 1908, General Board Papers, File 420-1; Morison, *Roosevelt Letters*, volume 5, p. 709; for a recent account of the fleet's voyage, see James R. Reckner, *Teddy Roosevelt's Great White Fleet* (Annapolis: Naval Institute Press, 1988), passim.

Four days later, this decision was duly passed on to Secretary of the Navy Truman Newberry. Meanwhile, the Senate was also making recommendations on battleship deployments. To satisfy the west coast demands for naval protection, the Senate amended an appropriations bill to say that "there shall be kept, as far as practicable, one-half of the Navy . . . on the Pacific coast at all times."[40]

During his last weeks in office, Roosevelt defended the principle of concentration that he had championed since the beginning of his presidency. On 18 February 1909, in a letter to George Foss, chairman of the Committee on Naval Affairs in the House of Representatives, the president wrote that modern wars could begin with one side endeavoring "to strike a crippling blow before the actual declaration of war. . . . To divide our fleet between two oceans would be to invite attack, and if attack were made, to insure disaster." With the help of Foss, Roosevelt saw the House drop the Senate amendment.[41]

Those who favored concentration, such as Mahan, feared that once Roosevelt was no longer in office the battleships would be divided into two fleets. On 2 March 1909, Mahan sent an urgent appeal to Roosevelt to warn Taft not to divide the fleet. "Will it be in any sense improper," Mahan wrote, "that you should give a last earnest recommendation to Mr. Taft on no account to divide the battleship force between the two oceans." The popular outcry to divide the battle fleet was "a nightmare" to Mahan.[42]

Prompted by Mahan's appeal, Roosevelt wrote his famous strategic testament to Taft. "One closing legacy," Roosevelt wrote. "Under no circumstances divide the battleship fleet between the Atlantic and Pacific Oceans prior to the finishing of the Panama Canal." Indeed, Roosevelt advised Taft: "obey no direction of Congress and pay heed to no popular sentiment, no matter how strong, if it went wrong in such a vital matter as this."[43]

Mahan remained concerned, however, that the "suicidal recommendation" to divide the battle fleet might nonetheless be adopted. And, indeed, a group of naval officers, led by Captain Staunton and Commander Clarence S. Williams of the General Board, continued to agitate for a battle fleet for the Pacific during Taft's term of office. In a memorandum for the General Board, Williams called the "present plan of keeping all our battleships in the Atlantic . . . illogical and dangerous." He proposed instead that a force of 20 battleships should be transferred to the Pacific. The officers attending the 1910 summer conference of the Naval War College agreed with Williams' assessment that "conflicts of sentiment and interest, race questions and trade

[40] Memorandum by Captain Sydney A. Staunton, June 23, 1908; General Board Proceedings, February 20, 1909; Dewey to Newberry, February 24, 1909, General Board Papers, File 420-1; and George T. Davis, *A Navy Second to None* (Westport, Connecticut: Greenwood Press, 1971), pp. 190-191.

[41] Davis, *Navy Second to None*, pp. 190-191.

[42] Seager and Maguire, *Mahan Papers*, volume 3, p. 290.

[43] Morison, *Roosevelt Letters*, volume 5, p. 1543.

rivalries, appear much more likely to arise in the Pacific than elsewhere." All 39 officers at the conference called for the establishment of a battle fleet in the Pacific. In addition, these officers argued that the growth of Anglo-German antagonism greatly reduced the chance of a German attack on the United States. "Like two bar magnets of equal strength placed side by side with poles reversed," their report read, "each with all its force clinging fast to the other and the two thus joined together forming one single mass incapable of serious disturbing influence exterior to that mass; so today, firmly locked together, appear the British and German fleets." To many naval officers, the Japanese threat in the Pacific was far greater than that posed by Germany.[44]

The General Board as a whole did not agree with these recommendations. Although the General Board's members could not agree on whether the United States would face first Germany or Japan in the next war, they did agree that Germany represented the "more formidable" enemy. If the Germans attacked while a portion of the battle fleet was away in the Pacific, the General Board declared the naval situation "almost hopeless" for the United States. Despite still further attempts by Staunton to station a battle fleet in the Pacific, concentration against the German battle fleet remained the strategic fulcrum of United States naval planning.[45]

Of course, given Mahan's views about the threat posed by German imperial and naval ambitions, he considered concentration of the battle fleet in the Atlantic as a naval necessity if the United States was to have any chance of staving off defeat in a war with Germany. Whenever asked for his views on this issue, Mahan did not waver in his conviction about the necessity of concentration. Since he feared that a fickle and ignorant public might pressure an administration into dividing the fleet, Mahan made repeated efforts to publicize his views on strategy.

Thus, when the two Republican Senators from California, George C. Perkins and Frank P. Flint, solicited the opinion of the respected naval historian and commentator on what was the proper distribution of America's battleships, Mahan replied: "The division of the battle fleet into halves, separated by the whole distance between our Atlantic and Pacific coasts . . . is contrary to all sound military practice . . . the military necessity of sustained concentration is as absolutely certain as anything can be." Much as Tirpitz argued that the best way to promote and protect Germany's interests world-wide was by building a battle fleet for the North Sea, Mahan contended that naval concentration provided for the security of the United

[44] Memorandum by Commander C.S. Williams, March 16, 1910, General Board Papers, File 420-1; Committee Reports on questions submitted to the Conference, Record Group 12, Naval War College Archives.
[45] Dewey to the Secretary of the Navy, November 17, 1910, and Secretary of the Navy George von Lengerke Meyer's endorsement, November 17, 1910; memorandum by Staunton, April 16, 1912, and memorandum by Dewey, June 26, 1912, General Board Papers, File 420-1.

States not only in the Atlantic, but also for areas where no battleships were stationed. "The people of the Pacific slope might *feel* themselves safer with half the battle fleet in their harbors," Mahan counseled Perkins, "but *actually* they would be in greater peril, because they would have conditions favoring the destruction of our entire navy, in detail."[46]

The young assistant Secretary of the Navy in the Wilson administration, Franklin D. Roosevelt, also wrote Mahan in the spring of 1914 to enlist his support in the public campaign for continuing naval concentration. It was Roosevelt's opinion that, with the opening of the canal, "a great deal of pressure [would be] brought to bear—political and sectional—to have the Fleet divided, and to have one half kept on the Pacific and one half on the Atlantic." After visiting the west coast, Roosevelt "was struck by the total lack of any correct conception of fleet operations." But he thought the "people can be educated, but only if we all get together ahead of time and try to show the average 'man in the street' the military necessity of keeping *the Fleet* intact." He urged Mahan to write "an article or articles" on the issue, since his "voice will carry more conviction than that of anybody else."[47]

Mahan complied with Roosevelt's request in an article entitled "The Panama Canal and the Distribution of the Fleet," published in *The North American Review*. Mahan reiterated his conviction that "concentration should be the controlling factor in peace dispositions,—should be the normal state then,—is evident from the rapidity with which modern wars develop, and from the political fact that, when relations are strained, significant movements may precipitate hostilities." Even the opening of the Panama Canal did not relieve the United States of battleship concentration: "The Canal modifies the previous situation by minimizing all the difficulties of transfer [from one ocean to another], but it does not change the dictate as to concentrate."[48]

To Mahan, the outbreak of war in Europe confirmed the wisdom of naval concentration in the likely theater of war during peacetime. Indeed, he urged on Franklin D. Roosevelt "that the fleet should be brought into immediate readiness, and so disposed as to permit of very rapid concentration."[49]

Of course, the dogma of battleship concentration was not unique to the United States, but is a distinguishing feature of naval thought in this era. All the principal naval powers— Britain, Germany, and Japan, as well as the United States— refused to commit what was considered "an act of utter folly"

---

[46] Seager and Maguire, *Mahan Papers*, volume 3, pp. 371-372.

[47] Franklin D. Roosevelt to Mahan, May 28, 1914, Assistant Secretary of the Navy Collection, Box 137, Franklin D. Roosevelt Library, Hyde Park, New York. It should be noted that this extremely interesting correspondence between Mahan and Franklin D. Roosevelt is not reproduced in Seager and Maguire, *Mahan Papers*, but published in Richard W. Turk, *The Ambiguous Relationship* (New York: Greenwood Press, 1987), pp. 109-172.

[48] A.T. Mahan, "The Panama Canal and the Distribution of the Fleet," *The North American Review*, volume 200, number 706 (September 1914), pp. 409, 411.

[49] Mahan to Roosevelt, August 3, 1914, Assistant Secretary of the Navy Collection, Box 137, Franklin D. Roosevelt Library, Hyde Park, New York.

(as Theodore Roosevelt called it) and divide their battle fleet. Naval competition with Germany had compelled American naval leaders to copy Tirpitz's battleship concentration. Indeed, some turn-of-the-century naval reformers, like Rear Admiral Henry Taylor and Rear Admiral Bradley Fiske, wanted to go much further in copying German military methods by creating a General Staff to be the "brains" of the Navy. Of course, the United States was not unique in attempting to adopt German military institutions and strategic dogmas to their own circumstances. In this era Britain also massed battleships against Germany and adopted a Naval War Staff to be the strategic guide for the Royal Navy. As one historian has observed about French military reform after 1870: "in military matters, modernity acquired a distinctly teutonic aspect, and Germany was regarded as the tutor of Europe."[50] The same could be said about naval concentration in the decade before the First World War. Thus, Tirpitz's battleship concentration triggered a strategic chain reaction as the other major naval powers did likewise.

Indeed, Mahan was a rather late convert to the dogma of concentration. Whereas the Naval War College was advocating battleship concentration by the summer of 1903 in response to German naval developments, Mahan still did not subscribe to the principle. But the concatenation of shocks, caused by the Russo-Japanese War, the war scare with Japan in 1906, and the rapid rise of German naval power, caused Mahan to change his views. Once converted, however, Mahan became an ardent believer and advocate of naval concentration. From 1906 on, Mahan argued with all the eloquence and force he could muster in the debate over naval concentration. His writings helped encourage statesmen and naval planners around the world that naval concentration was the correct strategy. Mahan played an important role, then, in developing an international strategic style for the deployment of naval power.

Conclusion

Mahan made a signal contribution in his later years by helping to inform his fellow countrymen about world politics and strategy. He attempted to highlight the importance of the balance of power for the security of the United States. Mahan argued that the United States needed to play a role—indeed, an increasingly important role—in upholding the balance of power on a global scale.

In Mahan's view, the United States would face new external challenges from rival great powers in the twentieth century. Mahan was warning his American readers that "the age of free security"—to use C. Vann

---

[50] Allan Mitchell, " 'A Situation of Inferiority': French Military Reorganization After the Defeat of 1870," *American Historical Review*, volume 86 (February 1981), p. 49.

Woodward's apt phrase—was passing away.[51] The security of the United States could no longer depend, as it largely did during the nineteenth century, on latent military power buttressed by the natural moat formed by the Atlantic and Pacific oceans and the icebound wastes of the Arctic. Instead, the United States was moving from an era of inexpensive security to expensive insecurity—from the "age of free security" to the age of "the national security state." The signal contribution made by Mahan during the last decade of his life in educating the American public and its leaders about world politics and strategy should not be overlooked in the study of his writings.

---

[51] C. Vann Woodward, "The Age of Reinterpretation," *American Historical Review*, volume 66 (October 1960), pp. 11-19.

Chapter 14

Mahan and American Naval Thought Since 1914

George H. Quester

There are many ways to remember Mahan, and to assess his impact on the United States Navy. One could, for example, focus entirely or primarily on his 1890 *The Influence of Sea Power Upon History*,[1] the book which won Mahan instant fame, the work which surely is the most often read; or one could instead factor in all the other publications and advice Mahan proffered thereafter. Even if one focused mainly on this book whose centennial we are now celebrating, moreover, we could stress one part of its message or another; and we would then have to wonder whether all these parts hang together so perfectly.

Becoming a classic of military strategic writing perhaps inevitably requires that conflicting interpretations be possible, so that opposing sides to an argument can quote an author back and forth, so that students can derive stimulation by puzzling over the exact meaning of one chapter or another. To be very straightforward in military writing, or perhaps in any other writing, may leave one too easily understood, and hence soon enough passed over as "pedestrian," as offering something which "we all knew already."

Such an interpretation of the achievement of classic status would surely apply to Clausewitz[2] (whom Mahan does not introduce and cite in developing his 1890 arguments), and to Jomini[3] (to whom Mahan indeed does assign a great deal of credit).[4] It applies as well to Douhet[5] and Mackinder,[6] and to others whom we have to read and reread. And it also applies to Alfred Thayer Mahan.

---

[1] Alfred Thayer Mahan, *The Influence of Sea Power Upon History* (Boston: Little Brown, 1890).
[2] Carl von Clausewitz, *On War* (Princeton, New Jersey: Princeton University Press translation, 1976).
[3] Antoine Henri Jomini, *The Art of War* (Westport, Conn.: Greenwood Press reprint, 1972).
[4] Mahan, *op cit.*, pp. 18-19.
[5] Giulio Douhet, *The Command of the Air* (New York: Coward McCann translation, 1942).
[6] See Halford J. Mackinder, *Democratic Ideals and Reality* (New York: Norton, 1962).

This chapter will thus attempt to lay out several layers of argument that could be credited to Mahan, some less controversial and others more so, some inevitably congenial to any advocate of naval armaments and others a little more confusing or bothersome. After such layers of argument have been outlined, the policies of the U.S. Navy in the twentieth century would then be compared with these arguments, to ask where Mahan should be credited with influence, and where he can not.

Mahan's Arguments, I: The Importance of Naval Power

It surely is undeniable that Mahan comes out repeatedly and consistently as a believer in the effectiveness of naval power. Mahan may disagree on some other important points with Sir Julian Corbett,[7] but *The Influence of Sea Power Upon History*, and virtually all Mahan's other writings, would indeed join with Corbett in stressing this central theme, that the dominance of the seas will very much influence the general power distribution of the world.

It is thus hardly surprising that midshipmen of the U.S. Naval Academy would be introduced approvingly to the writings of Mahan, or that Admiral Gorchkov, as commander of the Soviet fleet in the 1960s and 1970s, would cite Mahan as an expert on naval strategy.[8] The message is that fleets are worth buying, that naval power is worth having, since its possession by others can threaten our freedoms and social systems, and since its possession by our side can further many or all of the causes of which we approve.

Kaiser Wilhelm thus cited Mahan's writings approvingly to all his own naval officers and entourage, arranging for a German translation very soon after *The Influence of Sea Power Upon History* was published, noting that he, upon first reading it (the Kaiser was quite fluent in English), was "devouring" it[9] (some of the American naval officers I know have responded that they had less appetite than the Kaiser in this regard).

The Kaiser wanted to build a large German fleet, perhaps to challenge and sink the British fleet some day on "der Tag"; more probably he hoped merely to play some kind of balance-of-power game on the high seas, whereby the *riskflotte* ("risk fleet") would be so large that the British would not dare attack it, lest they be too weakened in the process for confrontations with other fleets around the world.[10] (This was an iteration, of course, of the logic of the balance of power always endorsed by the British so much on land, where weaker states counted on each other to engage and draw down the strength of any potential hegemon. Britain approved of the balance-of-power on land, but not on the seas.)

---

[7] Sir Julian Corbett, *Principles of Maritime Strategy* (London: Conway Maritime Press, 1911).

[8] Admiral Sergei Gorchkov, *The Sea Power of the State* (Annapolis, Maryland: Naval Institute Press translation, 1977).

[9] On the Kaiser's response to Mahan, see William E. Livezey, *Mahan on Sea Power* (Norman: University of Oklahoma Press, 1981), pp. 67-75.

[10] See Jonathan Steinberg, *Yesterday's Deterrent* (New York: MacMillan, 1966).

If one wishes a flat-out contradiction of this "navalist" part of Mahan's argument, it would not come from Corbett (who certainly agrees on the importance of an investment in naval power, and will also be assigned reading for midshipmen around the world, albeit not as often as Mahan), but rather from the writings of Halford Mackinder, who saw the real source of military and political power now being not the seas, but rather the center of the Eurasian landmass.

Mahan's Arguments, II: The Importance of Counterforce Offensives

Beyond stressing the value of naval power, Mahan, in his 1890 classic, comes out almost doctrinaire in arguing that the first and most important goal of any serious navy must be to sink the opposing navy, thereby to establish a "command of the sea." This is what we would label counterforce operations in today's jargon of air strategy, operations designed not to inflict pain on an enemy, but to strike from his hands the ability to inflict pain on us, or his ability to attack our forces, etc.

There are indeed always several explanations for any such stress on counterforce, and it is not difficult to find predecessors for this kind of an approach in military writing; but few sound as doctrinaire on the question as Mahan did here.

First of all, among the explanations, there is something orderly and tidy about stressing the elimination of one's opposite number in counterforce combat, for (once one has established himself as having the *only* navy, or the only army, or the only air force) one can then at leisure provide support for a sister military service, or impose pressure on the opposing side's civilian population and government.

"Erst die arbiet, dann das spiel" is an old German saying pounding Protestant thrift into children, "First the work, and then the play." First make a success of your business, and only then buy your wife a fur coat. First win the contest of establishing the capital goods, *i.e.* command of the sea, and then shift to the production of consumer goods, exercising political power over the other side's material welfare.

Second, it is more moral to aim at military targets instead of civilian, and more consistent with traditions of western culture and philosophy. One does not violate the laws of war when one aims to sink an enemy battleship; one is in more trouble with these laws, or with the chaplain, when one aims to kill civilians by bombarding a city, or even when one sinks ships carrying food or medicine.

Third, we more persuasively bring home the value of a navy to one's own public when we stress over and over again how important a target the opposing navy is, how much damage it might do to us, how much it might facilitate their grasping for power. Air forces thus sell more of their own equipment to taxpayers by stressing how much the opposing air force needs to be aimed at, and tank generals can sell more tanks by touting the menace of the enemy's armored forces.

Reaching for a total counterforce victory requires taking the offensive, of course, and not being content to sit on the defensive, which in turn probably requires expenditures for a larger and more ambitious force on our side, all the more consistent with advocacy of expansion in this particular field of preparation.

Mahan, if read literally in *The Influence of Sea Power Upon History*, urges that no attacks be undertaken on the enemy's commercial shipping or on his coastal cities while the enemy's fleet remains in being, since all resources should be concentrated on first destroying that fleet:

> It is not the taking of individual ships or convoys, be they few or many, that strikes down the money power of a nation; it is the possession of that overbearing power on the sea which drives the enemy's flag from it, or allows it to appear only as a fugitive;[11]

He makes a passing reference to the immorality of such countervalue campaigns; Mahan here had to reflect somewhat the traditions and feelings of his fellow Americans, on whether neutral shipping and non-military cargoes should be exempt from attack or confiscation whenever a naval power like Britain had gotten into a war.

> "The evidence seems to show that even for its own special ends such a mode of war is inconclusive, worrying but not deadly; it might almost be said that it causes needless suffering."[12]

But Mahan's more major thrust seems rather to be that such countervalue approaches would be *ineffective*, compared to the returns of aiming first and foremost to win a totality of naval power. John Paul Jones in the American Revolution, and the *Constitution* ("Old Ironsides") of the War of 1812, may thus have been important parts of a tradition of American naval bravery and competence that Mahan wished to reinforce, but the lessons of such operations were all wrong, as Nelson's defeat of Napoleon's fleet at Trafalgar illustrated the only really meaningful kind of naval exploit.

Sinking the enemy fleet would of course very often require an attack, and Mahan was thus inclined to espouse a taking of the offensive. If the defense had any advantages in naval warfare, these were factors that would simply have to be overridden, typically by the exploitation of mobility and the massing of the larger numbers. Above all, the principle of concentration needed to be applied here. Mahan credited his thoughts on this to Jomini among others, recommending that we (who always think in the counterforce terms of who has a fleet left at the end of engagements) do better if we keep our fleet concentrated, while tricking or luring the enemy into leaving his forces divided.

---

[11] Mahan, *op. cit.*, p. 121.
[12] *Ibid.*, p. 119.

Mahan is among the many military writers who are much more often cited than read. Someone picking up the 1890 classic today is often disappointed by the ponderousness of the book, by the very long paragraphs, and the excess of detail. Bernard Brodie and others have argued that the U.S. Navy was much influenced by Mahan,[13] but typically in a more cryptic series of aphorisms or axioms supposedly extracted from the theorist's writings. Among these axioms, the most immediately relevant to the point we are sorting out here would be "don't divide the fleet."

Mahan would himself have disclaimed any originality for this proposition, with its elementary stress on concentration of force. *If* the only task for the moment was winning the counterforce contest, that of retaining a fleet and eliminating the enemy's fleet, keeping one's fleet together indeed made sense, and it might have made sense as well for, and been mouthed by all the British naval commanders between Trafalgar and 1890.

Mahan is committed to counterforce, and to concentration, and to seeking out the enemy fleet to sink it in order to win a decision. As such, he is committed to the taking of the offensive.   In a 1905 book, Mahan notes that the defensive may have advantages at sea, just as on land, but he overrides this with the factor of mobility and massing, arguing that it is no use "to get there first, unless, when the enemy in turn arrives, you have . . . the greater force."[14]

It is this particularly doctrinaire line of argument (which Mahan only very partially modified in later writings) that Corbett contradicted. Corbett begins by noting that the naval technology of the new twentieth century might favor the defensive, making a Nelsonian offensive and the winning of a total command of the sea impossible. One may thus have no choice but to begin countervalue operations *before* any total counterforce victory has been accomplished, since the latter may not at all be attainable.[15]

Corbett goes further, moreover, to argue that naval and military power become meaningless unless countervalue operations and a punishment of the opposing side's civilian population are an integral part of all this.[16] While Mahan initially reflected the American tradition of supporting freedom of the seas for neutral shipping and for non-military goods even during wartime, an important part of Corbett's argument was driven by the fears that the rules of international law which the Americans and the continental European powers had been proposing before World War I might constrain too much the application of British naval power.

It is important to note that Mahan, in the two decades between his achievement of fame as a naval strategist and his death at the outbreak of

---

[13] For example, Bernard Brodie, *War and Politics* (New York: MacMillan, 1973), pp. 449–450.

[14] Alfred Thayer Mahan, *Lessons of the War With Spain* (Boston: Little Brown, 1899), p. 181.

[15] Corbett, *op. cit.*, pp. 87–89.

[16] *Ibid.*, pp. 90–95.

World War I, moved away from his moral objections to counter-commerce warfare and from his disparagement of its military effectiveness.[17]

At least three factors could plausibly have been at play here in moving Mahan from the absolute priority he had voiced in *The Influence of Sea Power Upon History* for counterforce warfare, and to come out in opposition to the traditional American commitment to the freedom of the seas. He even endorsed the wisdom of the 1756 British orders in Council which had so much infuriated the Americans in 1812.

First, the same British "navalist" audience that had applauded Mahan's basic emphasis on sea power must have been telling him that they were concerned about restrictions on what targets they could attack.

Second, Mahan might have envisaged the United States Navy as growing to a preponderance comparable to what the British fleet had mounted in the past, and his country might then want to be free to impose such blockades of its own, disturbing the commerce of its enemies.

And third, discounting for the mutual flattery that was so visibly at work between Mahan and the British, and for any double-standards as the United States grew in power, it must have struck Mahan that he had overstated his case. One can make á reputation by staking a position too clearly and baldly, so that readers see a new and different cutting edge. Yet, the subsequent discussion will require blurring amendments and recognition of the intertwining confusions.

While Mahan acknowledged more and more the importance of countervalue attacks on commerce, he nonetheless did not recant his statement of priority for the destruction of the opposing fleet. To go that far, to admit, as Corbett had admitted, that there might be no gain in seeking to destroy the enemy fleet, would have been to recede to having nothing distinctive to offer.

As noted, we could in fairness remember Mahan entirely by *The Influence of Sea Power Upon History*, for this is surely his most widely read and quoted work. If we are to consider instead the influence of his total work, there is much more subtlety and complexity to be found on the issue of whether opposing commerce is to be viewed as an *important* and *legitimate* target. Yet even Mahan could not deviate so totally from his initial 1890 statement so as to make commerce the *first priority* target.

Mahan's Arguments, III: America Succeeding Britain

Putting Mahan's analysis and arguments together, one then gets to a somewhat complicated confusing bottom-line on what he envisaged as the American role in the future, *viz-a-viz* Great Britain. If Americans were to be enjoined to learn more from Nelson than from John Paul Jones, did this

---

[17] See Bernard Semmel, *Liberalism and Naval Power* (Boston; Allen and Unwin, 1986), pp. 90-98.

mean that they were to challenge the descendants of Nelson, just as Tirpitz wanted? As Mahan favored the offensive over the defensive, he was much more consistent with notions of hegemony and monopoly than of any balance-of-power at sea. Yet how could one expect any smooth transition from one hegemony to another?

The British after Trafalgar had a fleet larger than all the other navies of the world combined.[18] In the latter part of the Nineteenth Century, they still had a declared policy of maintaining a fleet larger in size than the next two fleets of the world combined. The United States in 1916, two years after Mahan's death, with Germany and Britain and all the European powers deeply involved in World War I, proclaimed an intention to build "a navy second to none."[19] If Britain could ever turn away from the German naval menace, this surely would have to be read as an explicit American challenge to all that British naval policy had stood for.

On this third question, of exactly *how* the United States was to imitate Britain, Mahan does not settle into any one clear answer. Certainly, he favored American naval expansion. Certainly, he also regarded Britain as a power with which the United States should very naturally have friendly relations. But the building of a modern battle fleet was classically the way that one got into tensions with Britain.

One version of Mahan's analysis would suggest some quiet transition whereby Britain simply lost the energy or the will to maintain the command of the seas, and the United States assumed this role. Another version might see the emergence of some sort of joint condominium, with Mahan even at points being pressed to comment on the possibility of a political union of the English-speaking world. And a third possibility, of course, amounted to an English-speaking version of "der Tag," whereby a war might eventually break out between the United States and Britain. When an Anglo-American crisis erupted in 1895 over Venezuela, Mahan noted that he would certainly regret having to fight the British, but that he very naturally would have to do so if his country's interests required it.[20]

Mahan did not suggest any kind of balance-of-power partitioning of the seas, as Tirpitz and the Kaiser had in their more moderate moments envisaged for Germany in the North Sea, indeed, this actually occurred in the Twentieth Century, as dreadnought battleships and the need for coaling stations (contrary to all of Mahan's strategic drift noted above) tended to reinforce the defensive, making every fleet around the world relatively stronger when it was close to its home ports and coaling stations.

---

[18] On the overarching implications of this accomplishment, see Paul Kennedy, *The Rise and Fall of British Naval Power* (London: Allen Lane, 1976), chapter 6.

[19] 19. See Harold and Margaret Sprout, *The Rise of American Naval Power: 1776-1918* (Princeton, New Jersey: Princeton University Press, 1939), pp. 334-344.

[20] Such statements are quoted in W.D. Puleston, *The Life and Work of Captain Alfred Thayer Mahan* (New Haven: Yale University Press, 1939), pp. 169-171.

The British reception for Mahan's writings was extremely complimentary, as he was to receive honorary degrees in the same week from Oxford and Cambridge, and was lionized by all the authorities of the British establishment. Was this only because Mahan's writings were so complimentary to Britain and things British? Or was it instead that British naval analysts saw serious dangers to their own position if the Americans became too enthusiastic about naval power, about joining in the world naval game in a way which would threaten Britain's hegemony?

The exchange of compliments probably related to deeper issues than the formality of making a potential trouble-maker feel good, and thereby perhaps co-opting him. Mahan expressed admiration not only for British naval prowess, but also for its commitment to liberal democracy, in which Britons and Americans could share. He worried whether naval power could be maintained by so free a society, noting that some serious contradictions were possible.[21]

Britain, at the turn of the century, was moreover discovering that it might inevitably have to give up her goal of being able to defeat *all* of her possible enemies on the sea, or frustrating them on land by the application of sea power. She was discovering that she might have to choose among possible enemies, settling grievances with some, perhaps settling with all but the most worrisome, Germany. Despite the protests of Foreign Office specialists, the British made concessions to the United States, actually committed themselves to an entangling alliance with Japan (which in effect handed over the regional naval preponderance in Japanese waters to the Japanese), then made concessions to Russia, and to France, all because the growth of the German fleet, the plausible German preponderance in land power, and the nature of German diplomacy, had now identified Berlin as the principal enemy.[22]

All of this may have made it much easier for the United States and Britain to get along, as Mahan desired that they should. Yet this political change was at the same time driven by developments in naval technology and naval strategy that were almost the opposite of what Mahan had preached as his major propositions. Corbett made the very telling point that, short of achieving a total command of the sea for one's self, one could at least profitably deny an adversary such command of all the sea.[23] It was Corbett's emphasis on the defensive in naval combat,[24] and on the likely unattainability of a total command of the sea that explains the British reluctant acceptance of a Japanese preponderance around Japan, and of an American preponderance in the western hemisphere.

---

[21] See *The Influence of Sea Power Upon History*, pp. 51, 58, 64.
[22] On this period, see Steven Rock, *Why Peace Breaks Out* (Chapel Hill: University of North Carolina Press, 1989).
[23] Corbett, *op. cit.*, pp. 33-36.
[24] *Ibid.*, p. 87.

Did Mahan thus rejoice, or feel sad, when the British at last removed their Caribbean fleet, because of the more pressing need for maintaining naval force massed in European waters? Many American naval officers were quite pleased at this development.[25] In the years after Mahan's death, some of the same officers speculated about a naval war between Britain and the United States. Mahan, as we have noted, could not have been enthusiastic about such prospects.

Impact on the U.S. Navy, I: Expansion

It is obvious that the first of Mahan's major propositions would always have been the very most congenial to his colleagues in the U.S. Navy, for whatever else it was, his body of theory amounted to a plea for a much greater investment in the naval service. No matter if he was, in effect, deprecating the significance of John Paul Jones, he was certainly highlighting the future significance of an Admiral Dewey.

Historians differ in assessing whether Mahan's writings were significant in convincing the American public that navies were now necessary, or whether he was merely a symptom of the times. A revisionist historian like Walter Lafeber would point to the closing of the frontier at about the same time as the Naval War College was founded, and would thus see capitalism as thrashing about to find markets, somehow to avoid the destabilizing possibilities of over-production and unemployment.[26] By this measure, it was inevitable that the U.S. Navy would grow, with another theorist like Mahan coming along if he had not.

Most of us would not accept quite such a materialistic or deterministic view of the evolution of events. To be an atomistic liberal is inevitably to find intellectual events somewhat less preordained than, for example, a Marxist would find them. If Mahan had not captured the attention and imaginations of so many Americans, the fleet might well not have grown as much as it did in the 1890s, and thereafter.[27] The United States similarly would have been less inclined to acquire naval bases and coaling stations through the Caribbean and out into the Pacific, and would not have been as ready to endorse Theodore Roosevelt's acquisition of the Panama Canal Zone.

The United States in the days of Jefferson and Madison had striven unsuccessfully to design special kinds of fighting ships which could function only close to its coasts, in an early version of "defensive defense," posing no threat to any foreign shores, but defending its own. But the same country would in the administration of Woodrow Wilson (also no militarist, eager

---

[25] On the final withdrawal of British naval forces from the Caribbean, see Kenneth Bourne, *Britain and the Balance of Power in North America* (Berkeley: University of California Press, 1967).

[26] Walter Lafeber, *The New Empire* (Ithaca, New York: Cornell University Press, 1963).

[27] For an extended discussion of the growth of the U.S. Navy, see Walter J. Herrick, *The American Naval Revolution* (Baton Rouge: Louisiana State University Press, 1966).

until the end to keep the United States out of World War I), commit itself to building an ocean-spanning *Dreadnought* navy "second to none."[28] It may be impossible to sort out the counter-factual situation of what naval expenditures would have been like if Mahan had never decided to write about the subject, but it certainly seems plausible that he should be credited with a considerable impact and influence here.

Impact on the U.S. Navy, II: The Counterforce Emphasis

When we turn then to the more complicated and controversial portions of Mahan's strategic message, we might find a much more mixed influence on the U. S. Navy. Did this U.S. Navy, when it at last entered World War I on the side of Britain, bring with it any strategic insights that could be traced to Mahan? To the extent that there were disagreements with the British about how to fight the war against Germany, the American input might have been seen as just the opposite of what Mahan's advice had been.

As we assess the impact of Mahan's theory on American naval thinking, we must note that Sir Julian Corbett is sometimes credited or blamed for having had a profound impact on British thinking as World War I began. Critics accused him of making the British less willing to take the offensive as Nelson would have done, for supplying the theoretical underpinnings of the British policy which was disappointing to those who remembered more glorious victories by simply waiting at the entrances to the North Sea, in order to strangle German maritime commerce.[29]

Earlier in the century, when the German fleet first began to emerge as a menace, there had been serious discussion in British naval circles of "Copenhagening" the German fleet, of preemptively attacking before it could be brought to completion, much as Nelson (indeed two times, in 1801 and 1807) had launched preventive attacks on the Danish fleet at Copenhagen which was about to be merged into the fleets available to Napoleon.[30] Such a preventive-war attack on the German fleet was rejected, not because it was immoral, but because closer study of the new shape of naval warfare, amid coastal fortifications and torpedo boats and mine-fields, suggested that the attacker no longer had any advantage when he plunged into enemy waters, even if the German fleet had only partially been completed. There were now more powerful advantages for the defensive whenever a fleet was close to its home ports as was illustrated in another way by the total defeat of the Russians by the Japanese at Tsushima.

---

[28] This defensive inclination of U.S. naval planning before the War of 1812, and then Wilson's naval shift to battleships, are discussed in Sprout and Sprout, *op. cit.*, pp. 50-72 and 332-346.

[29] These indictments of Corbett are discussed in D. M. Schurman, *The Education of a Navy* (Chicago: University of Chicago Press, 1965), pp. 179-192.

[30] See Semmel, *op cit.*, p. 128.

From 1914 to 1917, the British fleet could not follow the advice implicit in what Mahan had written, but had to be content with blockading German commerce, while frantically countering the German submarine attack on her own commerce. For month after month, especially in 1916 and 1917, the "naval" aspect of World War I, an aspect on which the war might even have been decided, took a form which Mahan's writings had not prepared anyone. No one had anticipated the threat that German U-boats might sink so much commercial shipping that Britain might have to leave the war.

Mahan's 1890 claim to fame was based on the advice that one should shrug off enemy attacks on one's own commerce during a war, and should not be enthusiastic about attacking the commerce of the adversary. The real make-weight would be the contest between the two side's capital ships. Yet, with the singular exception of the Battle of Jutland, at the end of May in 1916, no such counterforce combat was really undertaken, as each side feared the consequences of taking the offensive, while each waited for the other side to attack. Whether they had lost their Nelsonian flair for the attack and the initiative because of Corbett's theories, or simply because of the raw dictates of military reality, the British were consigned to keep their fleet in being for the moment, still largely concentrated in case the opportunity for battle with the Germans were to present itself, but with such opportunity not really coming.

The earliest fear of the British Admiralty with regard to German submarines was consistent with such a fixation on the power of the combat fleet. The British temporarily had to desert their more southerly bases until proper protection against submarine attack could be arranged. The Germans had similarly envisaged the first use of their U-boats as directed against combat ships, as when a single submarine caught three small British cruisers, The Hogue, Aboukir and Cressy, unprepared for such attack, and sank all three. Yet, after the British had revised their protective tactics here, the most promising target for the U-boats soon turned out to be the Allied and neutral merchant shipping carrying goods to Britain and France. It was these attacks that, in the end, brought the United States into the war; it was these attacks, despite the strategic assumptions of Mahan that threatened to inflict a defeat on Britain.

Was the American impact on allied naval calculations then to bring Mahan's theories on the importance of offensive counterforce operations into play? It was indeed more the opposite. The net thrust of U.S. advice was that the British organize convoy operations for merchant ships, and to assign to such convoys, destroyers and other surface warships drawn away from the main battle fleet concentrations.[31]

---

[31] On the American pressure for a convoy system, see Sprout and Sprout, *op. cit.*, pp. 359-368.

Such a convoy strategy turned the tide in the end, so that submarine successes fell and fewer ships going to Britain were sunk. The German expectation that the war could be won by an economic strangulation of Britain, and American entry into the war shrugged off, was thus disproved. An important immediate impact of the American entry into the war was the provision of additional destroyers for anti-submarine duties. Another important impact was the addition of American naval strategic advice, but not the advice that would have been derived from Mahan.

The United States officially entered World War I, not because it liked the British better than the Germans, or even because it was comparing the long-term German naval threat with whatever threats one could anticipate from Britain, but because of its moral objections to German attacks on high-seas commerce. Here we might have to attribute a less-than-total influence to Mahan on his countrymen. As noted, Mahan by the mid-1890s had begun to challenge his own country's moral commitment to the freedom of the seas, endorsing the British Navy's complaints that too much political leverage might be given away in the circumscription of what could be attacked.

President Woodrow Wilson was adamant on this question throughout World War I, resenting British interference with American and neutral commerce, and making "freedom of the seas" a major issue at the Versailles Conference. At the same time, he moved ahead with expansions of the American fleet—precisely to apply pressure to Britain on this issue.[32]

Mahan in 1890 had disparaged counter-commerce warfare because counter-fleet warfare seemed more important and promising to him. Wilson may also have spoken for his countrymen in 1916 and in 1919 in condemning counter-commerce warfare as immoral. Yet for how much longer would this be an American attitude? Barely two decades. If Mahan had begun scoffing at freedom of the seas in 1892, the U.S. would be unanimous on this in 1942.

The United States was not to be involved again in naval combat again until Pearl Harbor. In World War II, it outbuilt the Japanese fleet in both battleships and in aircraft carriers. Quite fortunately the United States lost none of its aircraft carriers at Pearl Harbor and discovered in the end that it had less use for the battleships than for carriers. The Japanese offensive at Pearl Harbor would have done Nelson (and Mahan) proud, analogous as it was to "Copenhagening." The aircraft carrier had indeed been perceived by Yamamoto, and by carrier specialists in the United States, as renewing the advantages of the offensive.

Dreadnought-type battleships had favored the defensive, as demonstrated by the counterforce stalemate that had dominated the North Sea from 1914 to 1918, and as demonstrated earlier by the Japanese victory at Tsushima. If there

---

[32] Wilson's application of naval options at Versailles is outlined in Harold and Margaret Sprout, *Toward a New Order of Sea Power* (Princeton, New Jersey: Princeton University Press, 1943), pp. 62-72.

had been a major crisis between Japan and the United States in 1921, when the battleship was basically still the only tested capital ship, it is by no means certain that Japan would have felt a need to take the military initiative, or to launch any kind of sneak attack timed to coincide with the delivery of a declaration of war. The introduction of the aircraft carrier had changed all this. In effect, new life was infused into Mahan's theories on the nature of naval warfare, as it was certainly always better to have one's own airplanes over the decks of the enemy fleet, than the reverse.

While lacking in larger numbers of aircraft carriers and battleships, the United States Navy in World War II had one other weapon to deploy in facing the Japanese advance: the submarine. She used this weapon very effectively against Japan from the outset, indeed more effectively than the Germans anti-British campaigns in either World War. U.S. submarines sought to sink Japanese naval vessels, but, as in the German experience, they had more and easier successes going after Japanese merchant shipping. While the United States had entered World War I in protest against Germans unrestricted submarine warfare, it was ironic that the United States Navy was directed, on the day after Pearl Harbor, to engage in such unrestricted submarine warfare against Japan.

Apart from issues of civilization and a moral regard for the rights of civilians, this departure, and the substantial accomplishments of the U.S. submarine attacks in greatly reducing the flow of food and oil and other materials back to Japan across the Pacific, raises a question about the impact of Mahan, the strategic theorist, on the U.S. Navy? The answer again seems fairly clear. This element of the war was more analogous to the exploits of John Paul Jones and U.S. commerce raiders in the War of 1812, than to the dramatic fleet actions of Nelson.

In the end, the U.S. Navy won its portion of World War II in the Pacific by a combination of counterforce and countervalue actions. In the Atlantic, it repeated its accomplishment in World War I, getting another round of convoys across to keep Britain alive and able to participate in the war.

The Navy also played a major role in assisting ground forces. Amphibious operations, involving the U.S. Army or the U.S. Navy's own Marine Corps, were conducted far more effectively than those of the British in World War I, as the invasions of Italy and Normandy and the island-hopping across the Pacific were crucial to the defeat of the Axis powers. Such assistance to one's partners a shore never had the *moral* problems associated with attacking cities or merchant ships, but they relate to similar problems of *priority*. The thrust of Mahan's emphasis on sinking the enemy's fleet was that it should be done early or even first. All the benefits of command of the sea, in terms of assisting sister services or dictating peace terms, could be extracted afterwards, at leisure.

In an analogous World War II situation, the U.S. Army Air Force was often accused by the Army Ground Forces of being too intent on winning command of the air, so that it neglected the needs for ground support. Believers in "strategic" air power could always respond that *in the long run* the destruction of the German Air Force would pay dividends for all the sister services, as well as for dictating peace terms to the enemy which would have to confront such a monopoly of air power. The U.S. Army Air Force is often described, somewhat inconclusively, as having been influenced by the theories of Douhet. It might be noted, to close our loop here, that Douhet's paragraphs about the proper approach to control of the air sometimes read as if they had been copied from Mahan, with the word "air" simply substituted over and over again for "sea." But could the U.S. Navy be accused of neglecting such sister-service support, when it was indeed so much engaged in amphibious operations? In at least one instance, it could.

For it is in the inherent juxtaposition of priorities, whether to concentrate on winning total control over the seas, or whether to implement and exploit one's existing strength at sea, that we come to what Bernard Brodie cited so often as a mindless U.S. Navy commitment to a maxim derived from Mahan (derived indeed from centuries of memories of grand fleet actions), the maxim of "don't divide the fleet."[33] We refer here to the Battle of Leyte Gulf, where U.S. Army units had been landed and still needed the support of landing craft, and of smaller escort aircraft carriers for close air support, but where reports came in that the main Japanese fleet was approaching from one direction or another for a last grand round of combat.

Concentrating on defeating that Japanese battle fleet indicated to Admiral Halsey that he should keep his own fleet concentrated, rather than leaving some units to protect the ships supporting the landing, and taking only a portion of his fleet out in search of the enemy. Yet even a portion of the U.S. force might have been sufficient to defeat the Japanese battle units. The consequence of keeping too much force thus bunched together was that the Japanese fleet was able to penetrate to the scene of the Leyte landings, and was almost able to inflict major damage on the ships supporting the U.S. Army forces ashore.

Just as focusing on the possibility of a fleet action had caused the British to postpone too long convoying merchant ships in World War I, such a fleet concentration risked the safety of the ships at Leyte Gulf supporting another very important part of the war. If Mahan played a role in making the concentration of force seem even more axiomatic and unassailable as a principle, it might be checked off as another illustration of his influence on the U.S. Navy. But it would be an example criticized more than praised.

---

[33] See Bernard Brodie, *Strategy in the Missile Age* (Princeton, New Jersey: Princeton University press, 1959), pp. 14, 25, 128, 352-353, and Brodie, War and Politics, pp. 449-450.

The principle of concentration of force is a very old one, enshrined by Jomini and by others. It is a principle that Mahan would hardly have claimed to have originated. The writings of F. W. Lanchester lay out a more elegantly mathematical derivation and illustration of the same principles.[34] Yet Mahan, if he added anything to the discussion, certainly amplified the emphasis on concentration of force.

Influence on the U.S. Navy, III: Conflict With Britain?

The American commitment to building battleships, and "a navy second to none," persisted at the end of World War I, and this might be regarded as quite consistent with Mahan's first principles. For a time, it brought rounds of speculation, in Newport and Washington and other places, about future naval battles between Britain and the United States.[35] The 1921 Washington Naval Conference, wherein the Harding Administration stunned the world with some total-surprise disarmament initiatives which would have done Gorbachev proud,[36] ended this kind of speculation. In the process, it lead to the termination of the Anglo-Japanese alliance, and for a time to a feeling that naval competition could be phased out around the world.

Was the prospect of a naval war between the two English-speaking powers ever real? Perhaps there was something even as early as the 1895 U.S. ultimatum to Britain about the border dispute between Venezuela and British Guiana.[37] In retrospect, however, one tends to agree with Mahan. These two nations were destined to have a "special relationship," rather than going to war again as in 1812. The logics of cooperation or conflict needed to be sorted out, and Mahan certainly was relevant to such a sorting.

Mahan, in The Influence of Sea Power Upon History and in his later writings, attached great significance to the liberal impulses of republican government and political democracy which were so much at the center of the American system, and which had also come to govern Britain by the end of the Nineteenth Century. Mahan's worries about whether such societies being too averse to war and to things military, to command the seas and their adjacent domains for such liberal values, applied to both these powers. While endorsing a few of the racist sentiments about "white man's burden" which so much influenced all of the western elites at the turn of the century, Mahan did not base his expectations of Anglo-American cooperation or understanding primarily on racial or ethnic characteristics, He emphasized rather more the liberal traits, traits which excluded rather than included the Germans.

---

[34] F.W. Lanchester, "Mathematics in Warfare," reprinted in James E. Newman, ed., The World of Mathematics (New York: Simon and Schuster, 1956), Vol.4, pp. 2138-2157.
[35] For examples of such speculation, see Sprout and Spout, Toward a New Order of Sea Power, pp. 77-87.
[36] Harding's initiatives here are described in Mark Sullivan, The Great Adventure at Washington (Garden City, New York: Doubleday, Page and Co., 1922).
[37] See Rock, op. cit., chapter 2.

It has now become fashionable again, at the end of the 20th century, to contemplate whether political democracies can ever go to war with each other.[38] It is difficult to find an example of such a war, with the nominal British declaration of war on Finland in World War II not really sufficing (a declaration which the United States did not match). It was central to Woodrow Wilson's project for the League of Nations to assume that nations which were governed by free elections would not be inclined to go to war with each other. Just as it is central to Marxist belief to assume that nations governed by Marxist regimes can not go to war with each other. The example of Vietnam and Cambodia obviously imposes a severe strain on their theory. Americans favoring the spread of democracy after World War II would have shared this assumption, and probably still share it.[39] Mahan's theories of how the United States might join or surpass Britain in naval power also seemed to accept this proposition.

Yet Mahan's theories of power, and naval power, thus do not mesh with his observations about national character and liberal democracy, as he was quite ready to admit. Perhaps it has been a fluke, and only a fluke, that no two democracies have come to violent conflict. Surely India and Pakistan might go to war, even if Pakistan is democratically governed, and surely the same might apply between Israel and any democratically-governed Arab state.

The United States went into the years of World War I with battle plans drawn up for a range of wars with all the major powers: "Plan Black" for a war with Germany, "Plan Orange" for a war with Japan, "Plan Red" for war with Britain. All of such plans were circumscribed by American ideology, in that they had to presuppose a foreign invasion of American territory. If anyone were thus, in the aftermath of World War I, to argue that only "Plan Black" could have been real, he would have to take account of how totally unrelated this plan was to be to the actual American participation in combat against Germany, since no German amphibious force had ever stormed ashore along the Atlantic Coast. Indeed, given that Britain at least had the Canadian beachhead as an invasion platform, to be worried about by the Washington planners, this war plan would have looked the more plausible. Since Britain still had an alliance in effect with Japan until 1921, this made the American plans for war with Japan merge with the possibility of a war with Britain.

How real could any of this had been? If Mahan had remained alive, would he not have written it all off as errant nonsense? But how much did the theories and policies put forward by Mahan make such war planning more realistic or unrealistic?

---

[38] See Michael W. Doyle, "Kant, Liberal Legacies, and Foreign Affairs," *Philosophy and Public Affairs* Vol. 12, nos. 3,4 (Summer, Fall, 1983), pp. 205-235, 323-353.
[39] For a much discussed contemporary example, see Francis Fukayama, "The End of History," *The National Interest*, no. 16 (Summer, 1989), pp. 3-18.

The speculation about an Anglo-American naval war after 1919 are interestingly matched in the planning done by the Royal Air Force for the air defense of Britain from 1919 until 1933. The problem for the RAF was always how to defend London and other British cities against air attack, but the enemy upon which all focus was directed was always France.[40] France and Britain came very close to war in 1898 over the crisis at Fashoda, when both were indeed already political democracies (another close call for the theory by which democracies do not war on each other), but what would have been the grounds for a later war? The French occupation of the Ruhr in 1923 brought an upgrading of alert among British planners, as British sympathies veered away from France and toward the Weimar Republic, but was an Anglo-French war possible?

One can in the same years find Canadian war plans for a possible war with the United States, and U.S. war plans for a war with Britain involving Canada.

Perhaps it is in the nature of apprenticeships for staff planners that we have war plans for every possible contingency, even for wars against other democracies. But perhaps it is less abstract than this, as the *realities* of power dictate that the United State should resent and worry about British naval preponderance, just as Britain would have to resent and worry about American challenges, deliberate or inadvertent, to that preponderance.

This leads us into a slightly more complicated question of what American attitudes would have had to be, the attitudes of the U.S. Navy and U.S. government and general public, with regard to the balance of power at sea. The analogy between the land and the sea can mislead one here.

On land, one tends to favor the balance of power, in that one does not want all the other territory or population of a continent to be united and coalesced into one military unit, but rather prefers to see a number of units checking each other. Britain thus always welcomed, and worked to maintain, a division of the military power of the European continent; and the United States, from a greater distance, also welcomed this division. In effect, under the balance-of-power system, every power might like to attain hegemony for itself; but each of these powers would also more normally be a *de facto* partner for most of the others in opposing any state which seemed to be moving toward hegemony.

But how does this transplant to the oceans? The German goal, under Tirpitz and the Kaiser, was to develop the same balance-of-power mechanism for the seas; and Berlin counted upon the Americans and the Japanese and Russians and French to be *de facto* partners in this project of cutting British naval power down to size. But would Japan have preferred a division of the seas among

---

[40] British air defense plans of the 1920s are detailed in Basil Collier, *The Defence of the United Kingdom* (London: H.M.S.O., 1957).

other naval powers, and would the United States have preferred such a division? Or might each of these states bizarrely have preferred British naval hegemony to a balance-of-power situation on the high seas?

One does not live on the sea, and one can tolerate a foreign hegemony over the sea without suffering very much disruption of one's own lifestyle along its shores. If there is a lively conflict on the high seas, moreover, this may disrupt commerce and fishing, *etc.*, much more than if there was a hegemonic domination of the seas by a single power. A competition on the high seas may also bring about a competition among the naval powers for on-shore coaling stations and naval bases. These enclaves would indeed be irritating to those who had to live along these shores.

Neither the United States government nor the United States Navy would have welcomed the appearance of German and French naval units in the western hemisphere, even if these could have been seen as a check and distraction for the British fleet, which had so long been the only plausible enemy for the U.S. Navy. The Japanese, similarly, did not welcome the emergence of German and Russian and French naval bases along the coast of China. Even if such great-power rivalry offered possibilities of playing one state off against the other, the influence on local life and politics of these on-shore enclaves was too troublesome. The Monroe Doctrine certainly geared Americans to be very alert and resistant to any German attempt to replicate the Tsingtao seizure along the coasts of Latin America.

The United States may thus have simply been accustomed to British naval power, preferring the devil it knew to the devil it did not know. More importantly, it preferred British hegemony to the prospects of a naval power contest among the European states in the Western Hemisphere. Yet, when the British withdrew their Caribbean fleet in the first decade of this century, the reaction of Mahan's colleagues was not to mourn the loss, but to welcome this change. The United States Navy, with Mahan providing the prompting, would not have minded displacing the British in the Caribbean or the Western Hemisphere, and perhaps in other corners of the world.)

As noted, the Washington Naval Conference of 1921 is remembered as one of the major successes of disarmament, in that significant numbers of battleships were actually scrapped by the United States and Britain, as well as by France, Italy and Japan. Cynics and skeptics can note that the battleship was the capital ship upon which this disarmament was focused, while the aircraft carrier was not as constricted. They will note also that Japan was not bent on a permanently peaceful path by these arrangements.[41]

Yet, if anything else were to be doubted, the conference sealed the end of any speculation about an Anglo-American naval war. Perhaps it was the

---

[41] For a somewhat critical assessment of the Washington and London naval conferences, see Raymond O'Connor, *Perilous Equilibrium* (Lawrence: University of Kansas Press, 1962).

emergence of Nazi Germany, and Imperial Japan, and then Soviet Russia, that so transfixed the two English-speaking powers that they could never find the time to consider a naval war with each other. The United States took Britain's place on the high seas. By 1945, she had in effect matched the British accomplishment after Trafalgar, having a larger fleet than all the world's other fleets combined. Perhaps we would have to turn to the political rather than military insights of Mahan here. As he had quite correctly suggested, these two states were destined to be friends, regardless of what more abstract geo-politics or power considerations would have predicted. The "navalists" in both Britain and the United States, *i.e.* those who took the first parts of Mahan's message most seriously, were all indignant with the provisions of the Washington Treaty.

One can find one more issue juxtaposing the contradictory aspects of Mahan's predictions. When the United States acquired a string of bases in the western hemisphere in 1940, in exchange for giving some over-age destroyers to Britain, few Americans regarded this as a clever advancement of American power at the expense of Britain (although a few British Foreign Office advisers told Churchill to see it that way, only to be overruled). Most saw the destroyers as a way of helping out Britain when it was to be sorely tried by Hitler's U-boats, with the bases being useful as an excuse to transfer the ships, by the terms of American neutrality.

In shaping the attitudes of the U.S. Navy, and of Americans in general, Mahan could have been quoted on either side of this "debate," but he would have come down personally on the same side as the 1940 Americans.

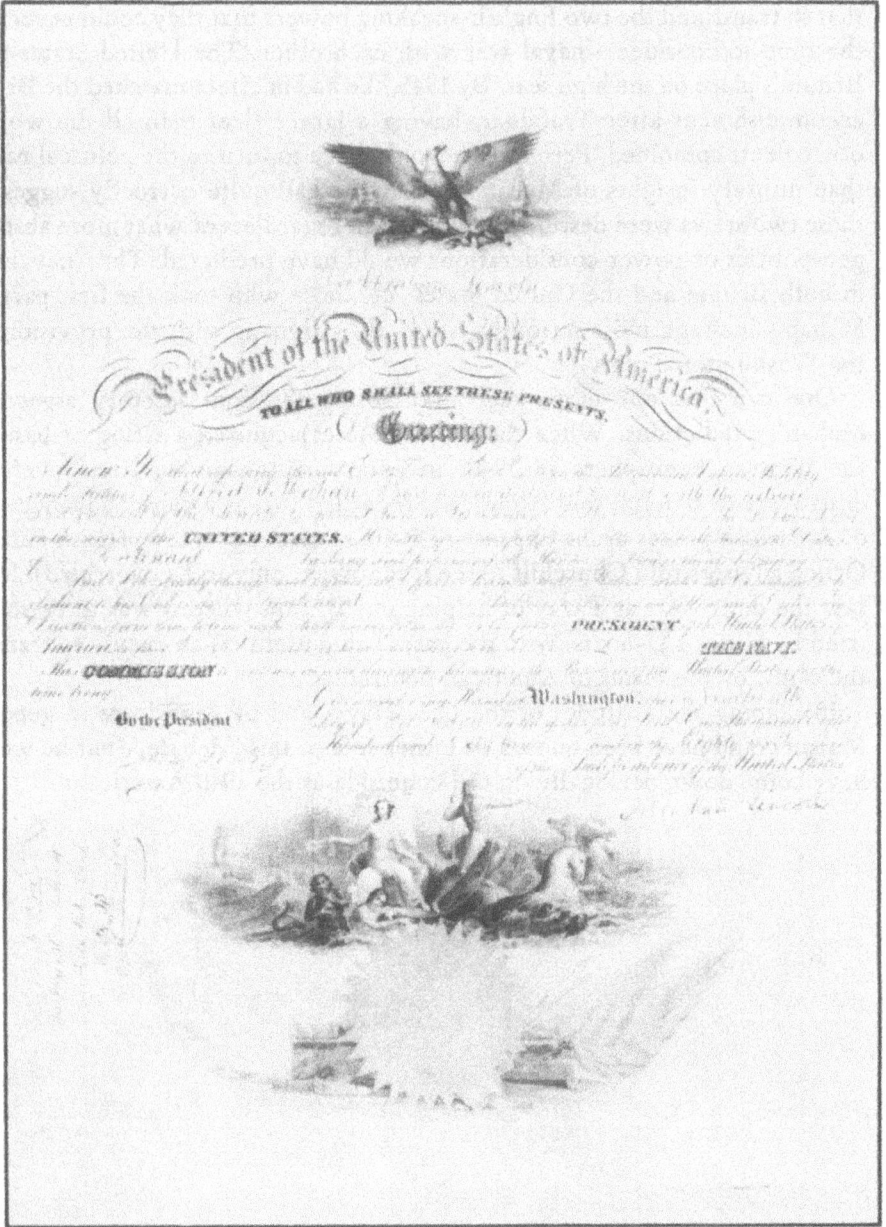

Mahan's commission as Lieutenant, U.S. Navy, signed by President Abraham Lincoln on 19 February 1862. From the Naval Historical Collection, Naval War College. Manuscript Item 83.

Chapter 15

Mahan, Russia, and the Next 100 Years

Clark G. Reynolds

"History has proved," said Mahan, "that a purely military sea power can be built up by a despot, as was done by Louis XIV; but . . . experience showed that his navy was like a growth which having no root soon withers away."[1]

Holger Herwig in his excellent paper has demonstrated that Imperial and Nazi Germany suffered similar fates as Louis' bid for supremacy at sea. Ken Hagan asks what might be the implications of the German experience for our own time and the future—meaning the Soviet Union. What indeed? Mahan's analytical framework offers important clues.

Mahan warned that no nation could be superior both on land and at sea; the expense has been too great for every power which has attempted it. "History," he declared in another telling dictum, "has conclusively demonstrated the inability of a state with even a single continental frontier to compete in naval development with one that is insular. . . ."[2] This held true for the France of Louis XIV and Napoleon and for Wilhelmian and Hitlerite Germany, each confronted and eventually defeated by powerful coalitions of continental powers and English or Anglo-American naval might. So it was for Imperial Russia.

On this May Day 1990, after a year of momentous political change in Eastern Europe which has heralded the fizzling out of the Russo-American Cold War, it is altogether appropriate that we look to Mahan for possible explanations of the Gorbachev phenomenon: dramatic military retrenchment, political-economic restructuring (perestroika), and socio-cultural openness (glasnost).

Mahan viewed the tsarist Russia of his day as a continental power oriented completely to the defensive. In his 1911 book *Naval Strategy*, Mahan saw

---

[1] Alfred Thayer Mahan, *The Influence of Sea Power upon History, 1660-1783* (London: Sampson Low, Marston, 1890), p. 88.

[2] Mahan, "Advantages of Insular Position," a 1902 essay excerpted in Allan Westcott, ed., *Mahan on Naval Warfare* (London: Sampson Low, Marston, 1919), p. 315. See also Margaret Tuttle Sprout, "Mahan: Evangelist of Sea Power," in Edward Mead Earle, *Makers of Modern Strategy* (New York: Atheneum reprint, 1966), pp. 425, 444.

Russia's Navy as no more than a "fortress fleet," the warships tied down in the passive role of augmenting coastal fortifications. For him this was "a dominant conception in Russian military and naval thought."[3] To this view I extend the time frame to eight centuries of a fundamentally defensive strategic posture, unbroken from earliest times down to the present.[4]

Much debate about Russian naval strategy, starting with Bob Herrick's fine book over twenty years ago,[5] has been generated in light of the Russian submarine and surface fleets of the Admiral S. G. Gorshkov era between the late 1950s and the 1980s and topped by the current commissioning of attack aircraft carriers.

The obvious question before us is whether or not Soviet General Secretary (and, as of 1989, President) Mikhail Gorbachev ever read Mahan. Or, if he did, did he misread Mahan and fall into the same trap as the despotic "Sun King," the *Kaiser*, and the *Führer*? Or, which is probably the case, has he simply faced up to the hard reality of experience that, as Mahan understood, no great continental power could afford to wield supremacy simultaneously on land and at sea, and, today, in the air *and* space as well.

During the past year, 1989-90, the Soviet Union has for all intents and purposes not only called off the Cold War, but has begun to crumble from within: its economy, its control over ethnic minorities, its frustrated youth and intelligentsia rejecting the old gods of communism, and its very people fed up with unfulfilled promises for economic prosperity as they finally join the global revolution of rising expectations. Gorbachev cannot solve these manifold challenges to the existence of the Soviet state unless he cuts back on arms. History abounds with examples of continental states seeking military retrenchment which select the navy as the first target for cutbacks. And, yet, the initial step was to discard the Warsaw Pact landward buffer states as expendable. Can the surface fleet be far behind? For apparently, the Reagan-Lehman naval offensive (as well as "Star Wars," the Strategic Defense Initiative), that saber-rattling Maritime Strategy of a 600-ship U.S. Navy aimed at assaulting Russia's northern flank in time of war, created a challenge Russia could not match economically. This offensive may well turn out to have been a key element of the bloodless American victory in the Cold War. Furthermore, even the Red Army, dishonored by the Afghanistan debacle, is under the budgetary knife.

---

[3] Mahan, *Naval Strategy Compared and Contrasted with the Principles and Practice of Military Operations on Land* (London: Sampson Low, Marston, 1911), pp. 383–401, excerpted in Westcott, pp. 256–275.

[4] Clark G. Reynolds, "Eight Centuries of Continental Strategy: Imperial and Soviet Russia," in Reynolds, *History and the Sea: Essays in Maritime Strategy* (Columbia: University of South Carolina Press, 1989), pp. 196–223. An excellent description of the defensive Russian "parade" fleet of 1839 may be found in the observations of a French traveller: Phyllis Penn Kohler, ed., *Journey for Our Time: The Russian Journals of the Marquis de Custine* (Washington: Gateway, 1987), pp. 52–64.

[5] Robert Waring Herrick, *Soviet Naval Strategy: Fifty Years of Theory and Practice* (Annapolis: U.S. Naval Institute, 1968).

These are of course mere events which, considered by themselves, could well turn out to be temporal. Rulers change, policies can be reversed, wars declared. Nor can Cold War caution be easily eradicated.

This is where a close examination of Mahan's broad historical theories can shed light on the depths of the Russian dilemma.

To understand these theories, we can thank Captain Wayne Hughes for his incisive paper redefining Mahan's nomenclature. What Mahan called "principles," his six "principal conditions affecting the sea power of nations," are not principles at all, according to Hughes. Principles are guides for action. Hughes ably demonstrates that Mahan's six points are actually trends and constants, descriptive of a nation's character and history. Mahan's actual principles were elucidated only when he tried to convince his own country to exploit its constants and trends to become a nation capable of commanding the seas.

The essential constants that a nation requires to become a major sea power are three, Mahan explained:

1. "production, with the necessity of exchanging products,"
2. "shipping, whereby the exchange is carried on," including warships to guarantee that exchange, and
3. "colonies, which facilitate and enlarge the operations of shipping and tend to protect it by multiplying points of safety," that is, overseas bases.

Despite variations, trends, in policy, "the history of the seaboard nations has been less determined by the shrewdness and foresight of governments than by conditions [that is, constants] of [geographical] position, extent, configuration, [as well as] number and character of their people—by what are called, in a word, natural conditions."[6]

By applying these 'constant' natural conditions to the Soviet Union of 1990, one hundred years after Mahan articulated them, the new 'trends' in Russia become clear:

1. **Production.** What Mahan surely meant was a flourishing economy able to produce manufactured industrial good and raw materials that would not only adequately supply the general population but would be competitive on the open international market. The Soviet Union has clearly failed in this regard, today devoting, we now know, at least 25 percent of its gross national product to military expenditures and thereby stifling civilian commercial production. Furthermore, Russia is turning to Western economic experts for advice.

2. **Shipping.** In this regard, Soviet Russia has succeeded, with a vast merchant marine, seagoing fishing factories, and a powerful navy. But against the overall trading might of the United States, Japan, Western Europe, and the ubiquitous "flag of convenience" merchant fleets headquartered in New

---

[6] Mahan, *Influence*, p. 28.

York City, Russian overseas trade is not a dangerous threat. Indeed, the Soviet Union has learned the efficacy of cooperating with the West in cartels, abiding by international law, and siding with other great powers against Third World countries to keep the sea lanes open. *Morflot*, the state shipping agency, even hires Western nationals to manage its foreign offices. And the Soviet Navy is focused not on trade defense but on protecting the coast and on nuclear deterrence. The Russian Merchant Marine is exposed.

3.   **Colonies.** The political character of "colonies" have changed since Mahan's day, when they were owned by European powers. Their economic and strategic characteristics have not. Today, the world runs on Washington time. Economic giants Japan and Germany (only the western half until 1990 but now heading toward reunification) were conquered and transformed into strategic-economic "colonies" of the United States during and after World War II. Britain and Western Europe, rejuvenated by the Marshall Plan, and much of the Third World, liberated from political colonial rule, have also been absorbed into this global "empire." The United States has worldwide naval bases and trading depots which would have dazzled Mahan. Russia has enjoyed none of this (granted, she utilizes overseas bases as in Cuba and Vietnam for stopovers and even trades at many great maritime centers, but these are mere ports of call, enjoyed by all trading nations under the strategic umbrella of the *Pax Americana*).

4.   Points 1, 2, and 3 equal a fourth constant, about which Mahan skirted and on which John Maurer touches in his paper: *Democracy*. For Mahan's model was Great Britain of the late Seventeenth, Eighteenth, and early Nineteenth Centuries, a model inherited by the United States in the 20th: democratic societies based on a liberal middle class of free enterprise merchants, bankers, and professional people. In a word, capitalists. Mahan had trouble with this 'constant' because of his admiration of the French through Jomini and the Napoleonic military examples taught by Mahan's father at West Point, especially Colbert's *forced* maritime enterprises (merchantmen, colonies, navy) of the late seventeenth century. Even the French have had difficulty in defining themselves, waffling through their turbulent history between being a continental empire and a republic. But neither France nor Russia ever settled on a dominant middle class of merchants, each relying instead on a two-class socio-economic-political system of aristocratic landowners and peasant-workers which is the mark of an agrarian rather than trading-industrial society.

Britain and America, in spite of fluctuating 'trends' in their history in which they have occasionally strayed into continental aspirations on land, both have shared a maritime 'constant.' In time of war, they have depended largely on continental allies to win on land while they commanded the seas (and the air in this century).

To conclude, then, it appears that Gorbachev, whether or not he ever read, much less understood, Mahan's historical theories, has realized that just shipping is not enough. To survive and to prosper among the family of nations in a free-market, democratic world, Soviet Russia must accept the economic constants of capitalism and global trade by restructuring Soviet institutions: *perestroika*. And it must accept the concomitant necessity of free political expression and open self-criticism: *glasnost*. To make these things possible, the Soviet budget must be rechanneled from exorbitant military expenditures to commercial pursuits. Gorbachev has already taken the first step by giving up his strategic colonies on Russia's borders, the Warsaw Pact nations. Can the dismantling of the expensive Soviet Navy be the second step?

Assuming, then, that the United States has won the Cold War by asserting Mahan's constants of global sea power, what 'principles' of action can guide us in the post-Cold War era? Mahan hinted at many of them, but the most articulate historical philosopher of such strategic and tactical matters was his brilliant British contemporary, Sir Julian Corbett. Let us hope that the Naval War College, in order to rediscover those principles, will examine both these savants of sea power anew in light of such a postwar strategic scenario.

The prospects for the future are exciting indeed, and we students of Mahan may well wish we could reconvene here in Newport 100 years hence to reflect on how well a triumphant democratic America and a restructured Soviet Russia will have fit into Mahan's historical scheme in the new era now beginning.

Mahan with his grandson, A.T. Mahan II.

Chapter 16

Under the *Influence*:
A Hundred Years and Around the World

George W. Baer

We must keep in mind that certain of Mahan's ideas changed over time, and certain stayed pretty constant, and we must keep straight which are which. There are several Mahans, and many Mahanians. The proponent in 1890 of naval power as a creature of commerce, had in a few years, become an imperialist for whom naval strength had an autonomous political importance. Luce, who put him on his original course, noted the shift. In 1897 he wrote of Mahan's third book, *The Interest of America in Sea Power, Present and Future*: "Mahan has allowed the views of a naval strategist to dominate those of the political economist. . . . Sea power, in its military sense, is the off-spring, not the parent of commerce."[1] We have to look at context as well as text. John Maurer helps us with the broad political constants in his discussion of structural constraints to Mahan's world view.

Mahan's pessimism seemed to extend to his view of human nature and the acceptance of war. Lyle Mahan's recollections of his father which John Hattendorf very ably edited leaves us with the impression of a cold fish father, or at least an unhappy and reticent son. Chaplain Leslie's study of Mahan's religion confirms why Lyle saw more of his father's austerity and his rectitude than his affect or his emotion. Mahan appears in his Roman guise here, more engaged by rational theology in its public exercise than the more emotional possibilities of the Christian religion. Of course, his confidence that the expansion of western civilization was the plan of Providence was shared by the prominent, western imperialists. Professor Quester is right to point out that Mahan's theory of power, his fusion of political and strategic elements, fits at best uneasily, even at the turn of the century, with American liberal constitutional democracy, or even the tenets of Clausewitz.

---

[1] Quoted by John D. Hayes, "The Influence of Modern Sea Power, 1945-1970," U.S. Naval Institute *Proceedings* (May 1971), pp. 279-280. The correct citation is *The Critic*, January 1898, for which see John D. Hayes and John B. Hattendorf, eds., The *Writings of Stephen B. Luce* (Newport: Naval War College, 1975, pp. 216-217.

But it does fit very well what Maurer described as Mahan's neo-realism. What struck me in Commander Leslie's paper, as it does with most of the 'neo-realists' I read, was Mahan's anxiety. "The world of civilized Christianity" stands out-numbered by the expanding civilizations of Asia. The West must either convert them, or perish "under a flood of outside invasion." The offensive-defensive strategy Mahan proposed, to gain time by organizing the West's material forces before embarking on an evangelical crusade, turns out to be less of Pericles and his funeral oration or Kennan and his X article, that is, stay true, trust in time and convert by example but more like a crusader's NSC-68: act or lose.

Professors Herwig and Dingman, Dr. Scheina, and Captain Montenegro tackled the vastly complicated matter of identifying an intellectual food chain for the transmission of a naval strategy. They wisely remind us that the adoption of sea power concepts was contingent. That was true in Japan, Germany, Latin America, and, I would say, in the United States as well. Mahan and his colleagues, Luce and Taylor at the Naval War College, Secretaries Tracy and Herbert at the Navy Department, and navalists like Roosevelt and Lodge, sought no less than to change the strategic culture of the United States, and the operations of the Navy. They wanted the ships that protected the United States to get out of harbors. They wanted them to mass their force in offensive forward deployment. They wanted an ocean going fleet. The offensive battle fleet, they said, was the only means of maritime defense in the modern age, a fleet that would protect both from invasion and commerce depredation. What the British did in the War of 1812 must not happen again.

To convert the Navy's strategy and to get the ships for the new doctrine of offensive sea control demanded a popular and professional consensus, one not unlike, in different contexts, that support which Dingman and Herwig show navalists sought abroad. In 1890 Mahan chose the phrase 'the influence of sea power' to rally public support. That phrase, more than his books, was the decisive rhetorical contribution to the campaign, so long as it was read as implying a forward deployed offensive battle fleet. Mahan needed an arresting slogan precisely because contemporary American experience did fit into his theory of history or his strategy for an offensively employed capital ship fleet. In 1890 most Americans did not think of the United States as dependent on its maritime interests, or vulnerable to maritime attacks.

A particular strategic conjunction was Mahan's main conceptual innovation, his combination of a purpose (protection of what he asserted was America's inevitably threatened maritime position) and a naval operation (an offensive, forward deployed concentrated battle fleet for a particular kind of sea control strategy). This strategic combination, however, was conjectural. There is no necessary connection between a maritime or insular culture, or a continental one for that matter, and a particular style of naval operations. Everything depends on time and place, the ends and the means. Navies are artificial, and they are contingent. Mahan himself, as Luce noted, ultimately admitted to the political autonomy of naval force, of sea power as naval strength. In 1890 Mahan had written: "The necessity of a navy, in the restricted sense of the word, springs . . . from the existence of a peaceful shipping, and disappears with it, except in the case of a nation which has aggressive tendencies, and keeps a navy merely as a branch of the military establishment."[2]

In 1911, at the end of *Naval Strategy*, Mahan wrote:

> More and more it becomes clear, that the functions of navies is distinctly military and international, whatever their historical origins in particular cases. The Navy of the United States, for example, took its rise from purely commercial considerations. External interests cannot be confined to those of commerce. There may be political as well as commercial; may be political because commercial . . .; may be political because military . . . may be political because of national prepossessions and sympathies. . . .

The United States . . . needs a navy both numerous and efficient even if no merchant vessel again flies the United States flag. [In short] a navy may be necessary where there is no shipping.[3]

There are also continuities. Mahan and the Mahanians moved from commerce to empire as the basis for their argument about sea power, and they defined sea power as naval strength. At the same time their plan of operations remained constant: to meet the enemy as far from American shores as possible, for a decisive battle between battle fleets. Everything about the new naval system led to and followed from that proposition.

It interested me how the Army accepted this. In the 1890s it cast its harbor protection philosophy in Mahanian terms. Lieutenant General John Schofield, formerly Commanding General, wrote in 1897:

> In a country having the situation of the United States, the navy is the *aggressive* arm of the national military power. . . . For this purpose entire freedom of action is essential. . . . Hence arises one of the most important functions of land defense: to give the aggressive arm secure bases of operation at all the great seaports where navy-yards or depots are located.[4]

This was meant to create what TR was to call "a foot-loose fleet," supporting the strategy of offensive sea control, and ultimately power projection, which became first the basis of naval, and then American, strategic culture.

Dingman searched carefully for evidence of direct causal connections between Japan's creation of a fleet strategy and Mahan's. He found none,

---

[2] A.T. Mahan, *The Influence of Sea Power Upon History, 1660-1783* (Boston: Little, Brown, 1890), pp. 26-27.
[3] A.T. Mahan, *Naval Strategy* (Boston: Little, Brown, 1918), pp. 445-447.
[4] Quoted in Graham A. Cosmas, *An Army for Empire: The United States Army in the Spanish-American War* (Columbia: University of Missouri Press, 1971), p. 38.

although there were plenty of parallels. Both the United States and Japan, and Germany too, as Professor Herwig shows, imitated. The new navalism in each country had to be taken as an act of faith in convincing the people. It did not spring indigenously from a nation of people who sat around on docks tying knots and imagining battle fleet tactics. In each case the new navalism was derived. Naval ideas, as well as navies, are more artificial than Mahan allowed. Or perhaps ideas follow technology and politics in the form that evolutionists call punctuated equilibrium. In an era of imitation, such as the 1890s, one can easily imagine a Mahanian who never read Mahan. In America, Mahan's countervalue offensive massed force as originally a deterrent, for a defensive political purpose.

What is interesting is how long the strategic and structural configurations lasted.

It certainly influenced Japan. By the late 30s, with the war against China, a case can be made, as Clark Reynolds has, that Japan was a continental power, with the military divided between the Army's attention to the continental north and the Navy's to the maritime and imperial south. What is interesting here, and which perhaps Professor Dingman lets slip by in reference to "sheer force of events," is the autonomy the Navy arrogated to itself and the persistence of its respect for the big battle solution. These were double blinds. The whole point of the Navy's southern advance, on this argument, was to get the resource base by which the beleaguered Army could win in China. Yet a sense of separateness, exemplified by its ideas of sea power and confidence in its barrier strategy, led the Navy to go it alone. The Army did not, until too late, give it the support it needed to maintain the island strongholds. Even worse, its Mahanian vision of decisive battle and sea control led it to neglect protection of its maritime commerce, the point of the whole enterprise. Japanese naval strategy was controlled by the sheer force of ideas, after all.

Tripitz and Scheer were too, as Professor Herwig shows. They had a hard row to hoe, to convince the Germans that they needed a high seas fleet. The contradiction is apparent in Professor Herwig's discussion, where he argues that Tirpitz used Mahan in a quasi-official capacity, but was evidently so uncertain of his stand, or his resource base, that he "had an imperial decree issued prohibiting public discussion of the basic tenets of German naval developments." There is something fundamentally wrong here. However artificial naval developments might be, there is something awfully wrong with a sea power philosophy that cannot go public or a naval strategy that cannot stand up to professional criticism. No matter how shrewd Tripitz was, he blinded himself. But perhaps not quite, for it appears that the Germans used Mahan as a public relations device, not as a guide to naval strategy. Certainly one would not have called it a "luxury fleet" if the true conditions of a maritime state existed, according to Mahan's conjunctural definition of sea power. The problem was, as Herwig showed, the conjunction did not in fact exist.

Without doubt, Professor Hughes is entirely correct in insisting that tactical analysis is a side of strategy. Of course strategy is a coin with more than two sides. In considering military efficiency one must look at purpose as well as action, at capacity as well as operation, and, always, at these dimensions with regard to the enemy. What is important is to look at the matter of combat as a whole.

Now, Mahan's effort to find historical principles did indeed run him into trouble. The all-big gun-many gun controversy with Sims, volume of weight versus volume of fire, is an example. When I look closer, I must say I conclude that Mahan probably did not think this was much of an issue. He did have history on his side, including the Yalu and Santiago. He did want to keep up morale with close encounter, but he conceded the point to Sims as soon as the evidence of big-gun, long-range accuracy was in. What was important, and on which fundamental power they both agreed, offensive concentration at the decisive point. It is true that Mahan often comes out looking like a technological ostrich with his head stuck in a history book on this matter. It was good to see Professor Hughes' qualifications about Sims' own use of evidence, and the openness of the debate, had Mahan cared to pursue it further. The key point is that both agreed it was only a functional matter: how best to build the decisive weapon for the decisive battle.

Hughes is right on the mark in the distinctions he makes in his discussion of blockades. Every tactic or strategy must be constantly subjected to the analytic perspectives he proposes. As to the discussion of trends, I suspect Hughes is singing to the choir that is here today. Historians seek context as second nature, or should, and although they might not use the term trends, they do what Hughes prescribes. I acknowledge in the audience today historians like Jon Sumida who showed British naval strategy had to be understood through the interaction of preferences, or trends, in the realms of administration, finance, technology, policy, and personality, and David Rosenberg who showed the connection of trends in nuclear weapons development to naval strategy and to the Navy's institutional self-definition, and Norman Friedman who has shown us the intimate relationship of technology and operational possibilities. Modern scholarship is far more alert than Mahan was to changes in modern warfare. Mahan was president of the American Historical Association, but he was not good at keeping up with trends, other than those which he declared, as principles. In this sense, we respond to Mahan as his own trendsetter.

There is one point I want especially to note in Professor Quester's paper. He shows the difficulties the British and Americans faced, especially in the 1920s, in moving from a Mahanian notion of absolute sea control to a balance-of-power on the seas. What strikes me is how the process of adjustment to an approximation of a balance of power came about. Ray O'Connor can remind us that the Navy thought there was no true 'yardstick,' but in popular, and political terms, agreement was made possible by Mahanian notions of sea control which were widely accepted, if perhaps misunderstood, and which rested on the idea of symmetry. The arms treaties were the mechanisms through which ratios, and hence a naval balance, was reached. And of contemporary importance, we may be seeing at the present time just such a process at work again, by which arms limitation treaties, which might come to include, as the Soviets want, some form of naval treaty, are used to establish a new relationship of strategic strengths which could otherwise only be found in battle or concession.

If so, we will see some radical changes in U.S. naval strategy, and we will need some Admiral William Pratts and Admiral Bill Wylies to remind us that sea power is not just absolute naval strength, that naval power is in fact provisional, and that a nation's maritime interests, which are necessarily part of international relations, may be protected and advanced by ways other than by absolute control of the sea. "The relationship between national and naval policy is one that is not always fully understood." Sea power and naval strength are not entirely synonymous terms," Pratt wrote after the Washington Conference. The Navy, he wrote, "is first, the statesman's tool, and second, the warrior's weapon." "Sea power and naval strength," Pratt concluded, "are not always synonymous terms."[5] This view cost Pratt many friends in the Navy, but it was true then and it is true today.

I conclude with reference to Admiral Wylie's address last night. Admiral Wylie is one of our foremost strategic conceptualizers, who has insisted that we never cease from looking at strategy whole. He reminds us of two fundamental facts. One is that sea power is not a policy in itself, but a basis for policy, according to the interests and situation of the country, and comprising many dimensions, only one of which, although it is an essential one, is naval strength. Secondly, if naval strength has to be used to an end, sometimes that end is sea control. People associate that with Mahan. Sometimes, it is projecting power from the sea on to the land. People associate that with Corbett. The truth is, as Norman Friedman reminds us in his recent book, this is a false dichotomy. Sea control and power projection ashore are associated and complementary. That was true in maritime strategy before 1890, as in the second Punic War, and it was true in 1890 when the purpose of the fleet ultimately was to assure blockade and access, or the reverse, and it is true for us today.

---

[5] Rear Admiral W.V. Pratt, "Naval Policy and its Relation to World Politics," U.S. Naval Institute *Proceedings* (July 1923), pp. 1073, 1083-1084, and, Gerald W. Wheeler, *Admiral William Veazie Pratt, U.S. Navy* (Washington: Department of the Navy, 1974), pp. 185-186.

www.ingramcontent.com/pod-product-compliance
Lightning Source LLC
Chambersburg PA
CBHW060047100426
42742CB00014B/2730